The Resourceful Mum's Handbook

The Resourceful Mum's Handbook

Bringing up a baby on a budget

Elen Lewis

SQUARE PEG
London

Published by Square Peg
2 4 6 8 10 9 7 5 3 1

First published in Great Britain in 2009 by
Square Peg
Random House, 20 Vauxhall Bridge Road,
London SW1V 2SA

www.rbooks.co.uk

Addresses for companies within The Random House Group Limited can be found at: www.randomhouse.co.uk/offices.htm

The Random House Group Limited Reg. No. 954009

A CIP catalogue record for this book is available from the British Library

ISBN 9780224082655

The Random House Group Limited supports The Forest Stewardship Council (FSC), the leading international forest certification organisation. All our titles that are printed on Greenpeace approved FSC certified paper carry the FSC logo. Our paper procurement policy can be found at www.rbooks.co.uk/environment

Typeset by Palimpsest Book Production Limited,
Grangemouth, Stirlingshire

Printed and bound in Great Britain by
Clays Ltd, St Ives PLC

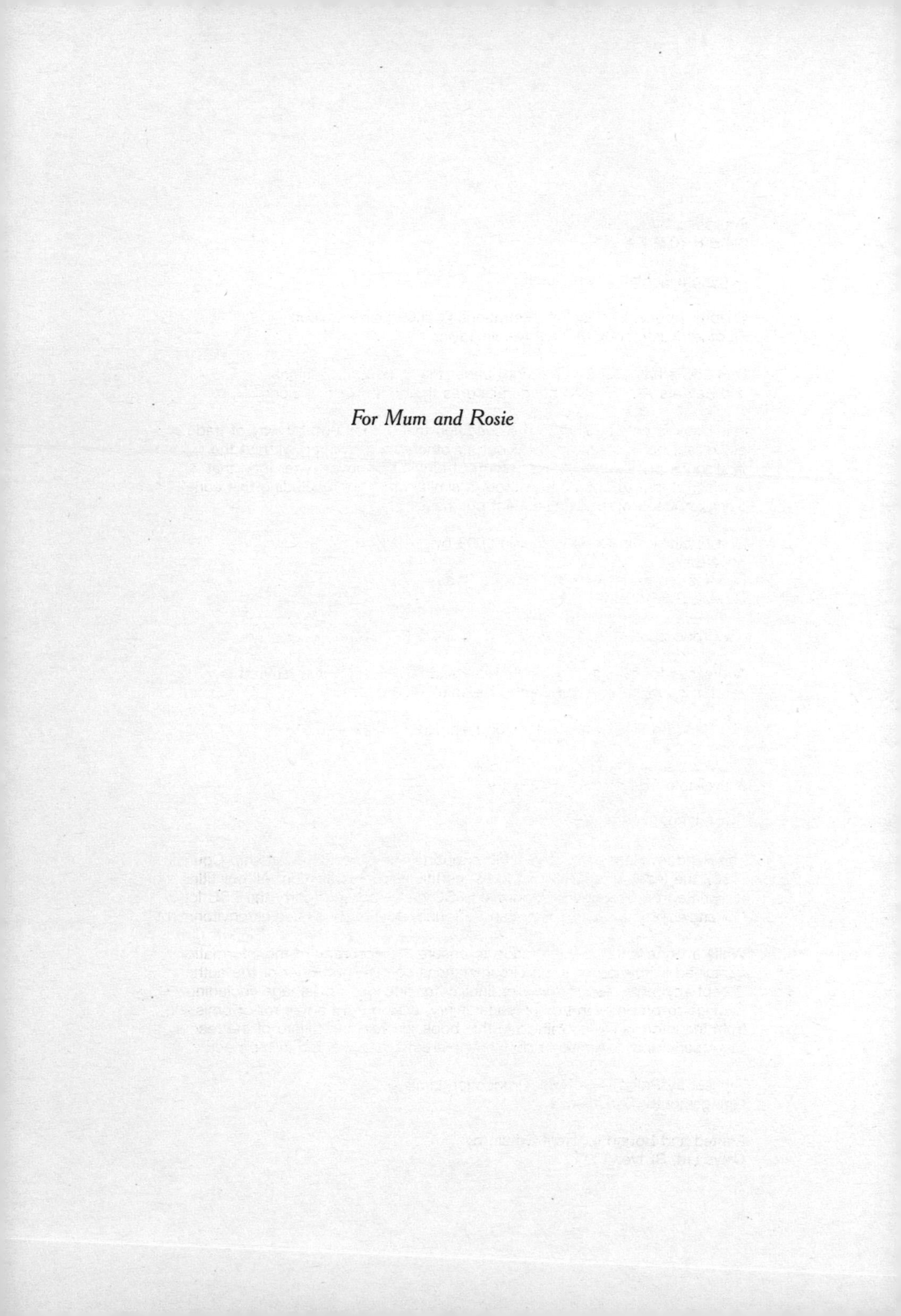

For Mum and Rosie

Contents

Introduction

From Bugaboo buggies to Burberry babywear and Bill Amberg designer sheepskin baby slings, bringing up baby is pricier than buying a house. The lifetime cost of raising a child is a staggering £194,000 – and rising. A typical family, bringing up a child from birth to the age of twenty-one spends £9,227 a year, £769 a month or £25 a day, according to research by Insurer LV, the UK's friendly society. The same survey said that parents can expect to shell out as much as £8,853 in the first year of their baby's life, once they have paid for nursery equipment, toys and clothing.

The marketing clout of the baby industry has got a lot to answer for. It has created a buoyant sector with healthy profits and a regular stream of new, impressionable customers that many other industries lust after. It's a market stuffed full of expensive, desirable, designer brands. Forget about women checking out your handbag when you're walking along the street – when you've got a baby they'll be checking out your pram.

Even the most sensible new parents feel emotionally blackmailed into buying the newest, shiniest, best-ever stuff for their children. It feels like a reflection of good parenting. The tiny cashmere cardigans, the cosy lambskin, the soft leather booties; some non-essentials are so beautiful that you can nearly justify the extravagance. Don't forget that once you've spent your life savings on the designer kit, there are still the mountains of nappies, bundles of toys and gallons of formula to pay for.

But having a baby doesn't have to be a costly business. When I was pregnant, one of the best pieces of advice I was given was that babies need very little stuff. Don't be strong-armed into buying all the things that the magazines and catalogues tell us that babies must have. A lot of this paraphernalia didn't exist when our own mothers were bringing us up and it certainly didn't in our grand-mothers' time. Why not return to a more old-fashioned approach to bringing up baby? Resist the powerful persuasion from marketing companies to buy expensive baby gadgets and gizmos or a new pram that costs as much as a second-hand car. Becoming a new mother is the perfect time to build, knit, sew, paint, craft, cook, recycle, mend and make do. And before you know it, you've had a baby on a budget, taken a more environmentally friendly approach to consumerism and satisfied some creative urges too.

CHAPTER ONE

Planning

Have no pride; beg, steal and borrow as much as you can from any friend/work colleague/neighbour who has had a child within the last three years – I even borrowed nursing bras and a breast pump, and so far have only bought about ten outfits, a buggy and a travel cot for my nine-month-old daughter.

Lynsey, mum of Amber

The budget

One of the first steps along the path of being a resourceful mum is setting a baby budget. It's a boring but important task. Don't put it off; spend some time sorting out your finances as soon as you realise you're pregnant. Then you'll know from the start how healthy your finances are to set a realistic budget.

- ✄ **Get organised.** Go through your bank statements and match up your income and outgoings. This will show you how much money you need for bare essentials like mortgage or rent, bills, food and travel each month.
- ✄ **Get in shape.** Make sure you're getting the best possible deals for all financial products and bills. By getting the best rate on your mortgage, mobile phone, gas and electricity, insurance and credit cards you could save hundreds of pounds a year.
- ✄ **Start squirrelling.** If you haven't already got one, open a savings account and shop around for the best interest rate. Before you go on maternity leave, both you and your partner should set up regular direct debits to pay money into the account as soon as you're paid. Save as much as you can afford.
- ✄ **Hatch a plan.** Work out a weekly budget that you can afford on one wage. Plan to have less income coming in than you expect. It's difficult to know how you'll feel about returning to work until the baby is born. You may want to work part time.
- ✄ **Pay cash.** Once your budget has been set take out weekly cash and avoid paying by cards to ensure you stick to it.

Being thrifty is not as difficult as it might seem. Once you've done the hard financial stuff, little steps can make a big difference. Planning weekly meals before shopping and making packed lunches will save money on food. Resisting treats like takeaway coffees and taxis makes an impact. You'll probably save money without even trying when you're pregnant because you won't be out late drinking wine or buying as many new clothes for yourself.

The budget planner

The best way of budgeting is to work out your income and subsequent outgoings to see where you can start to make savings. The more detailed you make it, the more accurate it will be. The financial website Moneysavingexpert has an excellent free planner you can download: www.moneysavingexpert.com/banking/Budget-planning.

Outgoings you should list include mortgage or rent, buildings and contents insurance, council tax, water, gas, electricity, home phone, mobile phone, broadband, TV licence, food and household shopping, eating and drinking out, gym and other membership fees, car, travel, credit card and loan repayments, savings and pensions.

A helping hand

There are a number of benefits for new families that can make a real difference. Free dental care and free prescriptions are available to all pregnant women and new mothers with babies under one, regardless of income.

All parents are entitled to claim child benefits. From January 5th, 2009, this was worth £20.00 a week for the first born and £13.20 a week for subsequent children. Within a week or so of the baby being born you'll receive a form from the government to fill in that you send off with a copy of the birth certificate. Although it's a busy time it's worth posting quickly because the benefit won't be backdated.

There is also a springboard for the baby's savings in the shape of The Child Trust Fund. New babies are given a £250 voucher to start their savings account; this will be followed by another voucher for the same amount on the child's seventh birthday. If your household income falls below £15,575 in 2009 your baby will qualify for a voucher worth £500.

All the money saved in this account is free of tax and you can top up the account by up to £1,200 a year. For example, if you could afford to save £10 a month, the fund would be worth around £5,210 by the time your baby is eighteen, compared to just £1,410 if the basic £500 was left in the fund. The account belongs to the child and can't be touched until they turn eighteen.

If you want to set up a separate savings account for your baby, try to save in the child's name to avoid paying tax. If you can afford to save child benefit you'll save as much as £941.20 annually.

If you do have enough disposable income to put aside some savings for your baby's future then, bizarrely enough, pensions are one of the most tax efficient kids' savings schemes offering unrivalled incentives. Realising that my four-week-old daughter had a pension, when I didn't, finally made me sort one out for myself. If you can afford to invest up to £2,808 in a year, the tax relief will top it up to £3,600, instantly boosting your children's savings by nearly 30 per cent. Do bear in mind that your baby's pension can't be cashed in until they retire, so it's not going to fund university fees or a first car or travelling adventure, although it will protect them in old age.

Essential kit

Contrary to popular belief, a newborn baby needs very little, and hardly any of this stuff needs to be brand-new. The subsequent chapters go into more detail about kit, but your baby bare essentials are listed below.

Must-haves
Cot and new mattress
Pram
New car seat

Highchair (no need to buy until baby is about six months)
Breast pump (you can rent these) and feeding bras – for breast-feeding OR
Bottles and steriliser – if you're formula feeding
A reliable washing machine
Clothing
Bedding
Nappies
Sling or papoose

Nice-to-haves
Bouncy chair
Baby monitor (if you live in a huge house)
Travel cot, a resourceful buy because it can triple up as a Moses basket when the baby is newborn and a playpen when it's a toddler

Naughty but nice
Lambskin
Moses basket (try to borrow one)

What you and baby can live without
Wipe warmers
Baby walker (unless you own a ballroom)
Bath thermometer (use your elbow)
Lotions and potions (warm water will do)
A womb bear
A solid night's sleep!

Most of the items listed in baby catalogues, from the vibrating seats to the womb bears and baby-wipe warmers, are non-essential luxuries which will only be used for a few months. Don't take my word for it; ask parents what they found useful and redundant. Question each purchase – is it essential? And assume all gadgets and gizmos are cons until proved otherwise.

The only items to buy new are the car seat and the cot mattress. This is for safety reasons. A second-hand car seat may have been in a car accident, weakening its protection. Similarly, research suggests that second-hand cot mattresses can increase the risk of cot death. Plan those purchases ahead so that you can take advantage of sales. Shop around for the best price. Use a cheaper online retailer like kiddicare.com to make the actual purchase and you could also use dealtime.co.uk to compare prices.

Beg, borrow and birthdays

When you first announce you're pregnant, tell the world you want hand-me-downs. Good friends would love to lend you items that are gathering dust in their attic. Colleagues and acquaintances, especially if their families are complete, will be keen to pass on unwanted baby stuff.

This is often a chance to obtain all those nice-to-have baby items that you don't really need, like a Moses basket, an all-singing, all-dancing bouncy chair and a baby bath. I don't know any parents who list these items as essentials but they'd all love to free up some space in their cupboards and pass them on to a new family.

Once you know what you're going to be able to borrow, you may find friends and family begin asking you what you would like as a gift for the baby. If you're asked the question it's worth being honest and saying what you need. People will buy the baby gifts and without direction it will be yet another tiny, expensive outfit that will only fit for about four weeks.

Often the most useful gift is a contribution towards more expensive items like the car seat or cot mattress. Many parents and in-laws like to make a contribution towards a big item and this can be a huge financial help, even if you buy it second-hand.

All families and friends are different, but if you don't think yours would take offence, some of the larger nursery retailers like Mothercare and John Lewis offer a gift list service for new parents. It's just like a wedding list. I didn't have one, but I know some friends were able to use a gift list to buy larger items. Their family were pleased to be able to buy baby stuff that was really wanted.

When the baby is born it's likely you'll receive lots of unwanted gifts. Most retailers will let you exchange unworn items. Mothercare even gives you credit onto a gift card so that you can return at a later date for 'free' shopping. So keep the labels on and don't throw away any hangers or packaging if you think you'd like to swap an item.

Resourceful shopping

Use other parents and the experts in nursery stores to research your nursery items. You can then buy second-hand armed with as much knowledge as possible. There are a number of different places where you can buy baby goods second-hand, some online and some on the high street:

1. **Charity shops.** This is often one of the cheapest places to buy nursery items, although you're less likely to pick up well-known brands here.
2. **Small ads.** Look out for ads in your local shops, in local newspapers and on the local sections of websites like freecycle.com and gumtree.co.uk.
3. **Specialist baby websites.** Mumsnet.com, netmums.co.uk, ukparenting.co.uk often have classified sections. Nappyvalley.co.uk is a local online marketplace for nearly new baby items.
4. **eBay.** The online auctioneer has a huge selection of nursery items for sale. Sometimes, the auction system enables you to pick up a real bargain; sometimes, the excitement means you pay over the odds.

5. **Second-hand baby sales.** The National Childbirth Trust (NCT) and other local parenting groups often hold second-hand sales in church halls. They can be a wonderful source of bargains.

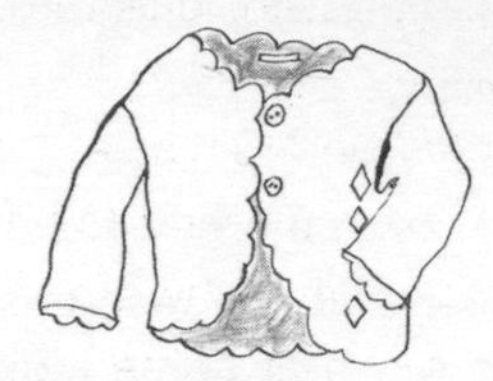

Tips on buying from charity shops

Specialist children's charity shops like The Shooting Star Children's Hospice, Save the Children or Barnardo's are often a good place to start, as parents seem to be more likely to donate their nursery items here.

Visit stores in more affluent areas where the quality of donations may be higher. Charity shops are a great source for plastic toys and board books. They can also sell larger items like pushchairs, high-chairs, travel cots and cots, although these will be snapped up fast.

Visit them regularly as the good stuff sells fast and the turnover of stock is swift. Some charity shops will let you put your name on a waiting list for desirable items like pushchairs and travel cot. They'll then give you a call when something suitable comes in.

Visit charity shops in affluent areas and visit them as regularly as possible as they have fast stock turnaround. Don't hoard too-large-sizes and too-grown-up buys just because they're cheap. Buy things for now and pass them back when you're finished.

Annabel, mum of Molly

Tips on buying from second-hand sales

Local NCT nearly new sales are a wonderful chance to stock up on quality clothes and equipment for not much money at all. In the last sale I went to, I bought a trike for £5 (£50 new), a wooden truck for £2 (£25 new), some wooden blocks for £3 (£15 new), a babycarrier rucksack for £25 (£100 new) and some clothes. Check out www.nctpregnancyandbabycare.com for lists of your local sales. You should also look out for children's second-hand sales in church halls and nurseries.

The first time I attended an NCT sale, I was shell shocked. I was about eight months' pregnant and my husband, Simon, was so intimidated by the hordes of pushy buyers that he had to wait in the car. So now I leave him at home looking after Rosie. The sales tend to be quite boisterous affairs, full of bargain-hunting elbows, so be prepared. The first time I only managed to buy a couple of babygros, but once Rosie was born I was able to attack them with more confidence.

Take your budget in cash so you don't spend more than you need. Make a list of what you're looking for and be really focused. The bigger items sell fast, so go for those before you buy clothes and toys. Arrive early so you can be first in the queue. Make a list of seasons and your baby's age so you can buy clothes for them to grow into. There's no point buying a snowsuit for a twelve-month-old if it's going to be a scorching summer when they reach their first birthday. Try to bargain. They can only say no. If you're buying a few items you might be able to knock down a few pounds or so. Check the condition of the item, check labels in clothes, check for missing items in toys.

If there's something specific you want or need, scan the room and try to find your item before someone elbows you out of the way. If you can, leave the baby at home. Remember to be nice to vendors, they're mostly mums themselves, but do not melt and pay more when they tell you; 'I can hardly bear to part with that . . .' Take cash with you; mostly that's all people will accept and it means you can set yourself a spending limit. Haggle – especially if you're buying more than one item from the vendor.

Annabel, mum of Molly

Tips on buying from eBay

eBay is a useful resource for new parents. As well as providing a marketplace to buy and sell items it also acts as a barometer on value. Use eBay to gauge the value of second-hand products; it will ensure you don't overpay.

Although eBay can be a source of good-value items, use with caution. The excitement of the auction often leads plenty of second-hand baby stuff to sell for 90 per cent of its retail price plus postage, which then becomes more expensive than buying from the shop in the first place.

Also, if you're tempted to buy something, check out the resale value on eBay. If the resale value is high it may be worth buying new and then reselling later. If the resale is low, buy it straight from eBay.

When you're preparing to make a big purchase email any queries to the seller to make sure you know as much about the product as possible. Gather information about the condition of the product, to ensure you're not disappointed. If you want to get a bargain it's worth bidding your maximum offer for something towards the end of the auction. That way you won't inflate its value too early on.

Decide beforehand how much you'd be prepared to pay for an item. I often bid with only ten seconds to go! In my opinion (unless you have no access to supermarkets and cheap new kids' clothing), it's just not worth buying the cheap labels on eBay. When you're buying toys and equipment always check if they come with any packaging or instructions. That can be important for safety issues and useful for age recommendations.

Annabel, mum of Molly

Tips on selling on eBay

If you've got some time to spare while your baby is sleeping, selling things on eBay can be the perfect way to make some extra cash. Providing you've got a digital camera, a computer and an internet connection, you can do it from home. It's an effective way of decluttering your home and enables you to make some cash from unwanted gifts so that you can buy things you really need.

If you have the space to stash them somewhere, keep all the hangers, packaging and instructions for baby clothes, toy and equipment, as this will help when selling them on eBay. Take clear pictures of the items – this will entice more potential buyers to click on your auction.

One of the most important aspects of running a successful eBay auction is to ensure it ends at a good time for your customers. Many auctions go horribly wrong because they end at 2 a.m., when no one is around to bid. When you start the auction think carefully about when you want it to end. Around lunchtime on a weekday or early evening between 7.30 and 9 p.m. is often a good time for new parents.

Research postage costs before setting a price. You don't want to be stung by the Post Office for a £10 postage fee when you've only charged your buyer £2.

Coupon queen

You may have shunned loyalty cards and coupons in the past, but these schemes can generate huge savings as well as a constant stream of free samples. One of my friends has saved enough Tesco Clubcard loyalty points to holiday in the new Center Parcs in France. Another has cashed in all kinds of useful free samples, from a nappy-changing bag to jars of baby food, baby wipes and bottles.

Sign up for Pampers, Bounty and Boots parenting clubs on the internet. You will get good vouchers for nappies and free samples for things like a weaning spoon, toothbrush and toothpaste.
Marcela, mum of Elly

Most of the big retailers and baby manufacturers, from the nappy companies to the formula milk and baby food producers, have their own loyalty schemes. If you don't mind volunteering your address and some personal information, you'll be sent more money-off vouchers and free samples than you know what to do with. Bounty, Boots, Tesco, Huggies and Pampers are just a handful of the parenting clubs on offer. They also send their members relevant magazines and pamphlets all about bringing up baby.

Finally

The easiest way to have a baby on a budget is to stay immune to the marketing messages from the baby industry. When you're buying anything don't always go for an item just because it is labelled 'baby' or 'maternity'. This often leads to a price premium. Play the baby industry at its own game by joining loyalty schemes for free stuff and money-off coupons, by becoming a savvy seller of baby brands and a wise buyer of second-hand baby items.

Being resourceful isn't just about saving money; borrowing, recycling and, especially, making baby things, are some of the most satisfying ways to opt out of today's disposable consumer culture. Use your maternity leave to fulfil some creative urges by crafting, customising, recycling, mending and making do.

CHAPTER TWO

Blooming

Make yourself a bandeau out of remnants – just get a nice piece of material about a foot wide that fits comfortably around your waist and either tie the ends or fasten with some poppers or Velcro. French mums do this all the time and it covers up the bulge if you're not wearing maternity clothes.

Becca, mum of James and Joseph

Pregnancy has traditionally been a time for indulgence, a chance to pamper and rest while you can. All these things are possible on a budget, too, with a little work. By swotting up on your rights and ensuring you understand what benefits you'll receive when pregnant and with your small baby, you'll be well prepared for the months ahead.

There's a whole new world of stuff you didn't even know existed until you've got a bump. The car seat-belt extender, the bump cushion, the maternity belt, the special pregnancy massage tool, the expensive, extensive wardrobe, not to mention numerous lotions and potions that promise to snap your body back into shape as soon as you've given birth. Needless to say, most of these items are not necessary at all, and if they are there's normally a cheaper solution.

Blooming essentials

Must-haves

Maternity jeans
V-shaped pillow
Bump bandeau
Long, stretchy vests
Big knickers
Raspberry leaf tea
Pineapple

Naughty but nice

Hot Milk maternity bra and matching knickers
A masseur!
A weekly hot spicy curry
Daily cream teas

What you can live without

Car seatbelt extender
Belly casting kit
Sound fetal Doppler (to listen to baby yourself)

Your maternity rights and benefits

Maternity rights mean that there's no need to rush straight back to work when your baby is born, even if money is tight. If you're in full-time employment, earning above a certain threshold, you will be paid at least £117.18 a week for thirty-nine weeks under statutory maternity pay. It's the legal minimum. Women who are self-employed, unemployed or have changed jobs during pregnancy can claim maternity allowance, which is also £117.18 a week.

Your Blooming Rights

- 26 weeks ordinary maternity leave, 26 weeks additional maternity leave
- 39 weeks statutory maternity pay at £117.18 minimum a week
- Paid time off to attend antenatal appointments and classes
- Free medical prescriptions and dental treatment
- £190 health-in-pregnancy grant. Go to direct.gov.uk/money4mum2be

Maternity benefit explained

Maternity benefit is called Statutory Maternity Pay, or SMP, by the government. There are just two criteria you need to fulfil in order to be able to claim:

1. You have been employed by the same employer without a break for at least twenty-six weeks by the twenty-fourth week of your pregnancy. (Part weeks count as full weeks.)

2. You are earning before tax an average of £90 a week. This is the amount you have to earn before you actually start paying National Insurance anyway.

Maternity benefit is paid for a continuous period of up to thirty-nine weeks, so the equivalent of nearly ten months' paid leave. You are entitled to basic maternity benefit even if you decide not to return to work and you can't be asked to repay it.

For the first six weeks you will be paid 90 per cent of your average weekly earnings and for the remaining thirty-three weeks you will be paid a standard rate or rate equivalent to 90 per cent of your weekly rate, whichever is lower. In 2008–9 the standard rate is £117.18 a week. This is the bare minimum that you will receive while on maternity leave, and many employers offer more favourable benefits, so talk to your HR team about what's on offer.

Step-by-step guide to maternity leave

As a pregnant employee you are entitled to a whole year off work, divided into twenty-six weeks' Ordinary Maternity Leave and a further twenty-six weeks' Additional Maternity Leave. Bear in mind that if you take the whole year off, that will leave around thirteen weeks of unpaid leave.

When you're around twenty-one weeks' pregnant you'll be given a certificate by your midwife or doctor called the MATB1. Give your employer a copy of this certificate as it provides evidence of when your baby is due.

When you're ready, tell your employer that you're pregnant, which is normally after the first scan, and should not be later than twenty-three weeks of your pregnancy. They'll also want to know when the baby is due and when you want your maternity leave to start. It's up to you when you start your leave; it can be from twenty-eight weeks of pregnancy. You can change this date as long as you give them twenty-eight days' notice.

Your employer is allowed to make contact with you during your leave, as long as it's not unreasonable. You may want to talk to them anyway about returning to work and they must keep you informed of any relevant promotions or job vacancies. You can also work for up to ten days during your maternity leave, which can be handy if you want to keep your hand in and earn some extra cash.

You can change the date of your return to work as long as you inform your employer eight weeks in advance. If you decide not to return to work at the end of your maternity leave, you are entitled to continue to receive your full amount of statutory maternity leave and pay. However, if your company offers more favourable maternity benefit read the small print, as you may have to return some of it if you don't go back. If you decide not to go back you'll need to give them the same amount of notice as you would if you were resigning under different conditions, which tends to be one month.

Dress your bump on a budget

While some women bloom during pregnancy, others find it a trial and feel frumpy. That's why it's worth investing in just one pretty dress that will make you feel on top of the world. The long, floaty maxi dresses currently in vogue are well-suited to pregnant ladies, accentuating your cleavage and bump, and you may be able to buy a stretchy one that will grow with you. As you get larger, dresses feel more comfortable than skirts or trousers because they don't press on your expanding bump.

Ghost dresses, though pricey, can be snapped up in the sales and will last you well once the baby's born as they're stretchy, machine washable and dry very quickly. I splurged on a black, soft jersey cowl-neck dress from Gap Maternity. I've continued to wear it regularly since Rosie has been born, so it was a good investment.

Customise, customise, customise

During the early days of pregnancy, you'll be able to wear a lot of your own clothes. It's just a question of customising them. Items like wrap-around dresses, smock tops, tunic tops, dresses and long tops made from stretchy material or anything with an elasticated waistband will become staple items in your maternity wardrobe.

With the fashion for smocks recently, I managed to get away without buying too many pregnancy tops. I bought things from the normal Top Shop sale rail that lasted right till the end just because they were baggy and floaty.
Amy, mum of Seth and Agnes

Invest in a couple of long, stretchy vest tops; you can wear these underneath your normal tops to stop your tummy peeking through. By the end of my pregnancy my normal-sized tops were beginning to look like crop tops pushed upwards by my huge bump, but I covered my tummy with long vests. You can achieve a similar effect by making your own bump bandeau, a wide piece of material to wrap around your bump. Expensive maternity wear shops sell these snazzy bits of kit for £30, but you can easily make one yourself.

Long cheap vest tops (you can get the tall size in Top Shop) were good. You can wear them under your normal clothes to cover your midriff and it will save you buying maternity clothes for that bit longer.
Abs, mum of Mae

The elastic-band trouser extension

In the early days, favourite jeans and trousers get a longer life by opening the top button – you can always hide the waistband with a longer top. Then you can start using the elastic-band method:

1. Thread the elastic band through the button-hole of your jeans.
2. Thread one end of the elastic band through the other end of itself and pull tight. This will attach the band to your jeans leaving the other end as an open loop.
3. Wrap the open loop of the elastic band around your button. You now have an extra one to two inches added to your waistband.

The essential blooming wardrobe

There will be a few essential maternity items you are going to have to buy, but remember you don't have to buy them new. I had one pair of jeans that I wore daily with oversized tunics and a stretchy, long black jersey dress that I smartened up with accessories and cardigans.

Pregnant women vary drastically in size. Some of my friends had tiny bumps and were able to wear tunic-style dresses and leggings right till the end of their pregnancies. (I did not fall into that category . . .)

Don't bother buying seasonal maternity clothes like special coats or jumpers. I wore unbuttoned coats and cardigans, with a big scarf to keep warm. Other friends wore ponchos instead of winter coats. And rather than buying a special maternity swimming costume I bared my bump in my bikini.

It's very likely that you'll still be wearing your maternity clothes once your baby is born. Very few women snap back into shape immediately and contrary to popular belief it seems to take even longer if you're breast-feeding. I was wearing my maternity jeans and some of my maternity tops until Rosie was at least six months old. That's why it's worth splashing out on at least one item.

Your maternity wardrobe will also depend on how smart you

have to look at work. If you're expected to wear a suit, for example, then you may need to look out for a smart pair of trousers or a skirt. So alter the list below depending on how smart your wardrobe needs to be. And don't forget you'll be able to use some of your existing tops over long vest tops or a bump bandeau for variety.

My wardrobe was very sparse. I would definitely recommend those comfy high-waisted numbers for lounging round the house, though I do remember I couldn't bear to take them off.

Abs, mum of Mae

Blooming wardrobe essentials

One pair maternity jeans
One black dress or black trousers or black skirt (something smart)
One pretty dress
One bump bandeau
Two long vest tops
One pretty smock or tunic top
Selection of oversized T-shirts and tops from high street
Big knickers!
Lots of accessories

Hello boys!

It's not just your bump that will be expanding, your bust will be too. For small-chested women like me, being given a brand-new cleavage is a wonderful thing; but big-busted women feel less excited. This means you may need to buy a couple of new bras. Pregnant women are not supposed to wear wired bras, as aside from the fact that your breasts feel more tender than normal, the wire can damage your milk ducts.

You can buy special maternity bras from places like Mothercare, but they're not very glamorous or sexy. They tend to look like they've been designed for ninety-year-olds, rather than pregnant women. I wasn't inspired by them at all. Instead I bought some soft, lacy Calvin Klein bras in the sales. There's a fabulous new maternity lingerie range called Hot Milk, that you can buy online, which does really pretty sets that double up as nursing bras too once your baby is born. You'll be wearing these bras all day – and night – for at least a year, so it's worth splashing out on something glamorous.

Buying oversized clothes

Today, there are a number of high-street retailers that sell good-value maternity clothes. If you can afford it, it's worth seeing what they've got for some of your staples, especially if you buy in the sales. Shops like Hennes, New Look, Gap, Top Shop, Dorothy Perkins, Next and Peacocks all have maternity ranges. Blooming Marvellous is a reasonably priced maternity-wear chain.

Depending on your size, it's often cheaper to buy tops around two sizes bigger than normal from the sales rails. Places like Matalan and Primark are great value. Some of my tall friends swear by men's jeans when they're pregnant. If you can find the right size they'll fit snugly under your bump and mean you don't have to succumb to elasticated waistband jeans.

I did buy an expensive Isabella Oliver top but it was so fussy with all the 'bandaging' you had to do that I never wore it! Hennes was my best find, as their pregnancy range is so cheap and I went to several weddings in dresses from there. Also, accessorising was my thing – I used bright scarves as belts and lots of necklaces and brooches to brighten up the usual all-black ensemble.

Amy, mum of Seth and Agnes

Be creative with sarongs, wrap-around skirts and dresses which you can wear when no longer pregnant, buy a couple of staples (i.e. one skirt, one pair trousers) which you can wear with anything and everything. Blooming Marvellous is a nationwide chain selling reasonable but stylish maternity clothes; they have regular sales and I have picked up some really pretty tops for a fiver.

Lynsey, mum of Amber

Beg, borrow and buy second-hand

It makes perfect sense to borrow and buy second-hand pregnancy clothes. Any of your friends who have had babies will be thrilled to see someone else use the maternity wear they bought. Otherwise these clothes just dwindle in a drawer somewhere. That's why it's also worth scouring NCT sales, charity shops, Freecycle and eBay for pregnancy clothes.

Buy second-hand! It's the obvious solution. Friends that I've made through having children have, with subsequent pregnancies, passed maternity dothes around the group. Everyone recognises particular pieces!

Ali, mum of Louis and Eddie

When buying second-hand check carefully for wear and tear. Although maternity clothes will only have been worn for a short period of time, they will have had a lot of wear, so make sure they're still in good condition.

There are even companies who specialise in hiring posh frocks for pregnant ladies, for example, www.doesmytumlookbiginthis.com. Don't panic buy if you need a posh frock. I squeezed my bump into some existing, floaty dresses for two weddings. Or glam up your smart work outfit with some sparkly accessories.

And . . . relax

The best piece of advice given to me when I was pregnant, and you'll be given plenty, was, 'Never stand when you can sit, never sit when you can lie down.' In your third trimester, as you swell bigger and bigger, finding a comfortable spot in bed or on the sofa will become a time-consuming preoccupation.

Towards the end of your pregnancy you may suffer from insomnia; 78 per cent of pregnant women do. This seems to happen for a lot of different reasons. First there's the baby pressing on your bladder, which leads to lots of night-time trips to the loo. Then there's the baby kicking and getting all lively at 4 a.m. It's also really tough to get comfortable in bed with a big bump. Then there's the indigestion if you had your tea too late.

When you do manage to drop off, you may be nudged awake by your partner disturbed by snoring. I developed a very noisy snoring habit when I was pregnant, perhaps because I was sleeping on my back. I think the excitement of what lies ahead leads to sleepless nights too; it makes it hard to switch off. Some people say that this sleeplessness is Nature's way of preparing you for broken nights once the baby is born.

Although it's difficult to do a rigorous exercise regime when pregnant, a brisk walk in the fresh air, a swim or some yoga will help relax you and make you feel more physically tired. Try to eat well before bedtime so your dinner is properly digested. Sip a small cup of chamomile tea, avoiding stimulants like chocolate, coffee or tea.

A hand, head and face massage using lavender oil will also aid relaxation. Mix two to three drops of lavender with two teaspoons of a base like grapeseed oil. Or drop a couple of drops into a warm bath before bed. (Lavender should be used with caution during your first trimester, although it's safe if you use it occasionally and no more than three drops at a time.)

Homeopathic remedies can help but are best prescribed by a professional. If your mind refuses to 'shut off', try one 30c tablet of the homeopathic remedy Coffea under your tongue before going to bed or if you wake in the night. Aconite is useful if you have vivid dreams and are restless, waking at the slightest sound.

The V-shaped pillow – a resourceful buy

Friends with babies may have an old V-shaped cushion to pass on. If not, scan second sources for one. It's easy to make a new pillow case if the outer covering is grubby. Or splurge on a crisp Egyptian cotton case in the sales from somewhere like the White Company. It's one of those resourceful items that is well worth buying (even new) because it's a multi-tasking pillow.

1. It will help all pregnant ladies get a better night's sleep. I used to coil it round my tummy and through my legs like a giant teddy bear to support my bump in bed.
2. It's a valuable breast-feeding companion. Propping your newborn on the pillow frees your arms and means you don't always need to find an armchair to feed in.
3. It is the perfect size and shape to prop up a baby who cannot yet sit on their own but wants to be able to sit more upright so they can have a nose around.

Pampering

It is important to pamper yourself when you're pregnant. As the birth of your baby looms closer take some time to treat yourself to a good haircut and maybe a manicure or pedicure, if that's your thing, as it will probably be a few months till you have the time and inclination to leave your baby for some more pampering.

My NCT friend Nikki was a very resourceful pregnant lady and contacted the local beauty school for some discounted pampering. These are great places to get good-value treatments from the students who are training to be beauticians. Some of the students were even prepared to make house visits so we could be pampered in our own homes.

Suddenly, being pregnant opens a floodgate of horror stories of angry, purple stretch marks across tummies, breasts and bottoms. At the time, it seems like the worst affliction imaginable, which is why the beauty industry has cleverly packaged some expensive creams to ward off the dreaded stretch marks.

Many doctors recommend drinking lots and lots of water and cutting back on caffeine to reduce your chances of getting stretch marks, as well as making sure your diet is rich in vitamins C and A, along with proteins from eggs, nuts and fish.

It's difficult to know if beauty creams work. Stretch marks do fade quite quickly into silvery lines barely visible to others, even if you think they're scored in thick purple marker pen. Do moisturise your expanding bump, but bear in mind that expensive potions and lotions will not necessarily be more effective than the cheaper creams. Cocoa butter creams, wheatgerm, almond or vitamin E oil will work just as well.

Time for a cream tea

As dinners and late nights out begin to lose their appeal, there's one new mealtime that should be honoured by all pregnant ladies – afternoon tea. There's nothing more satisfying and reviving than a nice cup of tea (herbal if you can no longer bear the normal stuff) with a scone, jam and cream. If a friend wants to take you out for dinner, ask them to take you out for afternoon tea instead. It's the best time of day for blooming women; morning sickness has passed and night-time nausea hasn't yet begun.

Once you've reached your thirty-second week of pregnancy, you may want to start sipping raspberry leaf tea as well as your regular Earl Grey. You can buy raspberry leaf tea online or in health food stores and it's widely considered to help strengthen and tone the muscles of the uterus, helping them to contract more effectively during labour.

Some research has found that taking raspberry leaf prior to delivery helps to shorten the second stage of labour by making contractions more effective. Some studies have even found that it reduces the need for an assisted delivery (like an emergency caesarean or use of forceps or ventouse).

There's been some confusion as to whether raspberry leaf can help bring labour on. This is not true. I was drinking it by the gallon when I was heavily pregnant, and Rosie was still two and a half weeks late!

Granny's scone recipe

My granny, Doris Lewis, made delicious home-made scones. Fortunately, she wrote down the recipe in a little notebook. I think scones always taste best with butter, jam and cream. If you are feeling virtuous you could skip the butter part.

230g self-raising flour
30g butter
1 egg
pinch of salt
¼ pint (142ml) sour cream

1. Sieve flour and salt into basin.
2. Rub in butter lightly with tips of fingers, to make an even crumbly mixture.
3. In separate bowl lightly beat egg and cream together.

4. Make a well in middle of the flour mixture, pour in egg and cream and mix from centre outwards using a fork and then hands to form a smooth dough.
5. Place the dough onto floured surface and knead lightly.
6. Roll out to 1½ cm thick, cut into rounds and bake on greased baking sheet in the oven for ten to fifteen minutes.

Getting ready for the actual birthday

Packing your hospital bag for the birth of your baby can be a palaver. I packed too much stuff, as usual, and after Rosie's birth when we were moved onto the ward there was barely any room for the three of us to sit and relax amidst the floating flotsam and jetsam.

Some of the redundant stuff I packed included:
A wooden massage tool – hands are fine
A special calming spritzer spray – use a cold flannel instead
Food to feed five thousand – a small packed lunch for your partner and some snacks for you is all you need
Three books – I didn't know what I might fancy reading, although it's unlikely you'll want to read anything when your baby is born
A huge toiletry bag – what was I thinking?
Massive pack of disposable knickers – they're horrible, use your own old knickers instead

The essential blooming birth kit
Two babygros for new baby
Newborn nappies (even if you prefer re-usables, disposables may be best for first meconium poo, which is like black tar)
Cotton wool for cleaning baby's bottom

Old shirt or T-shirt for birth
Nice PJs for breast-feeding and receiving visitors (don't expect to shrink immediately after giving birth)
Four or five pairs of your old 'granny knickers'
Pack of maternity towels
A good, easy book to read if you have an epidural or have to wait to be induced
Toiletry bag and towel – shampoo, shower gel, hairbrush, a bit of make-up for visitors
Packed lunch, reviving snacks and water for partner
Painkillers for partner (Simon insists I put this in as he had a migraine (!) after Rosie's birth and had to walk to a local petrol station to get some headache pills . . .)
Hot-water bottle
Mobile phone
Digital camera
Loose change for the car park, coffees and phone (the hospital car park can cost a fortune; ask your local midwife about cheaper alternatives. We were able to park on a side street for free . . .)

Once your baby is born, the adventure's just begun. And for the first time as you gaze obsessively at your newborn's every breath, you begin to understand how easy it might be to spend all your money on stuff for them. Stay strong, hold your nerve and learn the pleasures of indulging in some baby-thrift instead.

CHAPTER THREE

Nesting

When I was expecting Claudia I was determined to have Winnie the Pooh pictures in the nursery, as we didn't know which sex we were having. I found it really hard to find decent pictures and those I did find were expensive. My mum and I ended up buying some greeting cards with Winnie the Pooh and Tigger, we got some cheap frames from IKEA and they did the job perfectly! They cost me around £2 each. I saved myself a fortune and got the pictures I wanted.

Lorna, mum of Claudia and Gracie

In Western culture, decking out your first baby's nursery is as important a ritual as choosing a white wedding dress. And despite the fact that many babies don't sleep alone in their own rooms at night until they're six months old, it's a room that most new parents like to decorate before the baby's born.

Some people go crazy when decorating a nursery for their new baby. The average nursery costs around £2,628, meaning collectively British parents are spending £1.8 billion on decorating nurseries, according to research from Halifax Home Insurance. Some parents even install plasma televisions, designer furniture, rare film memorabilia and signed football shirts into their new baby's room!

These luxury nurseries are often created more for the parents' benefit than the baby's. Better to return to the days of hand-crafted mobiles, painted murals and simple nurseries. All your baby needs is a relaxing, calm place to sleep and rest. Set yourself a budget before you start to make sure you don't get over-excited about expensive wallpaper and curtains. Most of your budget will probably go on the cot. (See Chapter 5 on **Sleeping** for more information.)

Bare boxroom essentials

Must-haves

Cot
Shelves for storage
Chair (if room)
Bin with lid
Black-out curtains or blind
Chest of drawers (can double up as changing table)

Naughty but nice

Portable radio or stereo – for playing soothing music and listening to the shipping forecast during night-time feeds
A lambskin fleece

What you can live without
Plasma TV!
Bespoke art
Designer crib

The two best ways to save money when decorating a nursery are to think long-term and to think neutral. Plan for the room to last through childhood, rather than thinking of it as a nursery for a tiny baby. This should prevent you getting carried away by nursery gadgets and gizmos and ensure the decor is as interesting to a curious toddler as it is to a newborn.

The longer you can use the furniture, the better the value. Similarly, if you plan to have more than one baby it's worth holding off on the pink or blue paint. That way, the nursery won't need redecorating with the arrival of your second baby.

We painted the walls cream in Molly's nursery
so if the next baby is a boy it doesn't matter.
Annabel, mum of Molly

Nursery safety

- Keep curtain and blind cords out of baby's reach from cot and changing table
- Put plug protectors in unused electrical outlets
- Keep baby powder and other supplies out of baby's reach when changing
- If you use a night-light, make sure it's not near or touching curtains where it could start a fire

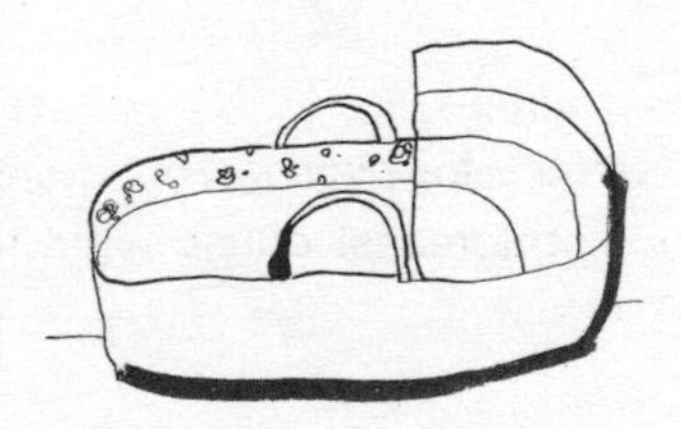

Wall to wall

Another easy way to save money when decorating a nursery is to use paint rather than wallpaper. We painted Rosie's nursery cream and jazzed it up with colourful animal curtains, a frieze and painted furniture. The alphabet frieze is made by a London artist called Judith Booth who also makes bespoke name cards. Her products can be bought online at www.notonthehighstreet.com.

If your heart is set on wallpaper, consider having a border instead, or wallpapering one feature wall. Do remember, though, that a wallpaper of pastel-coloured ducks, for example, will not be enthralling for a curious toddler, even if it suits a newborn.

If you do splash out on wallpaper it's worth finding one that's scrubbable to protect it from crayon scribbles. Very early on, when Rosie was just a few weeks old, she projectile pooh-ed onto her nursery wall, door and cream carpet. (I'm just glad we've since moved house . . .) These scenarios are impossible to imagine when you're still pregnant and decorating an immaculate boxroom.

We painted all the walls basic, cheap white and did just one wall with wallpaper. We only needed one roll so it was as cheap as chips but it made the room look that bit more special.

Emma, mum of Charlie

Stickers are also a cheap and easy way to brighten up a room and make it more interesting. Retailers like B&Q, Homebase and online stores like eBay all sell nursery stickers featuring licensed characters like Winnie the Pooh or generic themes like zoo animals. Pedlars catalogue and website do a funkier range with space invaders, colourful dots and flowers. An online sticker company, funtosee.co.uk, does giant stickers like murals.

These stickers can be either self-adhesive, and therefore removed at any time, or applied permanently like wallpaper. Just throwing a few of them on one nursery wall can totally transform the look of the space. The best part of these stickers is that they're much less expensive than wallpapering and are easy to change once your baby grows out of them. Mural stickers are also an ideal option if you're renting your home as most are completely removable.

Keep it simple

A cream- or white-painted nursery can be transformed with some pretty padded coat-hangers placed on the walls displaying baby clothes. Look out for antique baby clothes in car-boot sales and antique fairs to display in this way. A similar approach with vintage toys and puppets would work, too. Bare walls and ceilings can also be jazzed up with bunting, using odds and ends of fabric. Drape the bunting across the ceiling or the walls.

Make your own

Make your own padded coat-hanger
140cm x 10cm wadding or batting
Wooden coat-hanger
Needle and thread
Iron
60cm x 15cm fabric (gingham or vintage floral prints work well)
Pins
Ribbon

1. Wind the length of wadding around the coat-hanger, keeping it even. Sew the ends in place. If you want a scented coat-hanger tuck some lavender sprigs inside.
2. Iron a small seam around all edges of your piece of vintage or gingham fabric.
3. Fold the fabric around the coat-hanger, with the open edges at the top, and neatly sew the seam, gathering up each end so it curves around the hanger.
4. Wrap the hook in ribbon to cover.

Make your own bunting

Some stiff card
A coloured pencil
A ruler
A selection of different fabrics
Scissors
Pinking shears
Garden twine or string
Sewing machine and thread
Iron
Pins

1. Mark out a triangle on the stiff card, with the coloured pencil and the ruler. The base of the triangle should be 23cm, and the two sides should measure 28cm. Cut out the card triangle. This is your template.
2. Using the template, draw lots of triangles on the wrong side of the different fabrics with the pencil. Cut out the fabric triangles with the pinking shears. Take two of the matching fabric triangles and put them right sides together. Then sew around the V-shape, about ½cm from the edge.
3. Trim around the point of the triangle, close to the seam. Turn the fabric triangle the right way out and iron flat. Turn in the top edges of the fabric triangle, and press with the iron.
4. Make a whole heap of these triangles. Pin them to the garden twine, and hand sew them in place on to the twine. You can let the triangles nestle against each other, or leave a gap between each – either way looks lovely.

Paper chains are another effective way of decorating the nursery's walls and ceiling. As well as hearts and daisies you could experiment with shapes of your own. How about brightly coloured paper baboushka dolls or monsters?

Make your own hearts and flowers paper chain
Thick white card
Thick red card
Sharp scissors
Pencil
Garden twine or string
Ruler

1. Fold the card into two. Carefully stencil or draw a heart shape onto your red card with the curves of the heart at the fold.
2. Cut out the heart around the fold, being careful not to snip the heart in two. The shape should make two hearts attached at the top. Repeat to make as many hearts as you need.
3. Repeat the steps above, this time tracing and cutting simple daisy shapes from the white card. Again, the daisies should be drawn around the folded card with the top petals attached.
4. Carefully hang alternate daisies and hearts onto your garden twine or sting and hang in the room.

Discovering the Degas in you

Painting a feature wall with a mural or strong pattern will make your nursery stand out and offer hours of fascination to your baby. Don't be intimidated. Some murals are easier than others, so it's just a question of finding one you feel comfortable with. The easiest way is to use shop-bought stencils. Or you can make your own templates by tracing and pencilling outlines on the wall first to guide your paintbrush. Find inspiration from the internet or from the simple shapes in children's colouring books. Generic scenes are going to have more staying power than licensed characters.

Make your own murals

1. Choose a theme
2. Find pictures you like on the internet or in colouring books
3. Draw a pencilled grid over the picture
4. Draw a pencilled grid over your wall
5. Sketch the lines in pencil in each square
6. Start painting using sample paint pots of emulsion paint

Another method would be to copy a picture onto a transparency and then use an overhead projector to trace the outline onto the wall. It's a great idea if you can borrow an overhead projector from work.

Theme wall ideas

Easy

- Invite friends and relatives to come over and dip their hands in a bucket of paint and place their handprints on the wall. They could even sign their names underneath
- Draw hundreds of happy smiling faces with coloured markers
- Paint simple patterns like polka spots (use a pencil and a compass) or stripes

Intermediate

- Using acrylic paint a few shades darker than the wall colour, hand-paint a tree trunk and branches, then add birds and leaves. It doesn't matter if this sort of mural looks imperfect

Harder

- Under the sea – paint a seascape filled with brightly coloured fish, anemones, shells and trailing seaweed. See *The Little Mermaid* and *Finding Nemo* for inspiration
- Jungle safari – decorate walls with lions, tigers, elephants and giraffes
- Four seasons – paint a season. Spring flowers and baby animals, summer holidays on the beach, autumn leaves or a winter wonderland
- Noah's ark – paint the animals two by two
- Outer space – shooting stars, space ships, rockets and planets
- Farmyard animals – sheep, cows, pigs, dogs, ducks, chickens
- Crafty space – use blackboard paint and magnet paint to create a creative space for your baby once they're a toddler. While they're young you could decorate the space yourself with any of the above suggestions

Baby's eye view

When you're decorating it's worth remembering that your baby is going to spend a lot of time lying on their back. So perhaps the feature wall you concentrate on should be the ceiling instead?

- Paint a skyscape – paint the whole ceiling pale blue and once dry, sponge on white, fluffy clouds
- Suspend a kite or Chinese paper dragons or lanterns
- Attach some hanging rings to the ceiling and billow brightly coloured fabric through

In the frame

Plain, cream walls can also be jazzed up with framed pictures and photographs. IKEA sells cheap frames. You could also scour charity shops and paint old frames in the left-over paint from the nursery walls. Painting large contrasting blocks behind framed art makes small pieces look larger and visually pop from the wall.

We painted simple pictures of jungle animals and got canvases and painted bright letters of his name on each canvas. They sell something similar in Blooming Marvellous but it costs about £10 per letter. You can do it yourself for half the price. Also, rather than spending a fortune on decorating walls with pictures, take some pictures of the baby's family and put them up near the cot in plastic pocket holders so it can be changed frequently.

Rachel, mum of Josh

We didn't actually buy any new pictures for Rosie but used ones we already had – a giant photo of some strawberries I'd blown onto canvas and a smaller pencil drawing of a giraffe. All sorts of different pictures work well in frames.

- Your own photos of animals, nature and everyday projects
- Greeting cards, postcards or pretty wrapping paper
- Ripped-out pages from old nursery rhyme books found in charity shops
- Colour photocopies from classic children's books from the library
- Blow up your favourite photos into brightly coloured Warhol-style pop art

We just got a few posters from the local library, £1 each to brighten up the wall.

Lynsey, mum of Amber

Make your own Matisse-esque line drawings
Go online and find websites that offer free, printable colouring sheets of your favourite nursery characters or scenes. Choose basic ones without too much detail. Print them out and lay them on top of a sheet of good quality paper. (You can buy paper in sheets at art shops or Paperchase.) Trace the lines of your picture with a Biro or sharp pencil using pressure so it indents your paper underneath. Using a black marker pen, go over the indentations left from your tracing. It should leave clean lines and a simple, black outline of your illustration.

Make your own fabric painting
Using colouring books again for inspiration for simple shapes, select a very simple scene. Cut leftover, co-ordinating fabrics in your desired shapes, then hand stitch the shapes to a square or rectangular piece of contrasting fabric. Stretch the fabric over the frames used for artists' canvas and staple the fabric to the back of the frame.

Furniture

Aside from a cot it's generally best to avoid buying special nursery furniture. In terms of price, it's a bit like the difference between a white dress and a wedding dress. Nursery furniture is a lot more expensive and a lot less enduring. So avoid changing-table contraptions and opt for a low chest of drawers; use a second-hand chair rather than the expensive 'gliding' rocking chairs.

As with all other resourceful mum purchases, scour charity shops, Freecycle and second-hand furniture sales for items. If you want to buy new, IKEA has some very reasonably priced furniture. If nothing else, IKEA can be good inspiration for decorating the room and shows how much a plainly painted boxroom can be transformed with colourful furniture, small rugs and accessories.

We knew what cot we wanted and we looked on eBay and bought it for a sixth of the price. Then we bought a new mattress. The rest of the furniture came from IKEA and was very cheap. We used the top of the chest of drawers as a changing table. There's no point buying a proper changing table; after six months you won't be using it any more.

Annabel, mum of Molly

Scour antique fairs and car-boot sales for vintage nursery furniture. A second-hand antique sleigh bed could be transformed into a day bed or nursing chair until your baby grows into his toddler bed. A vintage rocking horse or antique puppet could turn a plain white room into a stylish, original nursery. Websites like carbootjunction.com and yourbooty.co.uk provide a directories of car-boot sales in local areas, while dmgantiquefairs.com lists dates and locations of fairs across the UK.

It's also worth adapting existing pieces of furniture. A plain wooden cot could be painted white for a more vintage look. To get a nice clean look when repainting an old cot, sand it down first and then wipe with a clean, damp cloth before starting to paint. You will need to to apply more than one coat.

We didn't buy anything new for Rosie's nursery. I painted a chest of drawers in multi-colours using sample paint pots. The outer casing was painted white and each of the drawers was painted a different colour. Then I swapped the brass handles for zebras, ladybirds, lions and bumble-bees. (Replacing door knobs on in-built wardrobes, cupboards and doors can make a big difference too.) For the first six months, the chest of drawers doubled-up as a changing table with a changing mat laid on the top. Then my parents gave us an old chair with arms that I could use for breast-feeding, and as Rosie got older we used it for story time, milk and lullabies before bed.

Create additional storage with shelving lined with baskets or painted or gift-wrapped shoeboxes. Brightly coloured rubber tubs make brilliant storage for clothing, nappies, toys and laundry. They can be quite pricey in designer shops but you can buy them for far less online at www.tubtrugs.com, where they come in a rainbow of colours from pistachio to primrose.

Build a row of shelves above a chest of drawers to store nappies, wipes and creams. Dress up bookshelves by backing the wall behind them with papercut pictures. Choose simple landscapes like clouds and sunshine or a city nightscape.

Hang a mobile or stick pictures underneath the bottom shelf to entrance your baby while they're having their nappy changed. As they get older and more wriggly, anything that keeps them stlll while changing will be a bonus. A mirror attached to the wall next to the chest of drawers will keep a baby entertained and happy. Or dangle some S hooks from a curtain rail above the changing station and hang different toys and interesting items from the hooks. This way you can rotate the items, changing them when your baby gets bored. Create a similar look by running an out-of-reach wire with clips or pretty clothes pegs (Pedlars.co.uk has bird-shaped pegs) for displaying treasures and postcards that you can swap and change.

Make your own – transforming a chest of drawers

Remove the handles and take the drawers out of the casing. Rub down the wood with some sand paper – this will make it easier to paint. Wipe with a damp cloth to remove any dust and dirt. Gloss or eggshell paint works best. You may have to use emulsion if you use lots of different colours with sample pots instead. Keep adding coats until the colour gets the density you want. (I painted

four coats.) I finished mine off with some clear varnish for extra gloss. Buy animal, star, flower and other novelty handles online or in DIY retailers like Homebase and B&Q. Line the drawers with wrapping paper.

Make your own cot toy bag and/or bedroom tidy

By the time your baby is around nine months old and moving around, putting some toys in their cot may give you a precious twenty minutes extra in bed in the morning. Getting up at 7 a.m. feels so much easier than 6.40 a.m. . . . The following pattern can be made into a square cot bag – or you could make a long, thin bedroom tidy to hang on the back of the door. Measure the width and height of the cot or door for bag dimensions.

Flat wadding or batting
Backing muslin or calico
Fabric for the bag back
Furnishing fabric for the pockets (animal patterns work well)
Pins
Needle and thread/sewing machine
Iron

Cut out a large square for a cot bag or a long rectangle for the bedroom door tidy to form the base of your tidy. The square should measure around 45cm x 45cm, and the long rectangle should measure 22cm x 90cm, which leaves enough room for seams. Iron a hem around the four edges and sew with a sewing machine. Now the back is ready for its pockets. Cut out four square patterns from your furnishing fabric, allowing 1cm for seams. These four squares should measure 18cm x 18cm, but you may find your pockets are square-ish, rather than square if the motifs vary. Cut out four identical squares from the muslin and batting. To make the pockets, lay the muslin down first, cover with the batting and then the motif fabric. Pin the three layers of material together and either iron in a 1–2cm seam around all four edges or pin them. If you pin the seams, pin from the inside; this will make it easier to remove the pins when you sew with your machine. Sew the three layers together using the zigzag stitch on your machine. Now you need to attach the pockets to your large square back. Position them in place on the front of the fabric with pins and then sew, again with a zigzag stitch around three edges, making sure you leave the top edge open to make a pocket. Cut loops from the backing fabric 4cm wide to fit around the top of the bag and loop onto the cot or door. Fold the loops lengthwise and zigzag stitch to neaten the edges before firmly stitching them onto the tidy.

Soft furnishings

Scour second-hand shops, Freecycle and eBay for nursery curtains, cushions and material. Traditional street markets are a wonderful source of unusual fabrics, as they often sell the remnants from a designer consignment. I got great Antoni & Alison cowboy fabric at a snip in Walthamstow market in North London.

Making your own curtains and cushions can save a fortune and also means you don't have to compromise on material. Babies tend to sleep better in dark rooms so it's likely you're going to be adding black-out material to bought curtains anyway. Why not just make the whole pair from scratch? A large pair of curtains can easily be adapted to fit a smaller window. If you don't like sewing, you could always use that iron-on, sticky hemming instead.

If you haven't got your own sewing machine, borrow one from

a friend. If you like it, it may be worth looking out for one second-hand on eBay or Freecycle; you can buy a decent one new for around £100. I use an old-fashioned, hand-operated machine that used to belong to my granny.

Tips on making curtains

- Markets and eBay are all sources for good-value nursery fabrics, or buy from IKEA, John Lewis or independent material shops in the sales
- An even cheaper alternative would be to buy some plain cotton fabric and decorate with fabric paints, or sew a bright gingham border round the sides and bottom
- Look out for vintage French linen runners in antique or flea markets – they make lovely blinds
- Save on the amount of material you need by having less full curtains. This way you'll only need one and a half times the width of the window, rather than twice the width
- Hang curtains with curtain tape if you already have a curtain track or add material loops to the top of the curtain if you have a pole
- A good-sized hem of at least the size of the palm of your hand will give the curtains a heavy drop and make them look better
- Buy black-out lining from a retailer like John Lewis or online. You can buy white-coloured black-out for pale material or just use a dark lining for dark material
- If there's a radiator under the window, make sure the material rests on the window sill so the heat can still come into the room

We made a blind from a blind kit, rather than curtains, as it used less fabric.

Annabel, mum of Molly

Tips on making cushions

- ✄ Cushions are even easier to make than curtains and are a good first sewing project to grow your confidence
- ✄ Although it's more time-consuming, cushions can also be sewn by hand if you don't have a machine
- ✄ Buy material remnants for cushions; it's much better value. Or use leftover material from your curtains
- ✄ Look out for vintage silk scarf squares at car-boot sales and charity shops, to turn into cushions. Use a bright contrasting fabric for the back of the cushion
- ✄ Buy cheap cushion pads from IKEA
- ✄ You will need to wash the cushion covers regularly, so don't use unwashable fabrics like felt. The easiest opening for a cushion is an envelope. If you use a zip, you could have a different piece of material on each side
- ✄ If you make a cover slightly bigger than the cushion you can run a seam outside for a border
- ✄ Jazz cushions up by trimming with ribbon or frills, or sewing on simple shapes of animals or letters in gingham or bright contrasting felt

I wanted some nice bright cushions for the nursery. So my mum and I bought some end-of-line material, some cheap cushions and she got one of her friends to run up some cushion covers. This saved a fortune on buying ready-made nursery cushions.

Lorna, mum of Claudia and Gracie

The patterns for the two cushions and beanbag below can help you make a cosy corner in the nursery for you and your baby to enjoy books together before bedtime.

Make your own simple appliquéd cushion

Two large squares of colourful material (you can buy two remnants and have different fabric on the front and back of cushion)

2m of binding (stiff ribbon-shaped material for seams) in a contrasting colour
Remnant of contrasting fabric for motif
Cushion pad to fit dimensions of your cushion, or stuffing
Card
Pinking shears
Needle and thread
Sewing machine

1. Cut out a distinctive shape in card. Shapes like letters, apples, sheep and cupcakes work well. Use the card as a template and cut out the motif in your contrasting fabric using pinking shears.
2. Pin the motif to the right side of the front cushion cover, then sew on with zigzag stitch using your sewing machine.

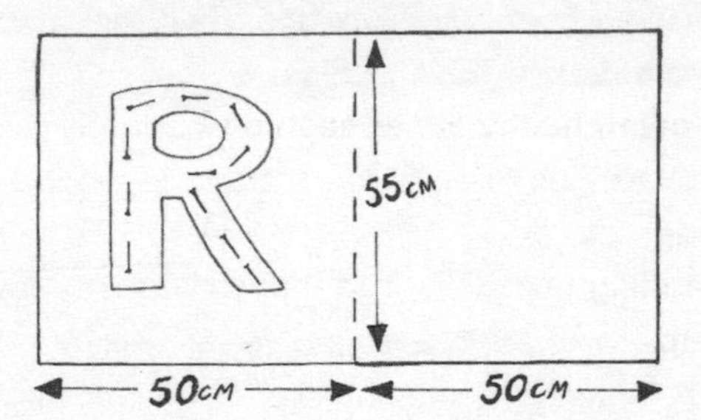

3. Next pin the length of binding around the front edges of the cushion leaving around 2cm on the outside to make a border. Again sew using the zigzag stitch on your machine.

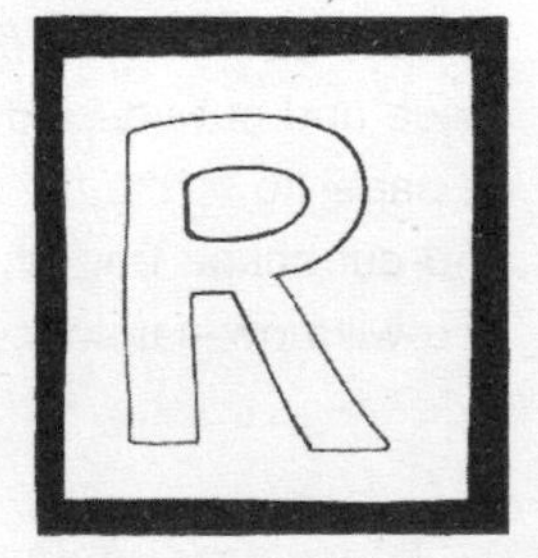

4. Pin the two large squares, right-sides together so the cushion is inside-out and hem along the three sides with a sewing machine.
5. Sew eight pieces of binding or strips of the same material around 5cm long onto the two sides of the open cushion, four on each side. These can be tied into bows to fasten the cushion cover.
6. Finally, insert the cushion cover or stuffing – if using stuffing, stitch up the seam by hand.

Make your own chunky-letter cushion
1.5m of material
2m of binding
Washable stuffing (available from haberdashery department)
Paper or card

1. Fold your material double and mark out dimensions to form a square 50 x 50cm.
2. Trace and cut your chunky letter (child's initial) onto a piece of paper to fit the dimensions of fabric. Use as a template and cut shape from the folded piece of material.
3. You will now have 2 separate fabric letters.

4. Cut out a strip of material 10cm wide and a length as long as the circumference of the letter.
5. Pin the long piece of material to the outside edges of your two letter shapes to form a 3 dimensional letter. The hems don't need to be turned inwards as the binding will neaten the seams up. Loosly tack all round the seams leaving a 10cm gap for the stuffing.
6. Iron the binding, folded in two lengthwise to make it easier to cover the hem. Again leave a gap for stuffing. With a machine sew on the binding to close up seams.
7. Stuff the cushion and sew up the gap. (This cushion does not have a removable cover so it's best to use a bold colour that won't get grubby easily.)

Make your own beanbag
One bag of polystyrene balls for stuffing
3m lining (use cheap material like calico or an old sheet)
3m colourful material
One zip, 50cm long
Sewing machine

1. Cut out two circles 46cm diameter and a long piece of material 70cm x 200cm from the lining material. Cut out three identical shapes in your colourful outer fabric.

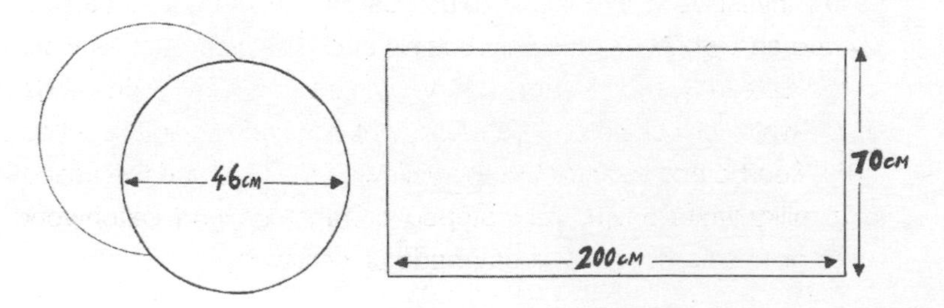

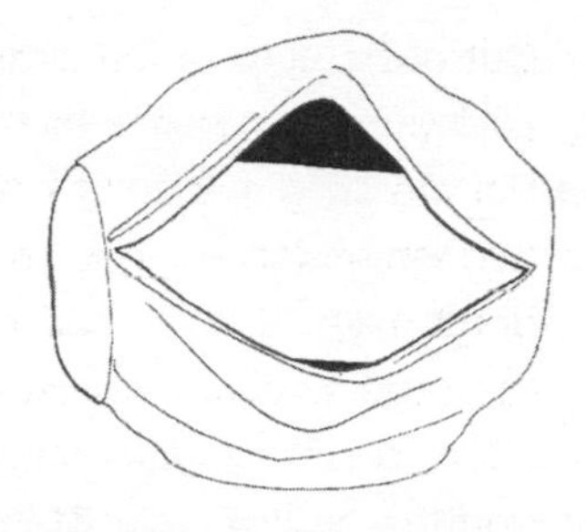

2. Sew the lining into a tube shape with the circles placed at each end. This doesn't have to be precise as it will never be seen, and once you've placed the polystyrene balls inside, it doesn't need an opening.
3. Sew the outer material together, inside-out to keep it neat and tidy, leaving an open seam along the straight edge for the zip. Sew the zip to attach the gap.

Flooring for the nursery

The nursery floor will get a lot of wear and tear, so think twice before investing in expensive, plush carpets. If there's no carpet, sanded and white-painted floorboards and rugs work just as well.

For a clean Scandinavian country-style nursery paint floorboards an off-white or use a lye treatment, which is when lye is applied to the floorboards to draw out the yellow of the pine and then oiled to a milky-white finish. Add striped or rag rugs and patchwork quilts or cushions to cover day beds or chairs.

A stylish effect can be achieved by painting rug-like patterns onto the floorboards themselves. Choose your colours carefully and paint a border around the outside of the room and/or a big circle in the middle.

Often using several small rugs can be more economical than buying one big rug. Again, IKEA has got all sorts of nursery rugs, from fish to big red hearts. Beyondfrance.co.uk sells beautiful vintage linen rag rugs for under £50.

Night-lights

Soft lighting is important in a baby's nursery. It enables you to do night-time nappy changes without waking the baby up too much and also feeding them before they go to sleep. In Rosie's first box-room, we opened the door wide to let the light from the landing flood in. A dimmer switch would also do the trick. We've since bought a small and very cheap lamp from IKEA. Energy-efficient light bulbs are perfect because they tend to be dimmer.

In the main light in the room, paper lampshades can be adapted to create a bespoke nursery lampshade. Use coloured paint to brighten them up with spots, stripes and swirls. Bold, bright colours will make the light shine less brightly. Or look out for big Chinese lanterns in Chinatown or online.

Make your own house doorstop

If, like us, you'll be relying on the hallway light to provide some soft, night-time lighting, this pattern will help prop open the nursery door.

A selection of fabric remnants – felt or other brightly coloured remnants
A bag of rice
Needle and thread (ideally a sewing machine)

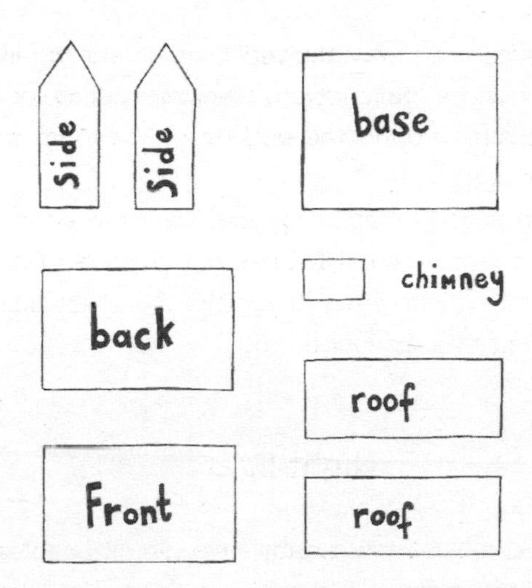

1. Cut out two equal sizes of fabric for the front and back, equal sizes for the roof, equal sizes for the sides and then one piece of fabric for the base and one piece for the chimney – as shown.
2. Fold your chimney piece in half right side in and stitch down each long side.
3. Turn right side out and fill with a small amount of stuffing so it can stand upright on the house.
4. Take your two roof pieces with right sides facing and sandwich the chimney between. Stitch the two roofs together with chimney poking out the top.

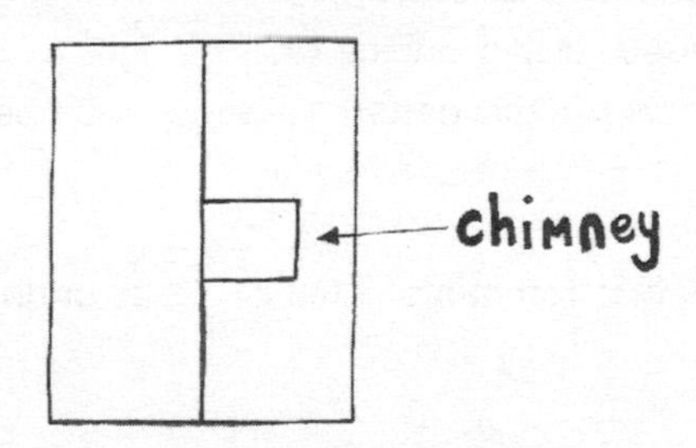

5. Take your front piece and, right sides facing, stitch long edge to long edge to one of the roof pieces. Repeat with the back piece on the other side.

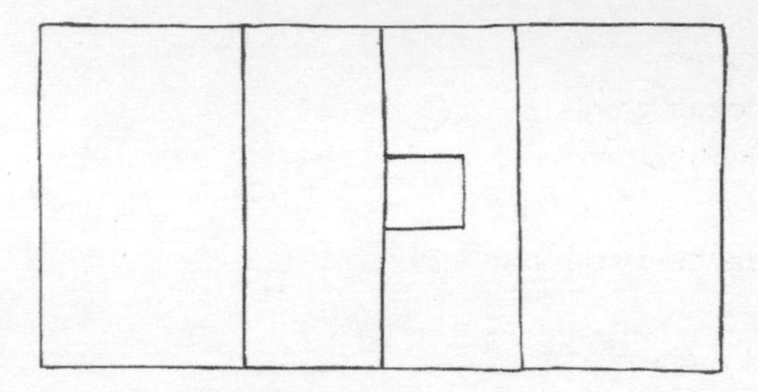

6. Take one of your side pieces and pin and sew to short edge of front piece, right sides facing.
7. Swivel your fabric so the slope of the side piece joins the adjacent short side of the roof piece. Repeat on the other side.
8. Turn the right way round and repeat with the other side piece. You now have a faceless house.

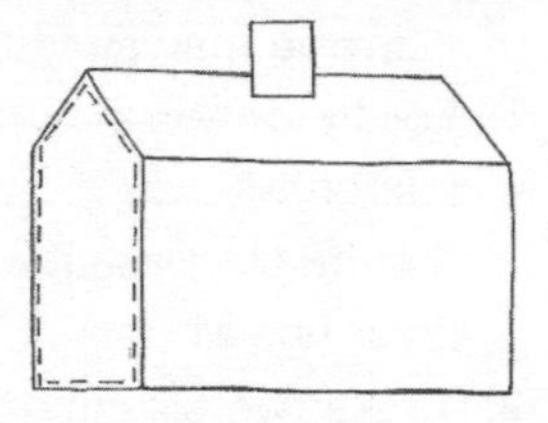

9. Add windows and doors with contrasting fabrics; you could use stitches to add window panes and door panels.
10. Turn house inside out again. Pin and sew the base piece to the bottom of the house, leaving a gap to turn the house right way around. Fill with rice and stitch the opening.

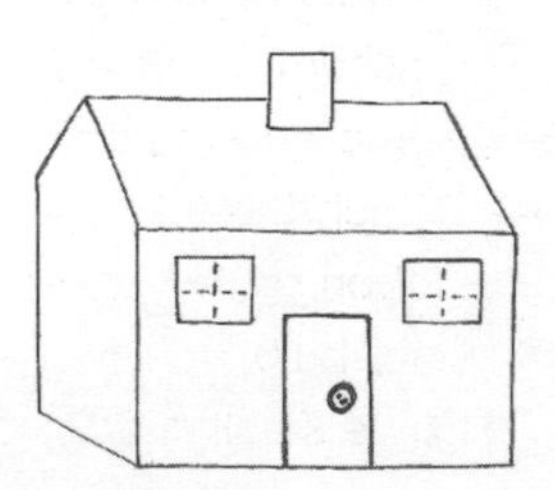

Make your own hot-air balloon lampshade

This lampshade works especially well if you've decided to paint a blue, fluffy cloud sky on the ceiling.

Paper lantern
Water colour paints
Margarine tub
Ribbon
Brown parcel paper and string

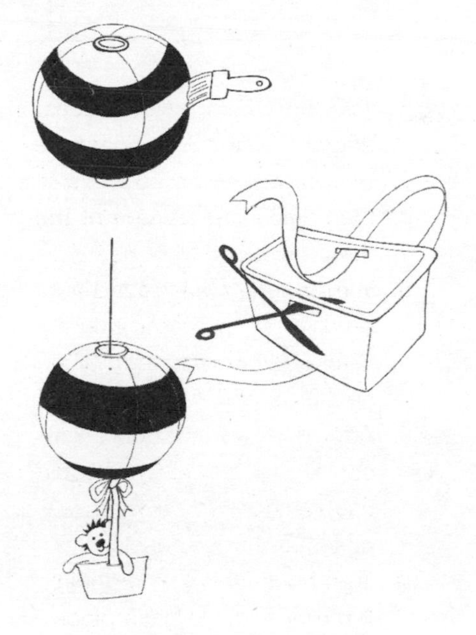

1. Paint a cheap paper lantern in bold stripes or patterns like a hot-air balloon. Use pale colours as these will allow the light to shine through.
2. Cover a margarine tub neatly with brown paper and string – this will be the basket of your hot-air balloon.
3. Make two slits in the top sides of the tub with some sharp scissors to thread some ribbon through.
4. Attach the tub to the bottom of the lantern by tying the ribbon to its wire frame, ensuring it hangs well below the light bulb.
5. Place small cuddly toys or peg dolls in the tub as passengers.

CHAPTER FOUR

Beginning

During the first three months, I was so grateful to have food in the freezer courtesy of my mum! She asked me at the time if there was anything she could do and voilà, eight meals or more in freezer containers. It felt a bit weird asking for food as a gift but, hey ho, needs must!
Emma, mum of Charlie

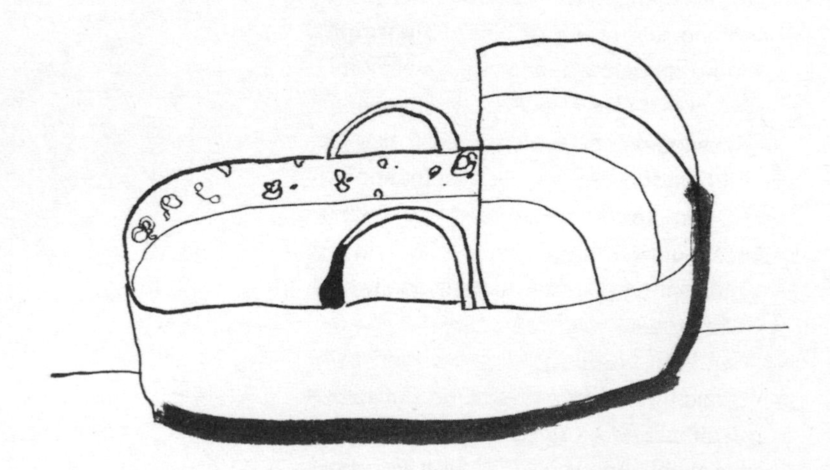

The Babymoon

Ayurvedic tradition in India encourages a new mother to stay at home and be pampered for the first twenty-two days after giving birth. She is cooked for, visitors are restricted and she is sheltered. In Indonesia, most women don't leave the family home or resume their regular household duties until the baby is forty-two days old. Then in Thailand, women who've just given birth are nursed by their mothers and mothers-in-law as they rest.

It sounds blissful. However, many modern women in the Western world have a much more hectic time when their newborn arrives. From the constant relay of visitors requiring cups of tea and slices of cake, to internal pressures that you need to be out and about carrying on as normal. When my mum gave birth in the late Seventies, she stayed in hospital for two weeks, a restful time she reminisces about, when she was fed good meals and cared for by a strict midwife who restricted visitors.

It's tricky when family, friends and colleagues are desperate to see the new baby, but try to make your first six weeks with your newborn as restful and peaceful as possible. It's a chance for you to all get to know each other. Day will merge into night and you'll need daytime naps to make up for being awake at night. The best way of feeling rested after a disturbed night's sleep is to sleep when the baby sleeps during the day. Sleeping and eating are really important for milk production, too, if you're breast-feeding. Once you start breast-feeding, you're stuck where you are, so make sure you have a big bottle of water, some snacks, the phone, TV remote, books, magazines at your fingertips – whatever you might need for the next forty minutes or so.

Be prepared to spend the first few weeks sitting feeding your baby a lot, if breast-feeding. Have phone, drink and snacks to hand. I also rented some good films and DVD box sets for cluster

feeding, when you breast-feed frequently in the evening, in the hope the baby will sleep longer at night.
Annabel, mum of Molly

In the very early days when I was literally up most of the night (and still breast-feeding), I used to have my Mozart in the CD player ready, snacks for me, bottle of water to hand, blankets for us both, the remotes to hand and fresh nappies nearby so I didn't need to move Charlie around too much.
Emma, mum of Charlie

Babymoon essentials

It's surprising how little kit you need in the first six weeks of your baby's life, especially if you don't go out that much, resting at home instead. Until Rosie was around four weeks old she wasn't very fond of her buggy. It also took her a few weeks to be persuaded to sleep in her Moses basket, as she much preferred to sleep on me or Simon instead. The later chapters focus on all the different kit in much more detail, from cots to buggies and baby baths. In the meantime, here's a short list of essentials.

Must-haves
V-shaped pillow
Baby sling (see p108, Make your own sling.)
Cosy blanket
Nice pyjamas for you
Lavender essential oil
Nutritious meals in the freezer
Lots of tea bags
Cabbage!

Naughty but nice
Cake and full biscuit tin
Guinness
A stack of your favourite DVDs

You and baby can live without
A constant stream of visitors
Expensive swaddling blankets; use a sheet or normal blanket

After Charlie was born my mum bought me some new 'relax at home' wear from Matalan. They were as cheap as chips but I was too big for my normal clothes. I was desperate to feel nice and not just fat so it was lovely to have a couple of pairs of what now feel like boring trackie bs and tops. At the time, they were the best and most comfortable thing in my wardrobe.
Emma, mum of Charlie

Sustenance

When you're impatiently waiting for the baby to be born fill the freezer with one or two meal portions of your favourite home-made food. My freezer was chock-a-block with lasagne, lamb curry, spaghetti bolognese, chilli and fish pie. These meals are fantastic for those evenings when it's hard to get the baby to settle and you're doing everything one-handed.

Breast-feeding makes you feel starving, and sleep deprivation even more so, so your appetite will be huge. You'll be wanting hearty meals like chunky soups, sausage and mash or steak and chips, even if you used to be more of a salad girl. Better to eat healthy, home-cooked food than lots of takeaways and ready meals.

First time round I stacked the freezer with pre-prepared meals like stews, tomato-based pasta sauces (I just fried some onion and garlic and mushrooms in olive oil, added some tinned tomatoes, tomato purée and dried herbs and if I had any other veg lying about like courgettes or carrots I'd pop that in too, simmer it for about twenty mins and then blend it), casseroles and soups (chuck some red lentils into a pot, add water, a stock cube, some carrots, an onion or leek and a couple of cloves of garlic and simmer for about thirty mins and then blend) in those little tin-foil dishes which could easily be re-used or just chucked away.

Lorna, mum of Claudia and Gracie

Recipe for baby cake

This cake was made by one of our neighbours when Rosie was born. It is precisely what you feel like in those first few exhausting days after having a baby – sweet, filling, energy-giving and nourishing.

2 apples, peeled and sliced
185g dates
125g butter
250g caster sugar
225g plain flour
1 beaten egg
1 tsp bicarbonate of soda
1 tsp vanilla essence
Topping – 60g sugar, 60g butter, 70g desiccated coconut, 2.5 tsp milk
Greased 22cm spring form tin

Soak the dates and bicarbonate of soda in a cup of water for one hour. Preheat the oven to 180 degrees C or Gas mark 4. Cream the butter and sugar together. Add the beaten egg. Fold in the flour, vanilla essence and diced apple. Mix all the other ingredients and add the dates. Press into a greased 22cm spring form tin and bake for forty minutes. Combine the topping ingredients in a saucepan and stir until the sugar has melted.

Pour the topping over the baked cake and bake for another ten to twenty minutes.

Once Simon had gone back to work, I used to find myself missing lunch and filling up on biscuits or crisps instead. Then he started making me an easy-to-eat packed lunch the night before, which really helped.

Stock up on easy-to-eat food like breakfast cereal, bagels and bananas, so you've always got something you can grab and eat on the go, even if your baby wants to be carried all day. This will save money and stop you from buying sandwiches when you're out walking.

I had loads of cereal in the cupboard and stacks of shop-bought pancakes to get me through tiredness and outrageous hunger pangs which breast-feeding created!
Lorna, mum of Claudia and Gracie

The first day Simon went back to work, my friend Sarah came to visit armed with lunch and home-made biscuits.

Sarah Mac's mackerel salad
Mix a bag of watercress and/or spinach with some flaked smoked mackerel, one peeled diced orange and a handful of pumpkin or sunflower seeds. Add lemon juice and olive oil for dressing and serve with bread if hungry.

Visitors

Although you're desperate to introduce your new baby to friends and family, indeed anyone at all, hosting the constant stream of visitors can be exhausting. Aside from close family, we didn't have any visitors for three weeks. Then once Simon had returned to work and I needed more company, my friends started making an appearance.

Other couples use their time in hospital to host visitors. This can be a good way of making short, sweet introductions to your newborn because you can always blame a strict midwife if you ask visitors to leave after thirty minutes.

We banished visitors for the first two weeks, apart from family, and when they did start coming, I always accepted help if it was offered and also explained the need to disappear for a sleep in the evening if people were there a while. Everyone always understands.

Emma, mum of Charlie

My friend Lynsey took a very resourceful approach to guests. While pregnant she made it very clear to family and friends that all visitors had to bring some kind of home-made food with them. When Amber was born, the well-briefed guests came along bearing useful gifts like soup, lasagne and stew for the freezer, carrot cake and muffins.

Accept help from anyone who offers, especially if they offer to bring you a lunch or dinner. Liz, my mother-in-law's beef and vegetable stew was just what I needed to keep me and the milk going in the first week. Be firm and clear with everyone about what you expect and tell them it's time to leave when it is.

Caroline, mum of Mae

When Rosie was about eight weeks old and beginning to settle better in the evenings, my friends Liz and Jack came round for dinner. What was wonderful was that they brought food and cooked dinner for us. It was a delicious lamb stew served on ciabatta with a splodge of crème fraîche, welcome respite from all the lasagne and spaghetti bolognese in the freezer. Even better was the fact we didn't have to do a thing. They even did the dishes before they left.

Liz's lamb casserole

Use lamb neck fillet, chop off the excess fat and then cut into chunks. First fry an onion in a tablespoon of olive oil: once cooked lay it in the bottom of a casserole dish. Then brown the lamb in the same pan. Once it's browned you add 2 tbsp of flour and 2 tbsp of paprika and fry together for a bit. Then you lay the lamb on top of the onions in the casserole and pour over one can of tomatoes and 2 glasses of red wine. Then you cook for 1½ to 2 hours until the lamb goes melty. Serve on toasted ciabatta rubbed with raw garlic and top with crème fraîche and parsley.

Some of my other friends with newborns purposefully wore pyjamas during visits from friends in the first few weeks. This ensures visitors don't overstay their welcome and also help as much as possible. Before you go into labour try to make sure you've got plenty of tea bags and packets of biscuits for visitors. When they arrive point them in the direction of the kettle; they won't mind making their own tea.

The constant stream of visitors was exhausting! I would sit on the sofa making chat when really I should have been in bed asleep – especially when some visits would be several hours long . . . so don't be afraid to point people in the direction of the kettle; fill a jar with biscuits that they can help themselves to and if they offer to tidy things away then let them! And accept all offers of help to do cooking, washing, ironing, etc., for you. I think it's easy to forget – especially if breast-feeding – how important it is to have your rest.

Lorna, mum of Claudia and Gracie

Road to recovery

It's important to be gentle with yourself when your baby is first born because aside from bonding with your baby and establishing feeding, you may also be feeling a bit bruised and sore from the birth. Arnica tablets, the homeopathic remedy, can help heal bruising and tearing after the birth: it also speeds up healing of stitches. Start taking the tablets immediately after the delivery.

There are a number of natural remedies that can help. Tucking a cabbage leaf inside each side of your bra can help to soothe sore, engorged breasts when your milk comes in. A hot flannel pressed on your breasts in the bath or before a feed can also help tenderness. Both these methods will help to ward off a bout of mastitis.

Lavender oil is wonderful, too, for head and face massage. Blend it with some rosehip or mild almond oil and massage the face, head and neck. A hand and arm massage will soothe aching arms after holding baby all day, too – and the lavender will help with stress and baby blues tearfulness.

Don't worry about the baby blues, everyone seems to get them after giving birth. One minute you'll feel ecstatically happy, the next minute you'll be crying. These symptoms normally start around three or four days after delivery, when your milk comes in, and may last several days. The baby blues normally go away around two weeks after delivery. If you or your family think you have more severe symptoms or they last longer than a few days, go and talk to your health visitor or GP in case you have post-natal depression.

Young babies do tend to have bouts of crying, when they can't seem to be settled. If your baby gets fractious in the evenings and pulls their knees up to their chests, they may be suffering from colic. Rosie had mild colic and seemed to be most unsettled from 7 p.m. to around midnight. We found that colic drops called Infacol, recommended by our midwife, helped.

We also visited a cranial osteopath when Rosie was six days old. Cranial osteopathy is a form of holistic and physical therapy that can help babies. Sometimes the experience of birth leaves newborn babies with overt or underlying pain or knock-on effects of the stress of birth, which can include colic, difficulty feeding or inability to settle to sleep.

During the thirty-minute treatment, Rosie was laid on her back on a bed while the osteopath gently stroked her head and stomach. It's hard to say if the therapy made a difference or not, but that evening Rosie slept for six hours. When I have another baby I will be visiting him again.

Your babymoon is the perfect excuse to switch off the phone, close the curtains and cocoon yourself and your new family at home. The less you do, the easier the beginning becomes. See Chapter 13, **Healing**, for more detailed information on natural remedies.

CHAPTER FIVE

Sleeping

Mae did look very cute in the Moses basket so it probably would have been hard to resist buying one for her, but it was an expensive buy for something she was only in for three months. We could have put her cot into our room from the beginning.
Abs, mum of Mae

And so to sleep

The most common question you're asked as a new parent is a loaded one. How are they sleeping? they'll ask. Well, newborn babies sleep a lot, but not necessarily when you want them to. And, obviously, everybody else's baby seems to sleep better at night than your own.

Perhaps because of this dogged focus on sleep, some new parents find themselves buying so many different places for their precious baby to go to bed in. From the Moses basket to the crib to the cot to the cot bed and travel cot, not to mention prams, carrycots and special reclining, vibrating, rocking, musical sleep chairs – some newborns are spoilt for choice.

Before you go crazy, it's worth remembering that little babies can sleep in anything. They can sleep anywhere, at any time. And so they will. It's truly surprising. Newborn babies sleep in drawers, on sheepskin rugs, on beanbags, squashy cushions, and of course their favourite place, being cuddled in your arms.

Amber spent her first night sleeping in a drawer as we didn't have a crib yet.
Lynsey, mum of Amber

Sleeping essentials

Must-haves

Cot
New cot mattress
Travel cot
Baby sleeping bag
Hand-knitted baby blanket
Sheet for swaddling
Cotton cellular blanket

Naughty but nice
Moses basket
Lambskin fleece

What baby and you can live without
All-singing, all-dancing crib
Bundles and bundles of cot linen
A womb bear!
Cot bumper
Baby monitor

The Moses basket/cot debate

Admittedly, newborn babies do look tiny in a proper cot, which is why I think many parents are determined to buy a Moses basket. Similarly, a big cot may not fit next to your bed, whereas Moses baskets can often squeeze into smaller bedrooms when a cot just wouldn't. Plus, they can be handy because you can carry them around the house, so when your baby is tiny and you want to see them all the time, you can have them next to you in the living room, kitchen, even in the bathroom!

Remember, though, that a Moses basket will probably only last your baby for around three months, less if they're big. I think Moses baskets are precisely the kind of paraphernalia that should only ever be bought second-hand or borrowed from a friend, it's a waste of money to buy one new. You won't use it for long enough.

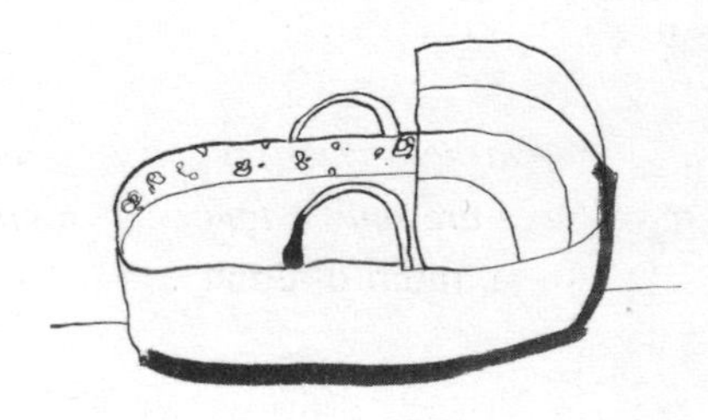

I shouldn't have had a Moses basket. £125 from Mamas and Papas and Charlie slept in it properly about six times. It still looks brand new. I would have just borrowed one and got a new mattress if I had known. But I had this thing in my head that everything had to be new!

Emma, mum of Charlie

Look out for second-hand Moses baskets in NCT sales, on eBay or advertised in your local paper. They often come with a stand that saves you from having to bend down low when you pick them up. Make sure that they're lined with cotton, or the sides of the basket can be too rough and scratchy for a little baby.

It's also worth asking friends to see if you can borrow a Moses basket or crib. Many will have fallen into the trap of buying an expensive new one and would be thrilled to see it used again. Even if they're planning on having more children, they probably won't mind lending it to you, because you won't need it for long.

Don't buy a new Moses basket. My friend lent me hers, and they use it for such a short time, it's quite easy to time-share with a friend!

Amy, mum of Seth and Agnes

We bought a second-hand Moses basket on eBay for £20 and a new mattress to fit from Mothercare for about £10. Rosie hated it. Every time she wriggled she hit the sides and it would wake her up. We moved her much more quickly than I imagined we would into her cot bed (a gift from my parents) and she seemed to sleep more soundly there.

Try to borrow a Moses basket or get one from a second-hand shop – new mattresses are only a tenner in John Lewis.

Anna, mum of Josh

And a Moses basket isn't the only option. Some friends used the carrycot attachments from their prams. You could even use a travel cot.

We used the carrycot as a Moses basket.
Marcela, mum of Elly

Another option would be to buy a crib, which is like a mini cot. They're often more expensive than Moses baskets and, again, would last a baby just six months. I think they're an expensive option, even if you buy second-hand.

The travel cot – a resourceful buy
Buy or borrow a travel cot. It's a multi-tasking sleeping station that will play many different roles during your baby's young life:

1. Use it instead of a Moses basket next to your bed.
2. Use it as a travel cot when you stay with friends and family.
3. Use it as a playpen.

Buying a cot

A cot is one of the few essential items that you'll need to invest in for your new baby. However, there's no reason why you can't buy one second-hand or ask friends and family to donate towards the cost of one as a gift. When your baby outgrows their cot, a second-hand sleigh bed makes a stylish toddler bed.

The key factor when you buy a cot is size. Do you want a standard cot, which will probably last a baby until they're around two to three years old? Or do you want a larger cot bed, which can be converted into a small bed for your toddler as they grow?

Part of your decision will depend on how quickly you want other children. A cot bed won't be practical if you're planning to have a small gap between your kids, as you need the cot for number two before number one has grown out of it.

I do think our small cot has been good because it's meant she's had more room to play in her bedroom but I've always wondered if she'd had the bigger one (with more room for toys and space to play) whether we'd have had more of a lie-in!

Abs, mum of Mae

We were given a cot bed from John Lewis by our parents as a present. It's worked very well for us, although Rosie did look tiny in it when she first slept there as a newborn. A cot bed has detachable sides so it can be converted into a toddler bed. They are normally bigger than cots, so may not work if you've got a small nursery or your baby is sharing your room. They're not normally more expensive than a standard cot.

Cot beds and cots have an adjustable base height. You choose the highest level for the first few months so you can lift the baby in and out easily, and then reposition at a lower level once they start being able to pull themselves up, to prevent Houdini-esque escapes.

Some cots come with all kinds of bells and whistles that you don't need. They can have drop-sides to help you lift out the baby more easily, or castors so you can wheel them from room to room, or a removable side so you can pull them close to your bed for night-time feeding. None of these extras are essential and can make the cot more expensive. If you want to buy a new cot, get one from IKEA for £29.

Buying a cot second-hand

As a cot can end up becoming an expensive purchase, buy second-hand or use a hand-me-down. Look out on eBay, NCT sales and your local newspapers. It's certainly worth inspecting the cot closely before you commit. Although this isn't always possible on eBay, most sellers are reasonable enough to give you a refund if it doesn't meet your standards. The best thing to do is ask detailed questions and request more photos while you're bidding.

There are some important points to bear in mind before you take on a second-hand cot. And remember that an old family heirloom may not reach today's safety standards, so scrutinise carefully using the steps below as guidance.

- Measure the bar spacing – it should be between 2.5cm and 6.5cm, and there must be at least 51cm between the top of the mattress and the top of the cot
- If it's a really old cot, it could be covered in lead paint. If you think this might be the case, or if there is any sign of peeling paint, strip and re-paint the cot. This is important because as your baby grows they'll love gnawing on the bars
- If there is a drop-side mechanism, carefully check it. It needs to work smoothly and stay reliably in the up position
- Scrape off any transfers or stickers from the inside of the cot; they could become a choking hazard
- Make sure there are no footholds or ledges in the sides or the ends of the cot where your baby could step on to climb out
- Make sure there are no indentations or protrusions on the top rail where your baby could get their clothing caught
- If your second-hand cot is an unusual size, it could end up becoming more costly, as you will need to get a new mattress specially made to fit

Buying mattresses

If you do buy a cot second-hand, you **must buy a new mattress**. Current guidelines on preventing cot death (Sudden Infant Death Syndrome or SIDS, when a baby dies suddenly for no known reason) suggest that babies should sleep on new, clean, dry mattresses. Research has shown an increased risk of cot death for babies sleeping on a mattress previously used by another baby. The risk was very small if the other baby was an older brother or sister in the same family but higher if the second-hand mattress was from another home.

Cot death is not common and mostly occurs when babies are less than five months. There are a few simple things you can do to reduce the risk, and the tips below come from The Foundation for the Study of Infant Deaths.

1. Lay a baby on their back to sleep.
2. Lay the baby 'feet to foot', which means their feet touching the bottom of the cot.
3. Ensure the baby's head cannot become covered by blankets or sheets.
4. Make sure the baby doesn't get too hot in bed. Use light blankets or a baby sleeping bag, rather than a duvet. A baby's room should be 16–20°C.
5. Your baby is safest sleeping in his own cot.
6. Sleep your baby on a new, clean, firm, dry mattress.
7. Don't let anyone smoke in your home.

Cot mattresses are surprisingly expensive, and are often not included in the price of a new cot. It sounds obvious, but do make sure your mattress fits your cot, especially if you've bought the cot second-hand. Mattresses normally come in two standard sizes; as a rule the gap between your cot and mattress should be no more than 4cm. Look for a cot mattress that is 8–10cm thick. Anything thinner won't provide the support your baby needs. One friend bought a hand-made-to-measure mattress for her second-hand crib from the General Workshop for the Blind. There may be similar workshops in your area.

There is normally a choice of three kinds of mattresses varying in price and materials. I remember being completely bewildered by the choice, and also quite shell shocked by how much it could cost if you bought the cot and mattress brand new.

First, foam mattresses tend to be the least expensive. They're normally made from a single layer of supportive foam covered with a wipe-clean PVC cover. Compared with the alternatives, they are good value for money.

Second, spring-interior mattresses have a coiled-spring interior with layers of felt and foam padding. They normally have a cotton cover on one side and PVC on the other. They are more expensive but do mean that if it's hot you could flip the mattress over so your baby sleeps on the cotton side.

Third, coir mattress are the most expensive option and harder to find. They have a core of natural fibre filling (made from coconut) with other layers of different materials and come with a wipe-clean covering. They are one of the firmest types of mattress and do tend to last longer.

Buying bedding

At some point during your pregnancy, you'll feel overwhelmed about all the different consumer decisions you're expected to make. So beware of your meltdown moment. For me, and many of our friends, it happened while we were out shopping for cot linen.

I had a total meltdown when we were buying sheets and my mum had to take me to the John Lewis café for lunch so I could calm down. I thought I was going to be a crap mum as I couldn't tell the difference between a Moses basket blanket and a pram blanket. I still don't, but Charlie doesn't seem to have noticed . . .
Emma, mum of Charlie

I was in Mothercare, overwhelmed by the different colours, sizes, materials and kinds of bed linen. How many sheets did I need for the Moses basket and the cot? Should they be brushed cotton or plain cotton? Fitted or flat? What colour? Would a little girl look boyish on a blue sheet? What if I wasn't having a little girl, as predicted, but a little boy? Would patterned sheets stop her from sleeping?

Should I get a waffle, wool, cotton or fleece blanket? Did I need different sheets and blankets for swaddling? Should I get different kinds of blankets for the buggy? What were these sleeping bag things and should I buy one? Needless to say, it ended in tears.

Hindsight is a wonderful thing. When Rosie was first born, a relation knitted us a beautiful, soft, white blanket. This is what she slept in: in my arms, in the Moses basket, in the buggy and now, one year on, in her cot bed for daytime naps. I had so many blankets that I'd either bought or been given as gifts that have never been used.

If you do have a friend or relation who's a good knitter, ask them to make you a blanket. It's such a wonderful gift. I think home-made blankets are much nicer than bought ones.

Cot sheets – I had loads of old single sheets which I just chopped in half and hemmed and they worked very well.
Catrin, mum of Theo and Cerys

Make your own cot sheets

Don't buy special fitted sheets for crib and cot mattresses. Cotton pillowcases will slip over most Moses basket or carrycot mattresses, and if you're at all handy with a sewing machine you can get about four flat cot sheets from one double or kingsize bed sheet – at much less cost. Or chop a single bed sheet in half and hem for a perfect cot sheet. The average measurements for the various sheets you might need are as follows:

Cot bed: 175cm x 122cm
Cot: 150cm x 100cm
Moses basket: 80cm x 35cm

Make your own fleece blankets

It's much cheaper to buy fleece from a material shop than to buy baby fleece blankets. Just buy one metre of fleece and cut to size. It doesn't even need hemming as it won't fray. I find fleece works best as outside blankets for the buggy or car seat or as a floor mat. Lay them on the floor of a friend's living room or café (even an airport lounge) so your baby has somewhere soft and clean to lie and play on.

Knitting a baby blanket

The easiest way to knit a blanket is to knit squares and sew them together. Keep the cost of wool down by raiding Granny's knitting basket and scouring charity shops for nice soft wool. You will need to wash the blanket, so bear this in mind when shopping around. Knitting a small blanket with chunky wool doesn't take long at all. You could ask friends and family to help by knitting some squares themselves too. You will need a large tapestry needle to stitch the squares together.

Remnants of different-coloured wool
Medium-sized knitting needles (size 5 or 6)

1. Cast on 20 stitches, 20 lines of knitting will make a square. For best results alternate one line of plain knitting with one line of purl.
2. Stitch the squares together using wool and a chunky tapestry needle.

How to knit

I'm a novice knitter – the last time I knitted something it was a scarf for Blue Ted in 1986. I found websites like www.knittinghelp.com and www.learn2knit.co.uk gave useful video tutorials. For me, casting on was the trickiest thing to do, then it seemed to get easier. For basic knitting, purl and the knit stitch is all you need.

Casting on

1. Dangle the wool between the thumb and index finger of your left hand, with around 50cm hanging off the end.
2. Enclose the two hanging pieces of wool with your other fingers.
3. With your right hand, take a knitting needle under the suspended wool and push it down with your RH index finger.
4. Feed the needle through the yarn on your thumb and then loop over and under the wool on your index finger.

5. Pull through and tighten both pieces of wool to make your slip knot on the needle. Repeat.

Knit stitch

1. The needle with your cast-on stitches should be in your left hand. Put the right needle through the loop on the left needle.
2. Wind the wool around the right needle.
3. Push the right needle down through the loop and use it to push the loop off the LH needle carefully. This is where it can go wrong and you can drop stitches.
4. If you need to remember how to knit a plain stitch try this: 'In through the doorway, run round the house, shut the door, and go next door'.

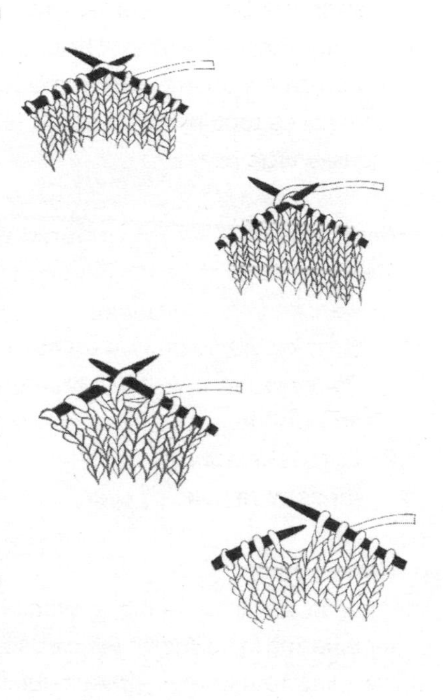

Purl stitch

1. Use the same principle as the plain knitting stitch but keep the wool in front of the knitting.
2. As before, the stitches should be in the LH needle.
3. Put the RH needle from right to left through the front of the first stitch on the LH needle.

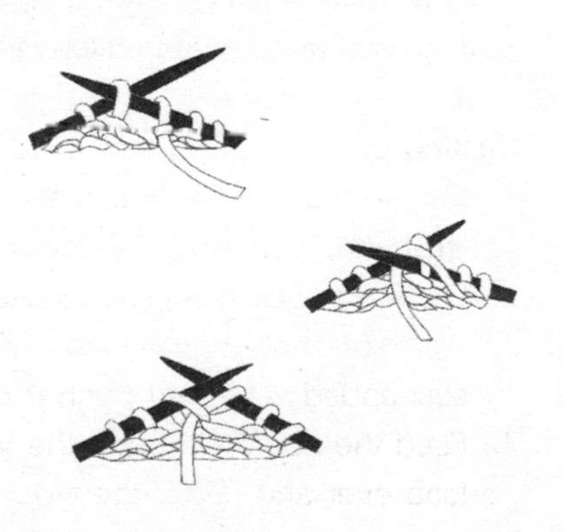

4. Wind the wool around the right needle.
5. Draw the loop through the back and gently slip old loop off the LH needle.

Casting off

1. Knit the first two stitches.
2. Lift the first stitch over the second and drop it off the needle.
3. Knit one stitch.
4. Lift the first stitch over the second and drop it off the needle.
5. Repeat.

Bare bedding essentials

Two home-made cot sheets

Two home-made Moses basket sheets (can also be used in pram), these can also be used to swaddle a small baby or as a cover on a hot day

One home-made fleece blanket for out and about

One cotton waffle blanket, handy if it's warm but you still need a blanket

One cosy, home-made woollen blanket for sleeps at home

Muslins – by tucking a muslin on top of a sheet where the baby's head lies, either in the Moses basket or cot, you'll cut down on washing. If they do dribble or are a bit sick, you won't have to change the whole sheet, just the muslin. Muslins also make lovely cool covers in hot weather.

One sleeping bag

I went for a 'one on, one dirty, one clean' approach, so bought three of everything (fitted sheets, flat sheets and blankets).

Mary, mum of Jack, Martha and Rosa

To buy or not to buy a baby sleeping bag, that is the question

Baby sleeping bags are a relatively new invention. They're widely regarded as a good investment. They look like a mini sleeping bag, with straps that normally button over your baby's shoulders to keep them in place. They're handy because it means your baby can't kick off their blankets in the middle of the night and wake themselves up when they are cold. You can also buy them in the same way that you would a duvet, in terms of togs, which just means that some are thicker for winter and thinner for the summer.

They can be quite pricey if you buy the brand names like Graco and buy them new – as much as £25. Cut the price by buying second-hand or a supermarket own-brand instead. They do last a long time though. They're normally sized as 0–6 months, 6–12 months and so on, and you'll find that your baby will initially have lots of empty sleeping bag at the bottom until they grow into it.

I've only ever bought one per size. If it gets dirty, wash it first thing in the morning to make sure it's dry by bedtime. I use blankets for daytime sleeps instead. I probably waited three months or so before I used a sleeping bag: partly because Rosie was so attached to her soft, hand-knitted blanket and partly because she was up so much at night that a blanket felt easier.

The sleeping bags are definitely essential – Mae used to wake up even more times in the night because she'd kicked off her covers and was cold! Soon realised!

Abs, mum of Mae

Swaddling

Swaddling is an ancient method for keeping a baby feeling safe and secure by wrapping them snugly in a sheet. Some midwives swear by this in the very early days of a baby's life as a trigger to help them sleep, as it mirrors the pressure they would have felt in the womb. It also stops them being disturbed by their own startle reflex and jerking themselves awake. It can also help settle down a baby when he's overstimulated.

Rosie didn't like being tightly wrapped up; she likes her arms free. It is possible to swaddle under a baby's arms too. However, even if your baby does love swaddling, there's no need to buy a special swaddling blanket, which is just a very clever marketing ploy. Experts say babies shouldn't be swaddled beyond four weeks old. When your baby begins to kick off the covers, it's a sign he no longer appreciates being bundled snugly.

We bought things like swaddling blankets and special baby towels with hoods – totally unnecessary!

Susan, mum of Madeline

How to swaddle a baby

1. Fold a sheet into a triangle with the widest edge at the top.
2. Place your baby on the sheet with their shoulder against the top edge.
3. Take the top right corner of the sheet and wrap it over the baby, tucking it under their left side.

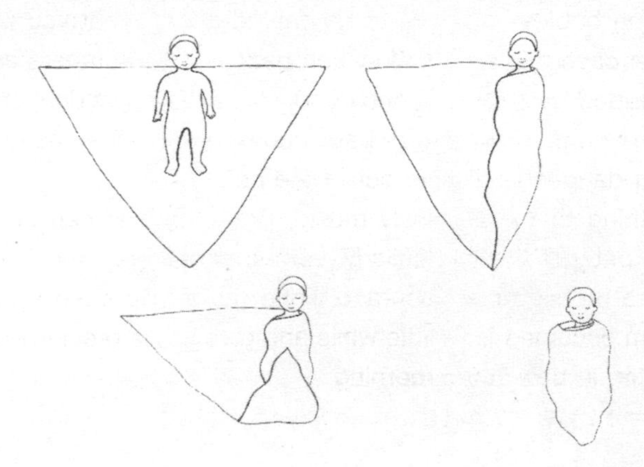

4. Take the bottom corner of the sheet and place it up over your baby's feet so it points upwards.
5. Wrap the left corner across the baby's body and firmly underneath and around again if it's long enough.
6. Check you can slip your fingers down the top of the sheet to make sure the swaddling isn't too tight.

What other cot equipment do you need?

There are so many extras you might buy for your cot, but try to restrict yourself. From cot bumpers and cot mobiles to cot toys that play tinkly music and cot books, there's even a cuddly bear that recreates the sounds of the mother's womb.

The womb bear. Now that was a waste of money. I think it cost me £30 from John Lewis and it played a tune that was supposed to sound like a mother's womb or it had a soothing music option. It was like being in a submarine and Charlie hated it. It wasn't very comforting. In fact, I was more concerned he would suffocate under the bear!
Emma, mum of Charlie

With young babies you have to be careful about what you place in cots, in case they're a suffocation hazard. Cot bumpers aren't recommended for newborns and cuddly toys can be as dangerous. Until you're confident that your baby can easily turn their head and roll out of danger, keep toys out of the cot.

Something that plays tinkly music, like a mobile, can help to soothe a baby to sleep. Similarly, something to grab their attention, like a mobile or a black-and-white pattern to stare at, may keep them occupied for a little while and give you a precious extra ten minutes in bed in the morning.

Mobiles – it's good to have one that you can just switch on and leave, rather than having to get up and wind it up all the time. But beyond that, go for as simple as possible – we got an all-singing, all-dancing one, and M was quite scared by it!
Susan, mum of Madeline

We took down the cot mobile when Molly was six months so I'm glad I didn't buy an expensive one.
Annabel, mum of Molly

Make your own simple cot mobile and play some soothing music in your baby's nursery as they go to sleep. Listening to Mozart is less likely to jangle your own nerves than the metallic, whirring, electronic version of 'Rock-a-Bye Baby'. Plus, it can play for longer – until your baby is properly sound asleep.

The light-and-sound wind-up thing that attaches to the bed was a waste of money. All it seemed to do was make the children unsettled when it stopped.
Ali, mum of Louis and Eddie

Make your own cot mobile
Coat-hanger
Wire cutters
Two lengths of ribbon (approx 30cm)
Cotton thread and needle

1. Bend the coat-hanger into a circular shape, cutting off the hook with the wire cutters (this will be used later on). Wind ribbon all the way around the wire to cover.
2. Attach one length of ribbon placing the ends 180 degrees from one another, and the same with the second piece. Use the hook of the hanger to loop the ribbons together.
3. The base is now ready for attachments. Aside from the

suggestions below you could also hang pom poms; CDs; leaves, pine cones and twigs; black-and-white felt-tipped patterns on card. A very artistic friend made one from bits of driftwood and seashells.

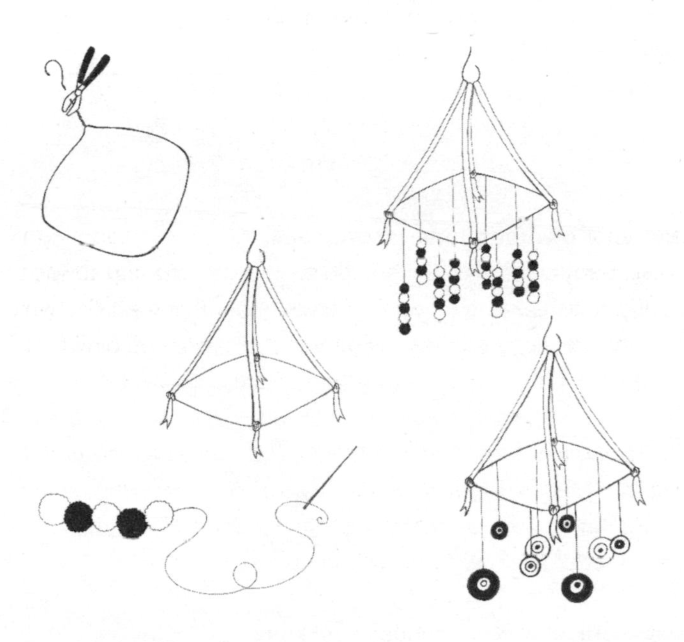

Feathers:

1. Bunch a few feathers together, simply bind them at the top with sticky tape. Make eight clusters.
2. Attach each feather cluster onto the hanging thread on the wire base of the cot mobile.

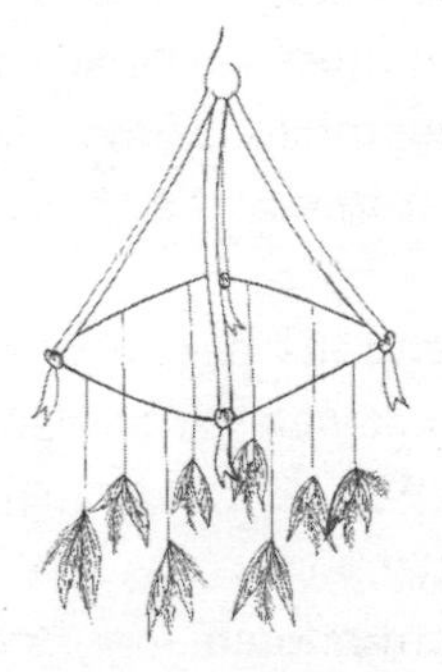

Ribbon:

1. Use two pieces of different coloured ribbon. Cut into four relatively short and four relatively long pieces.
2. Sew them on to the wire base of the cot mobile.

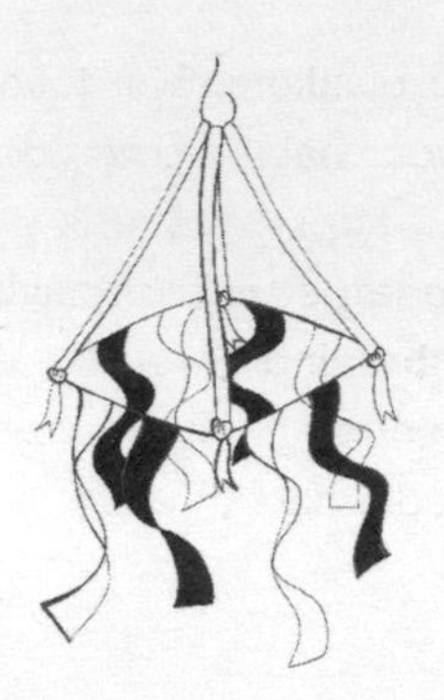

Make your own soothing music

Lots of companies sell compilations of soothing classical music specially formulated for young babies. Some of these CDs have even re-recorded the music using elevator-style electronic music. It's far better for both you and your baby to listen to the real thing. If you know classical music you'll be able to assemble your own compilation: if not, ask a musical friend to make one for your baby as a gift. Download your favourite soothing tunes from iTunes or look out for cheap compilations on Amazon. Here are some of Rosie's favourites:

'Clair de Lune' by Claude Debussy
'Canon in D Major' by Johann Pachelbel
'Gymnopedie No 1' by Erik Satie
'Cantique de Jean Racine' by Gabriel Fauré
'Lullaby' by Johannes Brahms
'Moonlight Sonata' (Sonata No 14, second movement) by Ludvig van Beethoven
'Winter' (*The Four Seasons*, second movement) by Antonio Vivaldi
'Nocturne for Piano', no. 13 in C minor by Frederic Chopin
'Piano Concerto in A Minor', movement two by Edvard Grieg

Make your own sleep comforter

Way before Linus dragged his security blanket through the stories of Snoopy and Charlie Brown, children have been getting attached to old blankets. The following pattern is for a soft fabric square that your baby will enjoy playing with as well as sleeping with.

Two large handkerchief-sized squares of soft fabric in contrasting colours
Selection of ribbons and remnants of different kind of fabric
Needle and thread

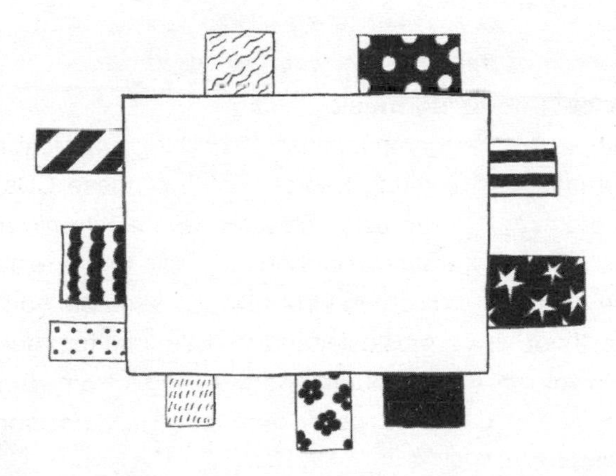

Choose soft tactile fabric like velvet, fleece, velour, soft cotton or soft towelling. Sew a selection of different ribbons and scraps of fabric into loops around the edges of one of the squares. These ribbons should be in different colours and different textures: try velvet, silk, satin, ribbed and textured ribbons, as well as lace and suede. Sew the two squares together neatly and firmly around the outside, turning them inside-out just before the last two stitches so the seams stays on the inside. These two squares should now create an 'empty pocket' that can be rubbed and stroked by your baby.

Make your own soft lopsided rabbit

Before Rosie was born, we bought her a soft flannel cat for the cot. It had a large crinkly label, which we foolishly chopped off, thinking it would get in the way. Babies love sucking, stroking and playing with labels, which is why the pattern for the soft lopsided rabbit includes its very own makeshift ribbon label.

Two large squares of soft fabric like flannel, brushed cotton (the rabbit can have contrasting fabric back to front)
Small length of thick silky ribbon (for label)
Needle and thread
Stuffing
Piece of stiff card

Draw the shape of your lopsided rabbit onto the thick piece of card. Experiment on a notepad first to get a shape you're happy with. (My lopsided rabbit looks a bit like a lopsided starfish.) Cut out the rabbit shape from your two squares of material. Place one of the pieces right side up, stitch on. Using bold, neat, coloured stitches, sew on the rabbit's nose in the shape of a diagonal cross and two eyes in contrasting thread. Place the fabric rabbits right sides together and hem along the edges with a sewing machine, leaving a gap for stuffing and ribbon label. Turn the rabbit the right way out and firmly stuff, ensuring it reaches the corners of the arms, ears and legs. Slip in the folded ribbon label and stitch the gap.

Baby monitors

Unnecessary – this is a bit controversial – baby monitors! Find me a new mother that doesn't hear their child's every cry.

Lynsey, mum of Amber

Unless you live in a huge house, you don't really need a monitor. Buying a baby monitor feels like buying a new mobile phone. There are so many new technological add-ons and extras, so many different models and variations to consider that it's tempting to blindly buy a recognisable brand with your fingers crossed behind your back. Some baby monitors will also measure the temperature in the nursery, others will check your baby's breathing, some are digital and some are not.

We had an all-singing, all-dancing monitor that even measured Leo's breathing. The alarm kept going off all the time, every time he moved off the mattress monitor. So we went out and bought a basic monitor for £10.

Hazel, mum of Leo

Again, there's no reason why you can't buy a baby monitor second-hand or borrow from a friend. It's simple to test they're working OK – just pop a friend in the baby's room with the monitor and walk around the house with the other attachment to ensure you can hear everything. Our monitor only measured sound, but I found it useful to be able to detach our section from its charger. This meant I could take it outside if I was sitting in the garden, while Rosie was sleeping.

Don't buy a monitor with an in-built thermometer. Ours beeps every time the temperature goes over 23 degrees, which means we can't have it on in the summer!

Annabel, mum of Molly

It obviously depends on the size of your house, but it is worth asking yourself whether you really need a baby monitor. Babies' cries are astonishingly loud – they measure up to 115 decibels, which is louder than a truck. As a new mother, it's not an exaggeration to say that your baby's cry pierces your soul. You'll be halfway up the stairs before they've barely opened their mouth to grumble.

Second time round we didn't bother with the baby monitor. Most people's houses are small enough that you hear a baby crying and they're in your bedroom with you for the first few months at least. However, a lot of people do feel more comfortable being able to hear baby breathing and moving.
Shonagh, mum of Daniel and Caitlin

Lullabies

Lullabies are a soothing way to help your baby go to sleep. They seem to have a miraculous calming effect from an early age. Even now, when Rosie hears 'Twinkle Twinkle Little Star', she knows it's time to go to sleep. When Rosie was first born I struggled to remember any of the words, so here are some lyrics to prompt your memory.

Rock-a-Bye Baby
Rock-a-bye baby on the tree top
When the wind blows the baby will rock
When the bough breaks the cradle will fall,
And down will come baby, cradle and all.

Twinkle Twinkle Little Star
Twinkle twinkle little star
How I wonder what you are

Up above the world so high
Like a diamond in the sky
Twinkle Twinkle Little Star
How I wonder what you are

Frère Jacques
Frère Jacques, Frère Jacques,
Dormez-vous? Dormez-vous?
Sonnez les matines, sonnez les matines
Ding ding dong, ding ding dong.

Hush little baby
Hush, little baby, don't say a word.
Mama's gonna buy you a mockingbird

And if that mockingbird won't sing,
Mama's gonna buy you a diamond ring

And if that diamond ring turns brass,
Mama's gonna buy you a looking glass

And if that looking glass gets broke,
Mama's gonna buy you a billy goat

And if that billy goat won't pull,
Mama's gonna buy you a cart and bull

And if that cart and bull turn over,
Mama's going to buy you a dog named Rover.

And if that dog named Rover won't bark,
Mama's going to buy you a horse and cart.

And if that horse and cart fall down,
You'll still be the sweetest little baby in town.

I Had a Little Nut Tree
I had a little nut tree,
Nothing would it bear
But a silver nutmeg,
And a golden pear;
The King of Spain's daughter
Came to visit me,
And all for the sake
Of my little nut tree.

Her dress was made of crimson,
Jet black was her hair,
She asked me for my nut tree
And my golden pear.
I said, 'So fair a princess
Never did I see,
I'll give you all the fruit
From my little nut tree.'

When the Boat Comes In or Dance ti' thy Daddy
Come here, maw little Jacky,
Now aw've smoked mi backy,
Let's hev a bit o' cracky,
Till the boat comes in.

Chorus:
Dance ti' thy daddy, sing ti' thy mammy,
Dance ti' thy daddy, ti' thy mammy sing;
Thou shall hev a fishy on a little dishy,
Thou shall hev a fishy when the boat comes in.

Here's thy mother humming,
Like a canny woman;
Yonder comes thy father,
Drunk – he cannot stand.

Chorus:
Dance ti' thy daddy, sing ti' thy mammy,
Dance ti' thy daddy, ti' thy mammy sing;
Thou shall hev a fishy on a little dishy,
Thou shall hev a haddock when the boat comes in.

Our Tommy's always fuddling,
He's so fond of ale,
But he's kind to me,
I hope he'll never fail.

Chorus:
Dance ti' thy daddy, sing ti' thy mammy,
Dance ti' thy daddy, ti' thy mammy sing;
Thou shall hev a fishy on a little dishy,
Thou shall hev a bloater when the boat comes in.

I like a drop mysel',
When I can get it sly,
And thou, my bonny bairn,
Will lik't as well as I.

Chorus:
Dance ti' thy daddy, sing ti' thy mammy,
Dance ti' thy daddy, ti' thy mammy sing;
Thou shall hev a fishy on a little dishy,
Thou shall hev a mackerel when the boat comes in.

May we get a drop,
Oft as we stand in need;
And weel may the keel row
That brings the bairns their bread.

Chorus:
Dance ti' thy daddy, sing ti' thy mammy,
Dance ti' thy daddy, ti' thy mammy sing;
Thou shall hev a fishy on a little dishy,
Thou shall hev a salmon when the boat comes in.

CHAPTER SIX

Travelling

I made in-car entertainment for Seth by hanging wide ribbons from the back of the passenger seat and attaching drawings to them – he loved just looking at them and now he's bigger he loves grabbing them.

Amy, mum of Seth and Agnes

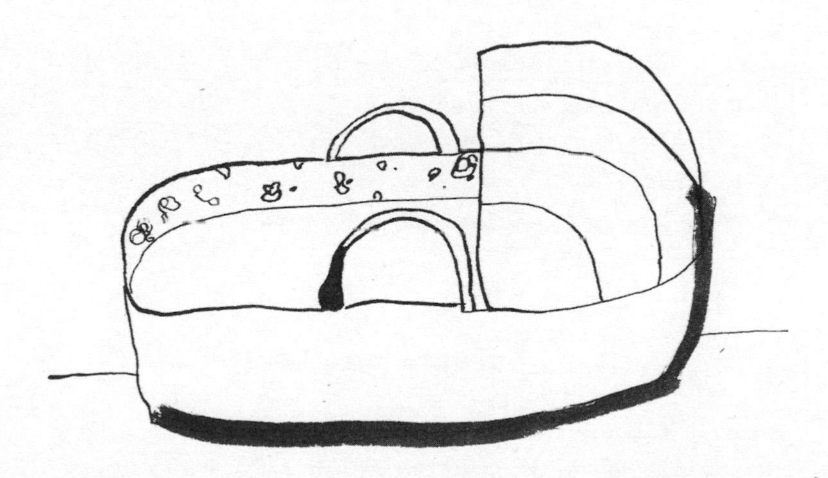

Buying travelling essentials for your baby, like a pram and a car seat, will probably end up being your most expensive purchases, alongside their cot. The choice is overwhelming and it's easy to be swayed by the fads and trends of the moment.

These two big purchases are crucial, because it's likely you'll be using them both a lot. And not only do they need to be comfortable for your baby, they also need to work for you and your lifestyle as well. A lot of new mums fall under the spell of a picture of a celebrity in a magazine with a designer buggy or are swayed by a nice fabric, rather than looking at the nitty-gritty technical elements and usability.

Must-haves
Pram
New car seat
Sling or papoose
Sealed packet of crisps!

Naughty but nice
Cosy lambswool fleece and/or
Sleeping bag

What you and baby can live without
All-singing, all-dancing travel system
Nappy-changing bag
Parasol
Pram cappuccino holder!

Buying a pram

In the old days, the word pram meant a Silver Cross-style traditional pram with large wheels, big, bouncy suspension and a carrycot for baby to sleep in, today, the term can also be applied to pushchairs or buggies. As a general rule, traditional prams are suitable for small babies but once they reach at least six months old and can support themselves upright, they'll be happier sitting in a buggy or pushchair so they can gaze around.

One of the first decisions to make is whether you're happy to buy a buggy or pushchair suitable for a newborn, which means it can recline flat, or if you'd prefer to buy a pram and then buy a buggy once the baby is six months old.

I bought a buggy, suitable for a newborn, for around £100. Eighteen months later Rosie is still happy in it, while my other friends have had to fork out for similar pushchairs once their babies grew out of prams. If I had my time again, I think I'd do exactly the same. And a quick poll of my friends, even those who were seduced by prams, says they agree. If your heart is set on buying a pram, it's worth buying it second-hand or borrowing from a friend and spending more on a decent buggy, because you'll need that for longer.

To make matters even more complicated, research published in November 2008 suggested that babies who sit facing away from their mothers in forward-facing buggies could be experiencing more stress than those in rear-facing buggies who have regular eye contact with their mothers. It's no surprise to hear that traditional, rear-facing prams are often much more expensive (at least £200) than their forward-facing counterparts. Unfortunately this is yet another issue that can make the purchase of a buggy an emotive and guilt-laden purchase. Although harder, it's still possible to interact with your baby in a forward-facing buggy, pointing out birds and dogs and stopping to chat.

The dangers of succumbing to peer pressure

I suspect it hasn't always been like this, but today the pram is almost like a fashion accessory. It's as if the brand of pram says as much about you as the car you drive. But it's not a fashion accessory, and if you fall into the trap of thinking it is, you're bound to spend lots and lots of money.

So if you're going to be resourceful, there are some expensive brands that you should make every effort to avoid – they're pricey, but many of them don't score highly in product reviews, so they're just not worth the money if you buy them new. For example, the Bugaboo Chameleon costs around £630, then there's the £69 foot muff, the £24.95 parasol, the £14.95 cup holder, the £69 frog bag, the £88.95 transport bag – and that's just for starters. So before you know it you've spent nearly £900! Designer brands like Bugaboo are expensive second-hand too, and often retail for around £300 on eBay.

My Maclaren buggy has been a dream. It was last year's colour so it was in the sale for £100. Mae does like to walk more these days but she does love snuggling in her fleece when she's tired and will still sleep in it if I'm lucky! The fact that it's light and easy to unfold has meant it's never been a dread to go out and about!

Abs, mum of Mae

Types of prams explained

Type 'pram' into Google and you get 5.1 million results. The choice can seem very confusing. The first decision you need to make is what kind you want, and there are four different kinds to choose from:

Prams
Buggies
All-terrain pushchairs
Travel systems

Then there are three-wheelers and four-wheelers, forward-facing and rear-facing, detachable carrycots, detachable car seats. Then there's how you want to look: like Mary Poppins pushing a big, old-fashioned pram or like Madonna jogging along with a three-wheeler off-roader buggy.

Pram

This is the good old-fashioned carrycot on wheels that conjures up pictures of uniformed nannies taking babies for fresh air.

Pros

- Very comfortable and cosy for a newborn baby
- Could easily double up as a carrycot/Moses basket
- Have lots of storage for shopping underneath

Cons

- Can be large and difficult to manoeuvre onto public transport
- Can they be stored in a car boot?
- They take up a lot of room
- The baby grows out of them fast, they'll probably only last around three months

Buggy

This tends to be the cheapest kind of pushchair and is commonly used to get out and about with toddlers. However, some models do fully recline to make them suitable for newborns.

Pros

- Good value
- Don't take up much room when stored in flat or car boot
- Easy to get on to public transport
- Lightweight and compact
- Can take you from newborn to toddler stage

Cons

- Don't look as cosy or comfortable for a newborn as a flat pram or carrycot
- Some models are not suitable for newborns: check for back support and ability to recline fully
- Small shopping basket
- Struggle over bumpy ground and rough terrain

We used the Maclaren Techno XT pram for £135 (found the cheapest deal on Kelkoo) for Seth from birth with a duvet attachment, and it is still so brilliant. I have never once yearned after anything more fancy.
Amy, mum of Seth

All-terrain pushchairs

These are the kind of pushchairs that celebrities get photographed in as they jog along the beach or in the park. They often have three big wheels and are bigger than standard buggies.

Pros

- Work well over rough terrain like bumpy roads, country lanes and beaches
- Suspension makes a comfy ride for baby, even over bumpy surfaces

Cons

- They're big and unwieldy, can be tricky to squeeze into a car boot or on to public transport
- They can be tricky to manoeuvre around steps and the kerb and also around shops
- The pneumatic tyres can get punctures!
- They're large to store

Second-hand buggies are also generally fine – we bought a second-hand 'off road' buggy from eBay for £25 and it was in very good shape.
Susan, mum of Madeline

Travel systems

Travel systems tend to be the most expensive option for new parents. You can clip a car seat onto them and a carrycot and they'll also transform into a pram and a pushchair.

Pros
- Enables you to transfer baby from car to shops and back home again without waking them
- The carrycot could double up as a Moses basket when they're little

Cons
- The price doesn't always include the car seat and carrycot
- A newborn baby should not be left in a car seat for long periods of time
- There's a lot of kit to store
- Danger you can end up getting an inferior buggy, carrycot and car seat just because they're all lumped together

The Graco Travel System was unnecessary in retrospect. The car seat was grown out of incredibly quickly, and was uncomfortable right from the start, and the buggy awkward and heavy. I switched to a decent car seat and the Maclaren buggy pretty quickly.

Ali, mum of Louis and Eddie

I wouldn't worry so much about something that converts from a pram into a pushchair. I bought one with a carrycot, but from three months we haven't used the flat pram and I feel we paid a premium. Half of the time in the first three months Molly was in a sling anyway.

Annabel, mum of Molly

Questions to ask yourself

There are so many prams to choose from that it can be helpful to ask yourself a few questions before you make the decision. While you're pregnant start researching all the pushchairs you see. Who is struggling on and off the bus? Whose buggy is overladen with shopping bags? (Could mean they haven't got much storage for shopping under the seat.) Who is struggling to manoeuve around shops or up and down the kerb?

Visit larger nursery stores to try out the different models, so you can physically see how big they are and how easy they are to push. Don't just push them in a straight line, try turning corners and manoeuvring them in small spaces.

Where will you store it?

You probably won't have the time or the inclination to fold up your pushchair every time you come home. So how much space will it take up unfolded? If you don't have much room in your flat or house, consider buying a buggy rather than a big travel system. When Rosie's buggy was delivered in a huge carboard box I was shocked at how much room it took, despite the fact I opted for a small buggy rather than a large pram or travel system.

Do you have a flat or house with lots of stairs to climb?

If you're not able to store your pram at the bottom of the stairs you may need to buy a lightweight buggy that you can safely carry upstairs.

We had a big flight of stairs up to our house and borrowed a modern Silver Cross pram with carrycot. It was so heavy I never took it out once. But I used the carrycot indoors. Then I used a sling for the first four months until she was too heavy.

Rosemary, mum of Florence and Spike

Will it fit in your car boot?

I've heard of quite a few new parents who've had to replace a brand-new pushchair because their chosen model was too big for their car boot. Remember that even if it does squeeze in, when you're going away for a weekend you'll need room for a travel cot and all the other kit that comes with your baby.

Will you often be travelling by public transport?

Smaller, more adaptable buggies are more suitable for families that travel on public transport a lot. Some of the big three-wheeler pushchairs can't squeeze down the bus corridor! Other models can be very heavy. If you travel by train and tube you may need to fold up the buggy quickly and carry it along with your newborn up and down steps. Or you might just pick up the whole thing. You'll be thankful it's light. You never notice all those steps leading up and down to platforms until you've got a buggy with you.

Our lifesaver was the Maclaren Techno XT buggy – suitable from birth to four, folds down really easily and can be put up with one hand and fits in your boot along with heaps of other stuff – and much cheaper than the Bugaboos of this world, which take up your whole boot and are shocking on buses. If a Bugaboo is in the buggy bit of a bus, no other prams can fit in!

Yvonne, mum of Scarlett

Will you be doing a lot of walking?

Whether it's manoeuvring your pushchair on and off the kerb or going for long, long walks, the lighter all-terrain pushchairs can make walking more effortless than the unwieldy travel systems or less robust buggies.

Do you live in the country or by the sea?

All-terrain pushchairs are specially designed to travel on bumpier surfaces like beaches and country lanes.

Tips on buying a second-hand buggy

Consider buying your pushchair second-hand. It's going to be one of your most expensive purchases and will save a lot of money. It's important not to be swayed by fashion and trends when you're buying second-hand. As long as your pushchair is comfortable and secure, your baby won't care whether it's fashionable or not.

A slightly jaded-looking pushchair in outdated fabric could be bought for a bargain price. If you're nervous about the idea of your newborn sleeping in a second-hand pushchair, buy a cosy new fleece or duvet to line the interior.

The best places for pushchairs are NCT sales, second-hand children's shops, charity shops, eBay and Gumtree. Also look out for ads in local shops and cafés. Pushchairs are normally in high demand at NCT sales so you'll need to be at the front of the queue if you want to snap one up – arrive around thirty minutes early to secure your place. Similarly, good second-hand pushchairs don't stay in charity shops for long. Keep checking them as regularly as you can, and you may be able to ask the manager to give you a call when something suitable arrives. (I know one good charity shop near me has a waiting list for double buggies . . .)

Don't feel embarrassed about checking out the pushchair thoroughly before you commit to buy it. Wheel it around and inspect the harness, wheels and brakes. If you're buying it online, scrutinise the pictures and email any questions to the seller. It's worth checking to see if accessories, especially a rain cover, are included in the price. It can be tricky (and expensive) to find a rain cover that fits an old model.

Things to look out for when checking a second-hand pushchair

1. Check the frame is rigid and sturdy and won't collapse unless the locking mechanism is released.
2. Check the frame for dents, sharp edges, corrosion and wobbly or badly worn wheels.
3. Check the brakes. They should operate easily and be able to hold a pushchair still on a slope.
4. Check the harness is working. You'll need a five-point harness.
5. Fold the pushchair down to make sure the mechanism works easily.
6. Make sure the material and seams aren't damaged.

Double trouble

Where a lot of my friends were struggling with double buggies and eventually ditching them, I moved my two-year-old straight onto a buggy board, which we have only just got rid of – he's five. Apart from the downside that the two can't sleep together when you're out, which you get around mainly by splitting the day in half and napping at home, we found this piece of kit invaluable.

Ali, mum of Louis and Eddie

There are two main types of double prams to choose from. A twin pushchair has two seats side-by-side and a tandem pushchair with one seat behind or below the other. Parents with twins tend to go for twin pushchairs, whereas parents with children born closely together seem to go for tandem pushchairs placing their toddler in the front seat and newborn baby in the back.

A twin pushchair ensures both babies get 'good seats' but can be difficult to navigate around the shops and on public transport. Twin buggies are normally lighter and more stable than tandems. A tandem pushchair is not as wide but means one baby gets a seat with limited vision. Phil and Ted's is a popular brand of tandem pushchair but the second seat is placed below the first, and looks cramped for a toddler.

Questions to ask yourself

Are you buying the double pram for twins or for two children born closely together?

Will you be able to navigate a wide twin pram around the shops?

How often do you use public transport and will your double pram fit?

Will your babies or toddlers fight about who gets the front seat if you have a tandem pushchair?

If you have two children of different ages, could the older toddler handle standing on a buggy board instead?

Measure your door and hallway: will the double buggy fit through?

Pushchair accessories

Check what accessories are included with your pushchair, for instance, a rain cover is optional on some models. You can only make meaningful price comparisons when you know what's included. While some accessories, like a cup holder, are not essential, others, like a rain cover, are.

Don't bother with parasols: it's impossible to keep your baby in the shade using them. You can either buy a pricey sun shade that looks like a giant mosquito net or clothes-peg a muslin or similar material to the hood of your pushchair to keep your baby out of the sun.

A cosy sleeping-bag attachment may be a worthwhile investment, especially for winter babies. They're handy for toddlers too, as it means they can't kick their blankets off. However, you can easily buy them second-hand or in a universal style, rather than specially fitted for your buggy. Buggysnuggles (buggysnuggle.com) retail for under £30 and fit all styles of prams; they can also be zipped apart and just used as a liner without blanket in the summer.

Make your own pram toy

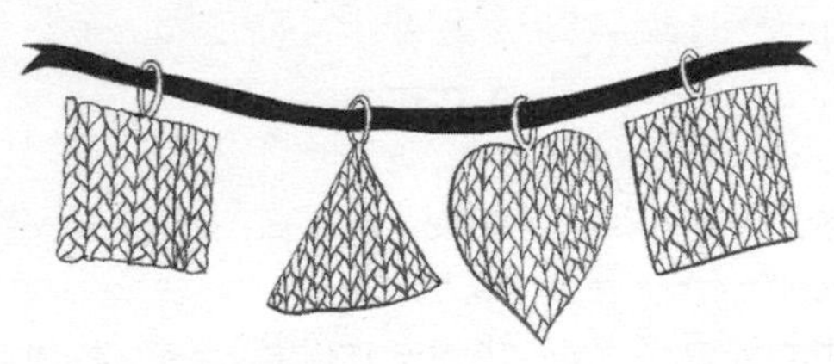

Remnants of leftover wool
Medium-sized knitting needles (size 5 or 6)
Ribbon length to form loops
Darning needle
Stuffing
Small bell or flat plastic squeaker (buy from craft shop or online at www.beinspired.co.uk or www.e.crafts.co.uk)

1. Cast on twenty stitches (see detailed how-to knit instructions in Chapter 5).
2. Knit one row with basic knit stitch and one row with basic purl stitch.
3. Continue alternating the rows for eighteen rows to make a square. Cast off.
4. Knit another square in a different coloured wool
5. Cut three 20cm lengths of wool, plait together, knot both ends to secure. This will form the string to tie across the pram.
6. Pin the two knitted squares together and place the ribbon loop at the centre, stitch the two shapes together and attach the loop, leaving a 5cm gap.
7. Stuff the square with stuffing and place a squeaker or bell in the centre; sew up the gap.
8. Make at least three knitted squares – or knit other shapes too, triangles, circles, etc. if you are more experienced knitter.
9. String the coloured shapes on to the plaited wool and hang across pram or buggy. This toy would also work well strung across a bouncy chair.

Buying a car seat

Buying a car seat is the one purchase where you can't cut corners to save money. It's important to buy the car seat new and it's the one investment that is worth the money. Visit a retailer that specialises in car seats and pick their brains. Also, get them to help you fit the car seat correctly. Hospitals insist that new babies leave their premises safely strapped into a car seat if you are driving, so you may need to buy it before your baby is born. Until babies are roughly six months old, their car seat has to be rear-facing.

Probably the only thing you should really buy new (for safety) is a car seat – unless it's coming from someone you know well.
Lynsey, mum of Amber

Our car seat Maxi Cosi Isofix, although expensive, is worth it for peace of mind and ease of fitting (comes top in safety, I think).
Rachel, mum of Matthew

I was given a car seat by my aunt. She had bought it very recently for my young cousin visiting from Canada, and it had been used just a handful of times. It still had the original safety leaflet with fitting instructions and I knew it hadn't been involved in an accident. The reason that official advice is so adamant about not buying car seats second-hand is the danger that their safety structure may have been weakened if they were in a car crash. It's also really important to fit them correctly.

There are lots of different bells and whistles to car seats, but the most important feature is their safety record. Check the latest *Which?* report to see which brands are scoring best. *Which*'s tests are more rigorous than the standard manufacturer tests, so well worth reading.

Rosie's seat reclines, which has been handy on long car journeys as it makes it comfortable for her to sleep in. For newborns, a car seat that you can take out of the car means you don't have to disturb sleeping babies.

The reclining car seat (when Mae was big enough) has meant that she sleeps for longer on journeys and mostly she always seems quite happy to get into it – so it must be comfortable.
Abs, mum of Mae

Car seats can be confusing to buy because they're classified according to a child's weight, rather than their age. Retailers often describe car seats in terms of 'stages': some car seats are capable of being converted as the child grows and, therefore, fit into more than one group or stage. The main types are:

Stage 1 = Groups 0 and 0+
Stage 2 = Group 1
Stage 3 = Group 2
Stage 4 = Group 3

There are two kinds of car seats suitable for babies, according to childcarseats.org.uk: rearward-facing for newborn babies and forward-facing once they're around 9kg and can sit up unaided.

1. Rearward-facing

Group 0 for babies up to 10kgs (22lb), roughly from birth to 6–9 months, or Group 0+ for babies up to 13kg (29lb), roughly from birth to 12–15 months.

Rearward-facing seats provide greater protection for the baby's head, neck and spine than forward-facing seats, so it is best to keep your baby in a rearward-facing seat for as long as possible. Only move them to a forward-facing seat once they have exceeded the maximum weight for the baby seat, or the top of their head is higher than the top of the seat. It's always safer to put babies in the back seat.

2. Forward-facing

Group 1 for children weighing 9–18kg (20–40lb), roughly from 9 months – 4 years.

These car seats can be used in the front or rear of the car, but it is safer to put them in the rear, especially if there is a passenger airbag in the front. Only move your child to a booster seat once they have exceeded the maximum weight for the child seat, or the top of their head is higher than the top of the seat.

Questions to ask yourself

Will the car seat only be fitted in your car, or will you be transporting it to other cars too?

If so, you need to make sure it will fit other car models too.

Will you need to take the seat constantly in and out of the car?

If so, a lighter model might work best.

Will you be taking a lot of long journeys?

If so, a reclining model could help your baby sleep.

Fitting a car seat

As this could be the only new baby purchase you make, take full advantage of the expertise of the retailer you buy from. Good retailers will recommend a car seat appropriate for your car and also help you fit the seat, to ensure it's been installed correctly. Alternatively, many local councils offer the same service.

Car seats can be fitted in the front or back of the car. It's always safer for them to be on the back seat. If you do fit the car seat in the passenger seat at the front ensure the passenger airbag has been disabled.

Slings

Even if you're not convinced before your baby's born, I promise you that a sling will be one of the most resourceful bits of kit you buy. Most newborn babies are much happier snuggled next to you in the sling than in their pushchair. In fact, it could help you solve the dilemma of whether to buy a pram or not. Don't bother, just carry them in the sling for five months until they're ready for a buggy.

They're also the unsung heroes for all those times when you

need two hands around the house with a grizzly baby to comfort. I've been able to cook a roast dinner, hoover the house, do some gardening, make numerous cups of tea and do a weekly shop, all thanks to the sling.

I didn't buy a good baby carrier (front one) – Ali lent me one but it wasn't very comfortable. I wish I had because I would have been freer round the house in the early days.

Abs, mum of Mae

Slings are also brilliant on public transport and mean you don't have to worry about escalators on the tube or steps on the train, or squeezing onto a bus. There's no need to buy a sling brand-new, you'll probably only use it for six months anyway, depending on how big and heavy your baby is. It's also the sort of kit that friends are likely to pass on.

There are two main types of sling. One is a structured papoose that looks like a padded harness; the other is a more traditional sling, a long piece of material that you swathe around yourself. Try them both out before you decide. Remember that anything too fiddly will be even trickier when you're carrying a wriggly baby. And do make sure it's machine-washable – it's bound to get covered in dribble. Women seem to fall strongly into two categories in terms of which they prefer. It's worth remembering that your partner might use it too.

The Baby Bjorn or sling is really useful in the early stages, particularly for dads, I think. Anna tends to be a little less settled when Martin is looking after her, but she is more than happy to be up and about looking out of the Baby Bjorn.

Nics, mum of Kate and Anna

The hippy sling was very uncomfortable for me and James hated being in it. And it was overpriced but looked really cute.

Becca, mum of James

I bought a second-hand Baby Bjorn on eBay for around £20 – it was well worth the money. Rosie loved being carried in it up until she was around nine months old. Even if we were out walking in the buggy, I'd put my sling under the pushchair in case she got grouchy. I could then place her in the sling for a 'cuddle' and still push the buggy easily with my hands free. One of my friends had a similar sling called a Wilkinet: she used it for both babies and passed it on to several friends in-between.

Make your own sling

It's easy to make your own sling with a long strip of cloth. It should be around 50cm wide and 1.5m long. Jersey-weave cotton material works well because it doesn't fray, so no need for hemming.

There are many different ways of tying a sling. Investigate different options online; there're even some videos on YouTube that demonstrate how to tie them! Here's a relatively simple technique. You'll need help the first few times before you get used to it.

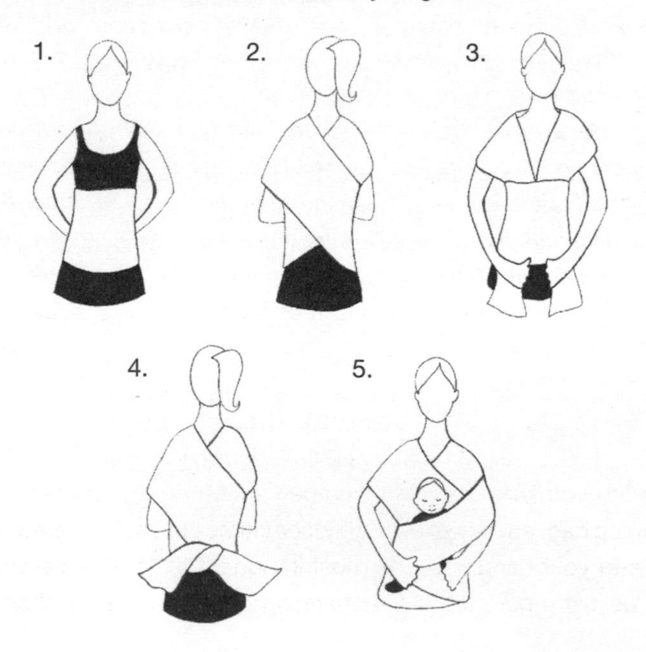

1. Find the middle of your strip of cloth. Place it on your belly button and wrap the material around your waist like a cummerbund.
2. Make an X at your back and bring the ends over your shoulders
3. Pull the cummerbund away from your body and drop these ends through it
4. Make another X at your stomach (this is where the baby will sit) pull the two lengths over your shoulders and then make another X on your back. Tie at your hips.

When your baby's outgrown the sling and if you do a lot of hiking and walking, you may want to buy a baby 'rucksack', which carries the baby on your back. These have metal frames and can be very expensive, so don't buy it new. And only buy second-hand if you regularly go on long country walks, or you just won't use it enough.

We got carried away with our baby rucksack. When we were travelling doing our four-day walks we had this vision that getting a really good baby rucksack would mean we'd still be able to go on really long walks! It obviously hadn't dawned on us that, even without a child, those days were over! Anyway, Mae has never been really that fond of it but I still think it's handy to have. But I would definitely buy a second-hand one – although getting a cheap but uncomfortable one wouldn't make a pleasant walk.

Abs, mum of Mae

Changing bags

By now, you may have succumbed to the novel concept of a changing bag, an oversized, bulky, sometimes plastic-covered alternative to your handbag. The most important thing to remember is that it's just a bag. It's not a changing bag. It's called a changing bag to make you part with £95 on a new bag that you wouldn't buy otherwise. Don't do it. Just buy a bag you like and put a nappy in it.

My work handbag, which was big enough for my laptop, is also big enough for nappies, wipes and muslins. Other friends use rucksacks, messenger bags, cloth shopping bags and plastic shopping bags. Some did succumb to the overpriced, oversized, heavy changing bag, but were using their own alternative very swiftly indeed.

Specially designed mummy bags are usually very, very expensive (between £60 and £100 in most baby outlets) and you find that you end up using your handbag for most things anyway, simply because you don't want to carry such a cumbersome, ugly-looking bag around with you all the time. And they normally tip up the buggy as soon as you take your baby out!

Nics, mum of Kate and Anna

When your baby is tiny it is quite easy to add their things to your handbag. However, it's worth having a separate bag packed and ready so you can run out of the door quickly when you need to. Also, always keep a spare blanket and your rain cover under the buggy. And if you remember, a plastic bottle of water for you.

I had a nice nappy-changing bag. Then it got poo on it. Then I got a cheap one. That got poo on it too. Now I use a carrier bag.

Tilly, mum of James

What to keep in your nappy changing bag:
When they're tiny:

Four nappies
Wipes (Or, damp flannel in a sealable plastic bag)
Plastic bags for dirty nappies

Sleepsuit and vest
Two resourceful muslins (bibs/blankets/changing mats/sunscreens/emergency nappies)
Sun hat (summer)
Warm hat (winter)
Small toy or book

If you're bottle feeding include:
Two ready-made feeds
One carton of formula for emergencies

Once they're weaned (from around six months):
As above but add:

Sealed plastic bag including two plastic spoons
Water beaker
Container of bread sticks or rice cakes (handy for unhappy babies on public transport)
Emergency tub of baby food in case you ever forget to pack their lunch
Handful of toys:
- an absorbing one like a book
- a chewy one like a rattle
- a non-toy one like a tea strainer

From around first birthday
You're less likely to need as many nappies or a change of clothes and you won't need an emergency tub of baby food. But add:

Snacks – dried fruit, chopped-up grapes, banana
Little bag with selection of toys and books, include crayons and paper

Make your own changing bag travelling mat

Don't splash out on a pricey changing bag; use one of your existing bags instead and slip this home-made changing mat inside, along with nappies and wipes.

Piece of washable material 56cm x 60cm
Cotton batting 56cm x 30cm
Piece of ribbon

1. Lay the rectangle of cotton batting inside your piece of material, which should be folded lengthwise.
2. Fold and iron the seams, tucking them inside by around 2cm.
3. Sew all around the outside of the mat, sealing the soft lining inside.
4. Take a length of ribbon and stitch it to the middle of the top of the mat.
5. The mat can be carried rolled up and secured with the ribbon.

Happy travelling

Travelling can feel so daunting when you've got a new baby, even if it's just your first ride on the local bus. There's a whole industry that has cleverly appeared, selling all sorts of different gadgets to keep your babies happy, but lots of things you can do yourself. The trick is to be prepared and make sure you've got things like a spare pair of clothes, emergency snacks or spare feeds and a couple of interesting toys, just in case. And although it may not feel like it at the time, small babies are often excellent travellers because they sleep so much.

In the car

It's best to time long car journeys around a baby's nap-time. As Rosie's grown older and slept less during the day, we now leave for most trips around 7 p.m., with her dressed in her pyjamas and ready for bed.

When she was very small and fascinated by black-and-white geometric patterns, we draped a patterned T-shirt that I bought in a charity shop over the headrest in front of her. It fascinated her for ages. Young babies can also be kept entertained by something as simple as a sealed packet of crisps: they are fascinated by the crinkling sound and texture.

From around three to four months old, more alert babies will need some toys to play with to keep them occupied during journeys. It's helpful if you can clip a toy onto their seatbelt or something nearby so they can't drop it, especially if you're travelling alone.

Make your own car entertainment
Wide ribbons
Black felt-tip pen
White paper
Double-sided sticky tape

1. Tie two or three wide, brightly coloured ribbons to the back of the passenger seat, or backseat (depending on whether your baby is still in a rearward-facing seat).
2. Using a thick black felt-tip pen draw some bold patterns and prints on some pieces of white paper. Young babies love the simple shape of faces, they also love bold geometric patterns like zebra print, a black-and-white swirl or some big black spots.
3. Using double-sided sticky tape, attach the drawings to the ribbons.
4. You can keep changing the pictures for variety: as your baby

grows add more colourful drawings or pictures of animals from a magazine or newspaper or even photos of them and their friends.

Music can really help on car journeys. Tune into Radio 3 or Classic FM for some soothing classical music or pop music for some light relief. Burn a CD of nursery rhymes and action songs and keep it in the car. If not, you can always just sing some songs yourself. On one memorable, nightmarish traffic jam on the M1, I must have sung 'The Wheels on the Bus', 'The Grand Old Duke of York', 'The Big Red Bus' and 'Twinkle, Twinkle Little Star' on rotation for nearly an hour, much to my husband's dismay.

The music tape has been totally essential for pacifying and distracting Mae when she's clearly had enough of being in the car!
Abs, mum of Mae

We wrap some of Charlie's toys in used wapping paper and put them in a bag, creating a lucky dip game. Pretty wrapped toys make each dip a surprise, even when the toy is an old one.
Emma, mum of Charlie

On the train and the plane

Depending on how busy it is, at least you can walk around on the train if you need to. So you can jiggle a newborn and rock them back to sleep and walk a restless toddler up and down the aisles. Take a sling with you; if you're on your own it will free up your arms when you're getting on and off. A car seat works well on quiet trains; you can put it on the seat next to you or on the table. This would work well on a coach, too, if there's enough room.

On planes, the trick is to ensure your baby is sucking during take-off and landing to help stop their ears from popping. Try to time feeds so you can breast-feed or bottle-feed them, or put a dummy in their mouth at the right time.

A small-ish blanket folded up in hand luggage can be invaluable, especially before your baby can walk. Lay it on the floor in airport lounges and waiting rooms when your baby is wriggly and wants to have a stretch and a play.

Make up nappy packs for your hand luggage: one plastic shopping bag with a nappy in it and a sealable plastic bag with some wipes in it ready to grab when you need to change their nappy and put the dirty nappy in the plastic bag.

Make your own train/plane baby entertainment

Make a strongly threaded necklace of different bits and pieces from the house to keep your baby entertained as you jiggle them on your lap. It might include pasta shapes, large buttons, scraps of ribbon, things they can twiddle with around your neck. (Just make sure you take it off again when you leave!)

Some toys that have been hidden for a while should entertain them, and use Emma's trick of wrapping them up first. I've always found that a train or plane journey is so exciting for your baby, so many new people to smile at, so many new things to stare at, that they normally turn into angelic creatures.

CHAPTER SEVEN

Feeding

I'm definitely in favour of making your own baby food. It's much cheaper and you know what's in it (even a lot of the organic baby food in the shops seemed to have added sugar when I was looking, as did some brands of baby rice). I used a blender and froze vats of the stuff so I wasn't cooking it up every day.
Catrin, mum of Theo and Cerys

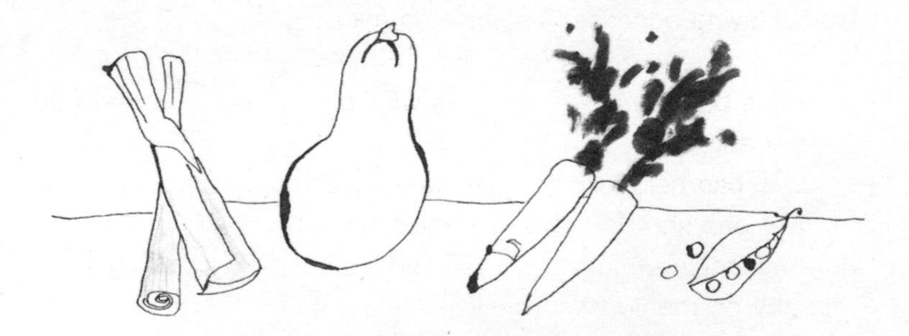

Must-haves
Compact, durable highchair like Tripp Trapp
Powerful milk pump
Muslins

Naughty but nice
Hot Milk nursing bras
Cath Kidston wipe-clean bib

What you and baby can live without
Colour-changing spoons
Bowls that stick down (they don't)

Feeding is so central to the well-being of you and your baby that it's easy to get carried away by all the gadgets and paraphernalia you might need. Stay strong and resist all these purchases; you just don't need half the stuff. The most important ingredient is the actual foodstuff, whether it's breast milk or puréed butternut squash, rather than the latest, whizziest steriliser or designer highchair.

Muslins – a resourceful buy
Buy lots of muslins. It's one of those resourceful items that is well worth buying because they have so many uses:

1. In the beginning, use them as winding cloths and to mop up milk and sick.
2. They can help with discreet breast-feeding by draping them over one shoulder and then over the baby.
3. As changing mats or a clean surface if you want to lay a baby on the floor somewhere.
4. Tuck a muslin over their sheets in the Moses basket or cot where their head lies; this stops you having to change the sheets so often.
5. They make light blankets in the summer.

6. Pin them to the buggy as impromptu sun shades.
7. Once you're weaning they make wonderful bibs, big enough to protect (nearly) a whole outfit.
8. They could even make emergency nappies if you ran short.

Below are the bare feeding essentials that will help nourish and nurture your growing baby, from the milk diet of a newborn all the way to a breadstick-chomping, banana-munching, pasta-throwing toddler.

Breast-feeding

Essential kit

Muslins
Nursing bras
Re-usable breast pads
One bottle
Steriliser or good dishwasher
Breast pump – you can rent one

Breast-feeding is a wonderful thing. Not only is it the healthiest, most nutritious food you can give your baby, it can also save you hundreds of pounds in formula milk, not to mention all the kit that bottle-fed babies need. The cost of even basic formula is around £800 a year, whereas breast milk is free, aside from the initial outlay of some nursing bras, breast pads and a pump.

Then there's the time and energy it can save. No need to wash and sterilise lots of bottles, boil the kettle, measure out formula every morning. Instead the baby's food is on tap, at the perfect temperature, when and where they're feeling at bit peckish. How clever.

There's really only one piece of essential kit that you need as a breast-feeding mother – nursing bras. They make it easy for you to breast-feed in public discreetly and also give much-needed support. You will need more than one because they need regular washing and you even have to wear them in bed. So buy at least two, more if you want to do washing less frequently. There's no reason why you can't buy them second-hand or borrow a friend's, but get yourself measured to ensure they fit correctly. I bought two from M&S and I lived in them for six months. More glamorous, feminine nursing bras from Hot Milk or Elle Macpherson can be bought online at underwear website www.figleaves.co.uk.

I even borrowed nursing bras and a breast pump.
Lynsey, mum of Amber

Breast pads are also important to prevent wet patches when your breast milk leaks onto your clothes. They normally slip into a pocket in your nursing bra. If you're stuck, a carefully folded muslin would work. (I used loo roll in emergencies.) Don't bother buying disposable breast pads, they are scratchy and uncomfortable. They're also a false economy because you'll get through loads. Instead, buy a pack of re-usable, washable pads. They're softer against your skin and tend to be more absorbent.

If you decide against expressing milk then you won't need a breast pump, steriliser or bottles. However, midwives often encourage new mothers to express as it can help increase your milk supply. And as your baby becomes a little older it can give you some freedom. It means someone else can do one of the night feeds while you sleep, or that you could pop out for a cup of tea or a swim and be away for longer than two hours.

It is worth investing in a decent breast pump whether you rent or buy one. One of the reasons many women don't get along with expressing milk is because some of the cheaper breast pumps are too time-consuming and a waste of money. I bought a second-hand electric breast pump and it suited me fine. It was called the Mini Medela Electric Breast Pump and retails new for around £50.

My editor, Rosemary, used an Ameda Lactaline Electric Breast Pump. It was quite pricey at £85 but afterwards her two sisters and several friends got great use out of it.

Another resourceful option would be to hire a breast pump from your local health visitor or NCT group. That way you'll get to try out a more powerful model that would be too expensive to buy yourself. You can then return it when you've finished. See www.expressyourselfmums.co.uk for rental options, sales and advice.

They say that the best pumps are those that mimic the baby's sucking action, starting off with a faster, lighter suction to stimulate the let-down reflex, and switching over to a slower, stronger, sucking rhythm to extract as much milk as possible.

Depending on how much you're into breast-feeding, using a breast pump was very time-consuming and the results never really made it worthwhile for me! I hear electronic ones are better than the manual one I used.

Shonagh, mum of Caitlin

Once you're expressing milk you will need a feeding bottle and something to sterilise it with. It's likely you'll only be giving your baby one bottle a day so you don't need more than one bottle. I hunted out a bottle specially designed for breast-fed babies, with a teat that's more like a nipple than standard formula bottles. Try and pick up a second-hand steriliser. Sterilising tablets and boiling water would work just as well, especially as you'll only need to sterilise one bottle a day.

The microwaveable steriliser seemed pretty painless – and I found these plastic on-the-go steriliser bags, which were useful if you were going away for the night.

Abs, mum of Mae

Bottle feeding

Essential kit
Six bottles and teats
One steriliser or good dishwasher
Lots of muslins

The formula milk and bottle manufacturers are clever at creating lots of different gadgets and kit for new parents to buy and use. The truth is you don't need most of them and it will certainly be cheaper to find non-baby alternatives. (For example, buy normal washing-up brushes or a new toothbrush, rather than expensive baby bottle brushes.) Obviously, hygiene for young babies is crucial and warm milk can be a ripe breeding ground for bacteria, so don't cut corners on cleanliness and sterilising, but you don't need to buy everything.

We inherited a microwave steriliser from a family friend. It was great. It just needed a splash of water in the bottom and then we popped Rosie's dummies, bottle and teat in for five minutes on high power. It all seemed very easy. And the added bonus was that we stored the steriliser in the microwave so it didn't clutter up our tiny kitchen.

If you're using formula exclusively you will have a lot of bottles to clean, sterilise and prepare. It can be time-consuming, and all the kit can take up a lot of room in your kitchen. So consider how much space you've got on your sideboards before you buy some expensive sterilising contraption that will dominate your kitchen – some of them look like spaceships.

If you have a good dishwasher or have the time to properly wash bottles in the sink with washing liquid and hot water, then you don't necessarily need a steriliser. Some doctors then recommend submerging bottles and teats in a pot of boiling water for a few minutes before using. Washing by hand could be a faff if you have lots of bottles to clean and sterilise.

Similarly, there's an American bottle system called Playtex, which doesn't require sterilising as the milk is dispensed from pre-sterilised liners. Apparently this helps to prevent colic, as the bags collapse as the baby feeds, reducing air bubbles. Playtex is not widely available in the UK, but you can buy them online at www.infantcaredirect.co.uk.

As someone who didn't breast-feed for long, I had to get the whole formula thing as easy as possible. I found the warming flask very useful in the early stages, although a waste of money down the line when I realised it wasn't going to harm Charlie to have his milk at room temperature! We bought an Avent bottle warmer and still use it now for his evening bottle but it is expensive and a kettle and jug will do the same job! I would not have bought the bumper Avent pack that is available at something ridiculous like £130 because you don't need half the stuff, but the large plug-in Avent steriliser holds six bottles and the job is done for the whole day. When you are bottle feeding, you need to feel organised, especially in those early days when you're dealing with the night feeds.

Emma, mum of Charlie

If you want to buy a steriliser, there's no reason why you can't buy one second-hand. Look out on eBay, in charity shops and NCT sales – and even better ask family and friends. I'd even buy second-hand bottles, a lot of them won't have been used, as many new parents buy loads of different types of bottles before they settle on a favourite.

You may end up spending as much as £15 a week on formula milk, so it's worth trying to save some money on the kit, if you can. For example, you don't need a bottle warmer, instead just use hot water and a large container to warm the milk. Similarly, although specially designed powder dispensers can be handy when you're out and about, you could just as easily measure out formula into a sterilised, small, plastic, sealed container.

Bottle warmers – you do not need these. Most cafés will be more than happy to give you hot water to warm milk and generally you will find that your baby will drink the milk however it comes.

Nics, mum of Anna and Kate

Weaning

Essential Kit

Highchair (don't rush to buy one, you can feed in a baby chair for a while)
Handheld blender
Ice cube trays
Recycled yogurt pots and/or plastic containers
Wipe-clean bib
Plastic bags for freezer

I vividly remember the day we gave Rosie her first spoonful of baby rice. I felt really nervous about it, I don't know why, and made the mixture so runny that it was the same consistency as breast milk anyway. Weaning your baby can be quite an anxious time: you feel as if you've only just got one type of feeding sorted and now you've both got to learn about another.

This is why you can be vulnerable to making all kinds of rash purchases, from the heat-sensitive, colour-changing spoons, to the all-singing, all-dancing highchair, special baby food pots and must-have baby recipe books.

Highchairs

The most expensive purchase in the kitchen will be the highchair. I think it can be difficult buying a highchair for your five- or six-month-old, knowing it needs to last them until they're around two years old. So don't rush; it's easy to feed a young baby in its baby chair. In fact, some little babies are just too small for highchairs and slump and slide down the seat anyway.

There's no need to buy a highchair ready for weaning. You can feed them in the bouncy chair or in the Bumbo.
Annabel, mum of Molly

A highchair can be lifesaver though. It's another safe place for your baby to sit while you can get on with two-hand pottering in the kitchen. Aside from eating, you may be able to persuade your baby to sit in their highchair for a little play. Especially messy play. And as they get older it can be the perfect place to sit when painting or drawing.

Many of my friends who bought highchairs perfectly suitable for their small babies, with lots of padding and gizmos and even a reclining function so they could snooze after lunch are now selling them to buy something more compact, like booster seats, for their toddlers.

Our highchair takes up so much space.
Hazel, mum of Leo

I regret buying our highchair. I thought it had to be height adjustable and that it needed to recline. But it's ridiculous and it takes up so much room. And it's hard to clean. Finding one that's easy to clean is really important.
Emma, mum of Charlie

Do consider buying your highchair second-hand. I've seen one white-pod designer highchair that costs £300; it looks like a swanky bar stool. Another hi-tech plastic highchair had seven different height adjustments. Second-hand, durable wooden chairs are a good buy, although you may find you need to buy a harness yourself and use cushions to support your baby while they're little.

If you do buy a second-hand plastic, multi-functional chair, inspect it closely for general grubbiness and old pieces of food. Also, make sure it's solid and steady. Before you buy, check it's easy to fold and put up again; remember you may need to do this one-handed. You can snap up some real bargain highchairs for just £5 in charity shops. They'll be perfect while your baby's little and then you can buy a booster seat if you need to when they're toddlers. If you want to buy new, IKEA has a well-designed, white plastic highchair (Antilop) with a harness for just £11.99 and a tray for £3.00 – a very resourceful purchase.

I splashed out on a wooden Tripp Trapp highchair for around £100 from www.stokke.com It was pricey but the chair adapts as your child grows, so your baby could still be using it at mealtimes when they're seven. The Tripp Trapp slots into your own table so your baby can feel as if they're eating with you. When Rosie was smaller, Simon made her a wooden tray to clip onto the chair. And I also squeezed a cushion behind her for extra support when she was little.

There are five main kinds of highchairs to choose from:

1. Wooden highchairs can often be adapted as your baby grows and some can even turn into adult chairs. They often don't come with padding, so you'll need to use cushions to support a smaller baby. Some don't come with trays – you can either make one or just pull the chair to the table. I protect our table with a brightly coloured PVC tablecloth and try to encourage Rosie to keep her food in her bowl.
2. Multi-functional highchairs are the all-singing, all-dancing chairs. They come with lots of padding so are comfy for little babies; however, this can make them hard to clean. They can recline and some have a removable tray that can be popped in the dishwasher, sometimes with separate compartments so you don't need to use crockery. They can take up a lot of room, so make sure you can fold them away.
3. Booster seats are clipped on to a normal chair and pulled up to the table or some come with a tray. They're often used in restaurants. They're not padded so are not as comfy for small babies. They're fantastic for travelling.
4. Table seats attach or clamp on to your table. They're

normally covered in fabric and can be folded down for travelling. Your table needs to be stable enough to support the weight of your baby and the seat. They can only be used by children up to a certain weight.

5. Convertible highchairs are made up of a table and chair that combine to form a highchair. This enables you to transform them into a little table and chair for your toddler.

A poll around my friends with babies suggests there are two key questions they wished they'd asked themselves before buying a highchair:

Is it easy to clean?

The padded, all-singing, all-dancing chairs can have lots of hidden nooks and crannies making them difficult to clean. These chairs will become caked in food, so don't make life harder for yourself.

Is it easy to store?

Highchairs take up so much room. If you buy a conventional one, can it fold flat so you can store it when not in use? If you live in a small flat or house it might be worth considering buying a booster seat or a chair that clips on to or slides under the table.

Feeding kit

The only essential piece of feeding kit you need initially is a special baby spoon and a couple of plastic or melamine bowls. The spoons are normally plastic, presumably because they're softer on a baby's gums than a metal one. You can get whizzy ones that change colour if the food is hot, but there's really no need. You'll be tasting and testing the first few spoonfuls yourself anyway.

Don't bother buying spoons with a coloured temperature gauge – just taste the food before giving to baby.

Nics, mum of Kate and Anna

You may already have some plastic Tupperware containers to use as baby bowls. I use some brightly coloured, melamine ice-cream bowls that I had before. Sometimes, providing I'm closely supervising Rosie, I just use one of our pudding bowls. If I'm using the microwave I prefer heating and defrosting her food in non-plastic containers.

Mess-control

Bibs are essential during weaning. Goodness, it's messy. If you're at home, feed your baby in their nappy and then hose them down! In the early stages I bought a long-sleeved bib from the supermarket to use or I would have had to change Rosie's clothes every time she ate. When we're out and about I find a muslin knotted behind her neck offers more coverage than a conventional bib. A wipe-clean bib will save your washing load too. I splurged on a pretty Cath Kidson Mini Cowboy bib for £6. Rosie's worn it for every meal since, so it was worth splashing out on. You can also buy solid plastic bibs with a little trough to catch the food, but I think they can be uncomfortable around the baby's neck.

Make your own bib

(Make sure the material you use is machine-washable)

Piece of material 35cm x 28cm – cotton towelling is ideal as it's absorbent and washable
Contrasting strip of material 5cm x 130cm
Contrasting remnant for motif
Two squares of Velcro

1. Either use an existing bib as a template or trace an oval 34cm x 26cm on some newspaper. Fold in two before cutting to ensure it's symmetrical.

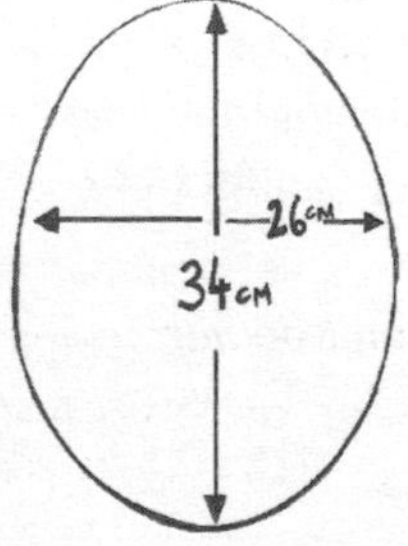

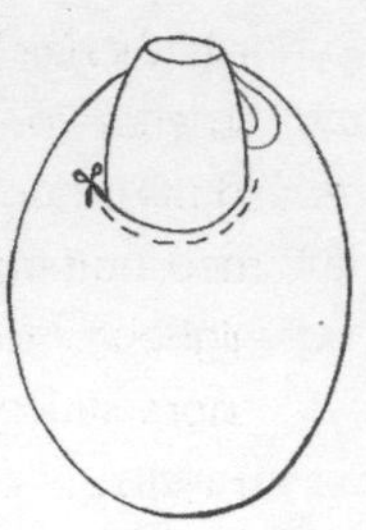

2. 5cm below the top of the bib, use a mug or coffee jar to trace a circle of 10cm diameter onto your pattern.
3. Cut out the circle by snipping through the top. These will be your neck straps and will be attached by Velcro. Now you have your pattern. Use this to cut out the material.
4. Using a contrasting piece of fabric to make the edges, cut out one long length or several pieces measuring 50cm x 130cm.
5. Rather than pinning the edging from scratch, fold it first using an iron. Fold the fabric in half lengthwise, open the fold and fold each edge to meet in the middle and fold in half again and iron.

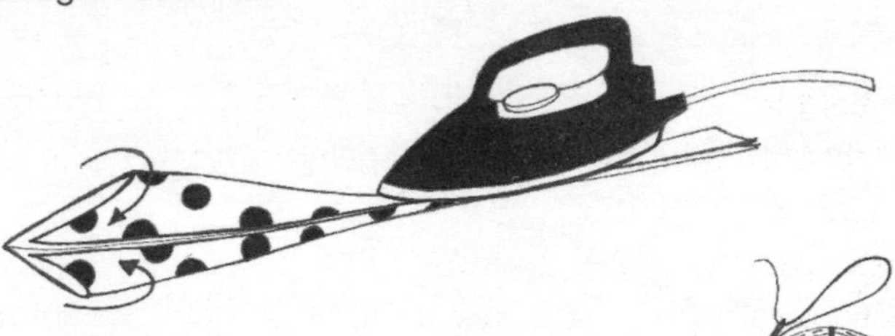

6. Pin your folded edge around the bib.
7. Stitch the binding in place by hand or with a sewing machine.
8. Using the same edging fabric, cut out a simple motif like an apple or a duck or a fish and stitch onto the middle of the bib, either by hand or with a zigzag stitch on your machine. If you're unsure, trace the shape onto newspaper first to make a pattern.
9. Stitch two pieces of Velcro to the neck straps to fasten the bib.

If your highchair is going to be placed on a carpet or rug, rather than an easy-to-clean floor, protect it with some plastic sheeting. Instead of buying a specially made mat, just buy one metre of PVC patterned material. You can do the same to protect your table if your highchair doesn't have a tray. I find friends and family are very appreciative when I take this protective floor covering with me on visits. (A bin bag would do the trick.)

Head chef

Make your own baby food. Don't spend a fortune on ready-made organic heavily packaged stuff when you can easily make your own version and freeze it.
Ali, mum of Louis and Eddie

Essential kit

Handheld blender or mini mouli-legume or potato ricer
Ice cube trays
Plastic bags for freezer
Plastic pots and lids (cheaper to buy from supermarket rather than baby shops)
Microwave – not essential but handy

The handheld whizzers were totally essential for puréeing food, as was the steamer and ice cube trays and plastic bags.
Abs, mum of Mae

One of the most effective ways of saving money with a growing baby is to feed them on your own food rather than on expensive jars of baby food. It's a lot more nutritious and saves stacks of money. Posh organic baby jars can cost as much as £1 each, meaning you can spend around £5 a day, if you're using them for breakfast and pudding too. That's £35 a week, £140 a month and £840 from six months until their first birthday.

Home-cooking baby food means you know exactly what your baby is eating. It also means that they're less likely to be fussy eaters when they move onto family food, although I've got no evidence to back this up, aside from anecdotal stories.

In the early days when you're getting your baby to try lots of different fruit and vegetables it couldn't be easier. In fact, it's not really cooking. All you need to do is steam the vegetables and then purée them. I found it was best to work on batches. So I'd steam and purée a load of carrots one night, sweet potatoes the next, then butternut squash and courgette and so on.

An electric handheld blender makes making purées simple and less messy than a food processor, which has a hundred attachments that always need washing afterwards.

Nics, mum of Kate and Anna

I've just (belatedly!) discovered a fab gadget in the potato ricer and I'm sure that would be very good (and portable) for preparing baby mush.

Catrin, mum of Theo and Cerys

Blend the vegetables into a smooth purée, mixing with a splash of the cooking water to get the right consistency. Remember you can always make them smoother with some breast milk or formula if you need to or thicken them up with some baby rice just before you give them to the baby. Pour the purée into a ice cube tray and cool fast before placing into freezer. Once they're frozen, empty the cubes into a plastic bag labelled with date and contents.

As your baby grows and their tastes mature, cooking in bulk and freezing in batches means you don't have to be cooking all the time. Indeed, once your baby is around ten months old, there's no reason why they can't eat very similar meals to the rest of the family. Today, I double the quantity of Rosie-friendly meals like fish pie, spaghetti bolognese, cottage pie, chicken casserole and freeze half, divided into small pots for later.

You don't need to buy special freezer pots or ice cube tray – just a standard, 99p ice cube tray from the shop is perfectly adequate.

Susan, mum of Madeline

There's also lots of special baby porridges and breakfast cereals on the supermarket shelves. I delayed giving wheat and dairy to Rosie until she was nine months because my husband has eczema and asthma. However, once I'd introduced wheat, I gave her Weetabix for breakfast, rather than special baby porridge; it's much more economical to use adult cereals and porridge, rather than special baby ones. However, do scan the ingredients list for extra sugar and salt.

Food for thought

I have been making all Joshy's food fresh, which can be more time-consuming but cheaper and better for them. My mate told me she spent £50 on jar food in two weeks! Little Tupperware containers are cheaper from supermarkets rather than children's stores.

Rachel, mum of Josh

There are some excellent baby food recipe books, notably by Annabel Karmel. I found I used a recipe book constantly when Rosie was first weaned, probably because I was lacking in ideas and confidence. However, I haven't referred to it since. So do order these books from the library, or look out for them second-hand, rather than buying them new. I also used to copy recipes from friends' books and swap ideas for combinations when I was visiting.

Weaning guidelines

Age	Introducing foods
Four months	Baby rice mixed with breast or formula milk, mashed banana, avocado, papaya, puréed cooked apple or pear, mashed cooked vegetables like carrot, parsnip, potato, butternut squash
Six months (recommended age to begin weaning)	As above, along with more vegetable and fruit combinations. Gradually introduce wheat, gluten and full-fat dairy like yogurt, fromage frais and custard
Seven months	Adult cereal like porridge, Weetabix or Ready Brek. Mashed fish (plaice is a good first fish), mashed chicken, mashed red meat, citrus fruits. Mashed pulses like lentils. Soft finger foods like pasta shapes, cooked carrot sticks, cooked peas and sweetcorn, banana sticks, chunks of avocado
Nine months	Introduce lumps, chop the food, rather than purée. Introduce well-cooked eggs. If allergies run in the family, gradually introduce gluten and dairy. Harder finger foods like peeled apple. May want to try to feed herself. Have one spoon each
Twelve months	Whole cow's milk around one pint daily – any more and there'll be no room for food. Introduce honey, soft eggs, limited salt and sugar, soft cheese. May become fussy. Can eat same meals as rest of family now, providing not too spicy, salty, etc.
Five years	Whole and chopped nuts

There are lots of baby food recipes on the internet. Take inspiration from the combination of food in baby jars and exchange ideas with friends and family. There's nothing wrong with buying jars when you're out and about, but you don't have to. Even on a hot day, you can take some ice cubes from the freezer in the morning, they will have defrosted by lunchtime and you can warm them in a cup of hot water. Even easier is the ultimate transportable baby food – mashed avocado for mains, followed by mashed banana for pudding. (Rosie used to love them mashed together.)

It's up to you whether you buy organic fruit and vegetables or not. You'll certainly save money if you buy your fresh fruit and vegetables from your local greengrocer's, rather than a supermarket. This will ensure you buy in season and buy stuff as fresh as possible. There's also nothing wrong with using frozen vegetables. My freezer has always got frozen sweetcorn, peas, spinach and broccoli.

What is baby-led weaning?

In the past few years, a new concept called baby-led wearing has been gaining momentum, which can take the pressure off endless puréeing. Baby-led weaning means you let your baby take control of feeding themselves. Rather than puréeing and spoon feeding, you place a selection of finger foods on their highchair tray and let them help themselves. Many parents find themselves weaning their second children this way, just because it can be easier.

Baby-led weaning can only be introduced when a baby is six months old, as they need to be able to sit up straight in their high-chair. The food you give them needs to be things they can grasp in their fist, as babies this age haven't always developed their pincer grip. Soft-cooked vegetables that are chip-shaped or broccoli spears tend to work well.

As an anxious first-time mum, I didn't use baby-led weaning with Rosie, preferring to spoon feed her purées instead. However, it is something I might consider for my next baby, as it would be much easier to fit in with family meals. Here are some pros and cons for you to consider before you make a decision:

Pros:
- No need to purée meals, which can be time-consuming
- Fans say babies tend to be less picky eaters as they get older
- Baby is able to take as much or as little as they need
- Baby tends to avoid food that they're later found to be intolerant to

Cons:
- Parents may be nervous about the baby choking
- Parents may be concerned that baby isn't eating enough
- Baby will have a limited diet initially
- Messy

First tastes

Once you've tested out the different vegetables and fruit with your new eater, you can start to blend a mixture of vegetables for variety. As Rosie wasn't a big fan of solids, I found mixing the vegetables with fruit helped improve her enthusiasm. Sometimes it just meant I'd be putting her dinner and pudding into the same bowl. All babies are different, but I do think there are some vegetables that are more popular than others. I wish I'd puréed a lot more butternut squash, a lot more sweet potato, a lot more courgettes and peas, for example, and a lot less swede.

Rather than making recipes, I found it was easier to do a 'pick and mix'. So I'd cook the vegetables, meat and fish separately, put them into bags and then take a mixture of whatever I fancied.

Abs, mum of Mae

Rosie's favourite purées
Courgette and tomatoes
Butternut squash and pear
Sweet potato, butternut squash, apple and cinnamon
Peas, spinach, pear and apple
Courgette, beans, pear and apple

I was a little too enthusiastic about puréeing and ended up with a freezer drawer full of vegetable cubes that Rosie was no longer interested in. However, you can use them to make delicious soups, either for adults or for your older baby. Defrost a tasty combination of cubes, add some vegetable or chicken stock to thin to the right consistency and add some lentils, cannellini beans or cut-up spaghetti for texture.

Tasty mush for babies
It all gets a bit more interesting once your baby is around nine months old and is becoming a well-practised eater. Rosie seemed to enjoy her food more once I was making her proper meals, rather than combination purées. I think she preferred the stronger flavours of herbs and garlic; perhaps she had grown a taste for it while breast-feeding?

Again, cook meals in bulk and start freezing sections of family meals (just make sure you don't add salt or too much chilli while cooking). My friend Annabel often adds a handful of cooked quinoa to Molly's meals, instantly boosting its protein content.

The sort of family meals that translate well into baby mush are 'nursery food': cottage pie, spaghetti bolognese, fish pie, ratatouille, roast dinners and casseroles. Traditional puddings like rice pudding, crumble and custard, apples and custard and bread and butter pudding go down a treat, too.

Yogurt and jellies are normally a big favourite for babies. However, it's healthier and more economical if you avoid the specially made baby fromage frais, yogurts and jellies on the market. Instead, mix a few spoonfuls of natural yogurt with some fruit purée or mashed banana. Similarly, make your own jelly with fruit juice, fruit purée and gelatine or agar (from seaweed).

Rosie's chicken casserole

Fry one chicken breast, one onion and a clove of garlic. Add one sliced sweet potato and one courgette. Add a tin of chopped tomatoes and some mixed herbs. Simmer until cooked, adding a handful of frozen peas five minutes before the end.

Molly's avocado surprise

Mash half an avocado with two teaspoons of creamy cottage cheese and whatever fruit is lying around; so far we've tried pear, papaya and mango.

Ruby's British veal casserole

Heat a little oil in a saucepan and cook a chopped onion, stirring occasionally for five minutes or until softened. Add 200g diced British veal and cook for another five mins until browned. Stir in two diced carrots, one small celery stick, tomato purée with some fresh parsley. Mix it all together and cook for another minute or so. Cover with water and cook, stirring occasionally for approx thirty minutes. Add a handful of long green beans (I use frozen) and cook for another ten minutes. You can serve it with potatoes, rice or even pasta. Ruby loves it and veal is a much healthier and lighter option than beef.

Kate's cheesy spinach

Kate loves spinach with cheese, which is surprising as she is quite a fussy eater when it comes to anything green. I just defrost frozen balls of spinach and melt them with cheese (generally cheddar), and she can't get enough.

Ruby's easy polenta with yogurt

Cook some polenta following the instructions on the pack. Once cooled to a warm temperature mix in some yogurt for a quick and nutritious meal. This can be eaten for breakfast or for dinner and instead of yogurt you can use just ordinary milk.

Rosie's speedy tuna tea

This is the perfect no-cook baby food if your freezer is empty and you need something fast. Mash two tablespoons of tinned butter beans (make sure you rinse well) with one tablespoon of tuna and a little milk or water for one portion.

Charlie's fish supper

Simmer some rice and water in a pan for ten minutes. Add a skinned, carefully deboned fillet of fish (cod or plaice works well), and a diced carrot and cook for another ten minutes. Add a handful of frozen peas and some parsley and cook for another five minutes.

Rosie's butternut squash ice cream

Bake a butternut squash in the oven, scoop out the flesh and mash, stirring vanilla extract into the mixture. Cool and pop into freezer. At the point it's beginning to freeze, give a good stir and serve. This 'pudding' will be especially popular for teething babies.

Oli's peas please

Mash a handful of peas with the same amount of cottage cheese. Serve spread on toast or rice cakes or as a dip for breadsticks.

Toddler tastes

By the time your baby has reached their first birthday, it's likely they'll eating a very similar diet to you. Indeed, there's nothing they love more than seeing that everyone has got the same things on their plate as they have. All of the recipes listed above for younger babies work well with toddlers; they just need chopping rather than puréeing.

Molly's ratatouille
Chop and fry one onion, one red pepper, one courgette and one aubergine. Add a sprinkle of herbs and a tin of chopped tomatoes. Simmer for thirty minutes. Serve with brown rice, pasta or as a filling for tortilla or pitta bread.

Rosie's pork stir fry
Chop some spring onions, half a yellow pepper, a handful of mushrooms and a fillet of pork into thin slices. Throw into a hot, oiled frying pan and stir quickly. Add a splash of water, a squeeze of lime juice and a teaspoon of soy sauce as needed. When cooked, add a handful of cooked noodles to mixture and a beaten egg. Stir vigorously.

Dino's chicken and barley casserole
Place a chicken piece (leg or breast or whatever you get from butcher or carve off whole chicken) in a pan with a couple of handfuls of barley, a diced carrot and diced celery. Cover in water, bring to the boil then simmer for around an hour and a half until the chicken is soft. Add some parsley for seasoning.

Dino's vegetable cake
Steam and mash some carrots, a potato and some peas. Serve the vegetables shaped like a three-layered cake with potato at

the bottom, then carrot, then peas, topped with some grated cheese.

Amber's big pasta surprise
Use big pasta shapes, toddler hand-grabbing size, and combine with the following toppings:

1) Home-made tomato sauce.
2) Pesto, plain yogurt (optional) and cheese.
3) Sauteed leek, mushroom, smoked mackerel and plain yogurt.

Finger food

Lauren's yummy pizzas
Slice a wholewheat muffin in two. Cover the surface with tinned chopped tomatoes, a sprinkle of herbs, pieces of ham and grated cheese. Pop under the grill for delicious, speedy pizza tea.

Molly's super veggie sauce
Roast a selection of vegetables in the oven with garlic and herbs, for example, red onion, green pepper, courgette, aubergine, sweet potato and butternut squash. When cooked, add a tin of chopped tomatoes and blitz in blender to make a sauce. This versatile, healthy, 'hidden veggie' sauce can be used as a topping for pizza and pasta or as a sauce for rice or couscous. It's worth freezing it in ice cube trays.

Rosie's cheesy feet
Pop some slices of brown bread in the toaster. Butter and spread with cream cheese. Using a foot-shaped cookie cutter, cut out some cheesy feet.

Charlie's cheesy dippers

Beat together two eggs and a tablespoon of milk. Dip brown bread into the mixture till both sides are covered and fry gently in a little olive oil until browned. Mix together some cream cheese and a tablespoon of tomato purée in an egg cup, serve with eggy-bread soldiers for dipping.

Gracie's snail sandwiches

Trim the crusts off a slice of brown bread, spread one side with a filling like jam, cheese spread or hummus. Carefully roll up the bread into a log shape, which you slice into pieces 2–3cm thick. Stand the spirals on their sides with the piece of bread poking out from the bottom. Add two thin carrot batons to make the snail's eye stalks. Serve on a bed of chopped lettuce.

Leo's chickpea dip

Put a tin of chickpeas in a blender with two tablespoons of extra virgin olive oil, lemon juice, one crushed garlic clove and black pepper. Serve with vegetables like cucumber, pepper, carrots or bread sticks and toasted soldiers.

Caitlin's picnic lunch

This works well for lunch on the go, when you don't want the hassle of a messy spoon-fed meal. Chop a chunk of cucumber, a handful of cherry tomatoes, a handful of olives, some raw pepper and cheddar cheese into bite-sized pieces. Add a handful of cooked sweetcom and anything else you've got lying in the fridge, from cooked chicken to ham. Rip a small, brown pitta bread into the mix. Your baby will love being able to dip into their lunch and select different bites to eat.

Dino's spinach pie

This is a delicious Bosnian recipe from my friend Maida for the whole family to enjoy. Mix some cooked spinach with some crème fraîche or Greek yogurt, spread the mixture on a rolled-out piece of filo pastry and repeat the process until you have three or four layers of pastry and spinach. Cook in the oven for thirty minutes.

Oli's Apple Fritters

My polish friend Monika gives this as a pudding to her little son Oli: sometimes he even gets it for his dinner (lucky Oli). You need two apples, one glass of milk and one glass of water, some flour, one egg and a pinch of salt. Mix everything together aside from the apples, enough flour for the mixture to have the consistency of a thick pancake batter. Peel and slice the apples into small flat chunks and add to the mixture. Heat some oil and add spoonfuls of mixture to the pan, when one side is honey-coloured turn it over. You should be able to make around four fritters each time in a regular-sized pan.

And finally, some wise words:

Some good food facts to remember as you struggle to get anything past your little cherub's rosebud lips:

1. It takes a toddler sixty-eight days to starve

2. Yogurt contains all the main food groups – fats, proteins, fruit and carbs in the form of fruit sugar, then there's always vitamin drops for the really fussy eaters . . .

Dr Lynsey, mum of Amber and GP

CHAPTER EIGHT

Dressing

Accept gifts graciously, but if you think brand-new snowsuits are never going to be worn (or if you've been given four) take them back to the shop and exchange them for something more useful. We were given four blankets, in addition to what we'd bought, and countless fleecy jackets and snowsuits! Mothercare and other big chain stores are usually happy to exchange if labels are intact and the garments are unworn. You can always say how sweet the baby looks in whatever item but watch out for friends and relatives who you see regularly and who will expect to see these items being modelled.

Annabel, mum of Molly

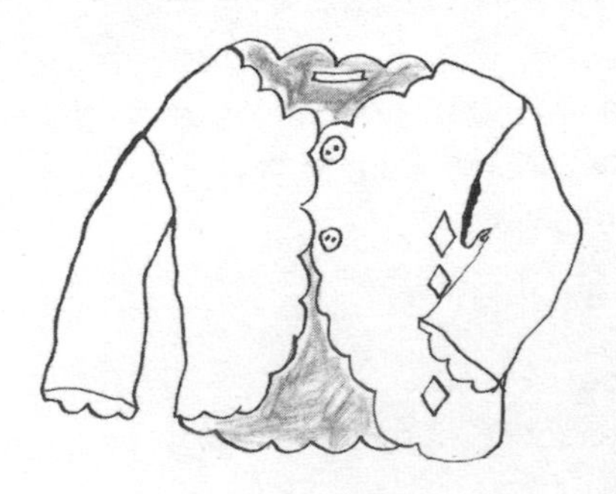

When the first person in my group of friends had a baby girl called Kate, I went to a posh boutique and spent a silly amount of money on an impractical, tiny, pink outfit. It even had wings. They wrapped it up with beautiful, crinkly tissue paper and enclosed it with coloured ribbons in a small, expensive-looking shiny box.

I should have known better. For starters, the 'wings' that had caught my eye would have been so uncomfortable for a little baby lying on their back. Then, there was the tininess of the outfit; if it hadn't been worn within days of Kate being born it would have been too small.

It's so easy to get carried away when buying clothes for babies. But the moral of this story, I suppose, is that you as a new mum don't have to, because everyone else will instead. Just focus on buying a few essential items and I promise you that everyone else will buy the stuff you didn't even know you needed.

I didn't buy loads of stuff in advance, just a few babygros and vests, and due to the amazing amount of clothing as presents we got sent from family and friends I didn't really need to buy very much for about the first year.

Catrin, mum of Theo and Cerys

Dressing essentials

Must-haves

Handful of soft cotton babygros
Handful of soft cotton vests
Hand-knitted cardigans
Warm hat

Naughty but nice

Soft leather shoes (once baby is mobile)

What you and baby can live without

Anything brand-new with a designer label

We all know at least one story about the total surprise of the sex of a baby, so play safe and buy white or brightly coloured babygros before your baby is born. Bright colours can look gorgeous and don't stain as easily as pastel colours. Healthy babies grow quickly, so there's really no need to buy too much in one size. Within days they may be in the bigger size anyway.

The most important thing to remember when dressing your newborn is their comfort. As they're going to be snoozing nearly all the time, they need to feel relaxed. Look out for natural materials like soft cotton, and opt for clothes that are easy to put on and off. I washed all of our baby clothes (both new and second-hand) before Rosie wore them with a mild, non-biological washing powder.

All-in-one sleepsuits or babygros and vests are all you need. The vests are really handy because aside from keeping your baby warm and snug, they also act as extra security for explosive nappies and can protect a babygro from getting covered in pooh.

Jazz babygros up during the day with a little cardi or a knitted tank top. Always opt for babygros with built-in feet; that way you don't have to worry about baby socks, which are so cute, but impractical because they always fall off. Babygros are also kinder on a baby's round pot belly than trousers and tops, especially in the early days before the tummy button has healed.

Make your own – customising white vests and sleepsuits

It's cheap and easy to jazz up plain vests and babygros into snazzy, bespoke outfits. Visit your local craft shop and buy a couple of small pots of fabric paint and a brush. You could cover them all over with patterns, but I think it looks best to stick with one motif or name. I drew a big, red, round 'R' on Rosie's vests, and also decorated some with her name. On others I drew a simple flower.

Spots are very easy to draw freehand and would look nice in a little square. The good artists among you could draw animals – sheep, ducks and fish are normally quite simple. Copy design ideas from baby clothes you see in the shops.

If you've received a bag full of hand-me-down, not-so-white babygros, you could give them a new lease of life by dyeing them in bold colours.

Babies seem to hate having things pulled over their heads, which is why cardigans are a good option. Also poppers are much faster than buttons, handy when your baby gets cross about being changed. Look out for buttons at the back of an outfit; they'll dig in when a baby is sleeping on their back.

I bought a really cute brown bear snowsuit for Rosie before she was born. It was from BabyGap and cost lots of money. It was so small that she soon grew out of it. However, the biggest issue was how difficult it was to get on. I couldn't simply lay her in it and then do up some press studs but I had to force her arms and legs into the suit, which she just hated. Needless to say, she only wore it about three times. And I personally think that lots of snug blankets in the pram or buggy are an easier alternative than a snowsuit for winter babies.

The essential items for a newborn

Six vests in newborn size
Three sleepsuits/babygros in newborn size
Six vests in 0–3 months
Three sleepsuits in 0–3 months
Two cardigans
One cotton/sun hat (if summer baby)
One woolly hat (if winter baby)

Buying new

If you want to buy the essentials new, then do shop around, buy budget brands and never miss a sale. Scan the sale rails in BabyGap, Next, M&S, Mothercare, and visit retail outlets for bargains.

You can buy the basics from supermarkets like George at Asda, Tesco or Sainsbury. I bought five white, short-sleeved vests for £7 and three sleepsuits for £5 in Tesco. And they were perfect. Budget retailers Primark, Matalan and H&M are all also good value.

We did get over-excited and buy a very cute babygro from Petit Bateau but it was way too small for him when he was born. My tip would be to go to Mothercare, buy a cheap pack of three sleeveless/legless vests in white and three white towelling babygros in size 0–3 months. Then, when the baby is born, you can always go smaller if necessary.

Amy, mum of Seth and Agnes

By the time your baby reaches their first birthday, it's likely you'll need to consider buying them their first pair of shoes. And if there's one thing you should buy new, it is shoes. Babies' feet are so delicate and grow so quickly that it's essential they wear a well-fitted pair of shoes. Go to a shoe shop that specialises in baby shoes and get their feet measured – and be prepared to pay at least £20. Providing your toddler has one good pair of well-fitting shoes, there's no need to splash out on other pairs, aside from a cheap pair of wellies for splashing in the puddles.

Buying second-hand

Buying second-hand baby clothing is not only kind on your wallet, it's also the most ethical and environmentally friendly way of buying clothes. Think of it as recycling. Babies grow so fast that they often barely wear an outfit before it's too small for them. This means that second-hand baby clothing is sometimes brand-new and nearly always barely worn.

NCT sales, charity shops, car-boot sales and eBay are all excellent sources of good value, good quality clothes for your baby. There's still a hierarchy of quality and price when buying second-hand – jumble sales and car-boot sales tend to be the cheapest, followed by NCT sales, charity shops, eBay and then second-hand stores. Church sales, bring-and-buy and school sales are a good source for gorgeous hand-knitted cardigans and jumpers.

I bought some beautiful soft newborn babygros from an NCT sale. It ended up costing me around £1 for five, so it was very good value. As I said earlier, the key for success in NCT sales is to be prepared to hold your ground against some pushy mothers. I was a little shell shocked by the way their elbows did not discriminate over my pregnant tummy. Parents in the know volunteer at NCT sales, so they can get first pick of the best items.

When you're shopping for baby clothes in charity shops, it's often worth hunting out the children-specific shops like the Shooting Star Children's Hospice or Barnado's. Travel to posher areas for your charity shopping. One of my favourite Oxfams is based in Hampstead Heath because the quality of labels there is much higher than your average charity shop.

Stock turnover in charity shops, especially the good stuff, is fast, so keep popping in for a browse. I've also found that smaller, independent charity shops like Fara are better value and often sell the real gems. The more established chains like Oxfam and Cancer Research are very savvy about the value of good stock and often siphon off the best quality labels to their designer outlets.

Tips for buying baby clothes at jumble sales and charity shops

- Check the labels – it's rarely worth buying budget brands second-hand, this is your chance to splurge on the 'designer' labels!

- Check carefully for stains; it's unlikely you'll be able to get rid of a stain that's already there
- Check the seams; check for missing buttons
- Make sure the garment will be comfy for your baby and easy to get on and off
- Look out for pretty buttons and remnants of material in charity shops, too, for resourceful stitching and crafting

Don't bother buying cheap labels in charity shops; they'll be almost as cheap new. Inspect carefully for missing buttons and stains; who has time to sew on buttons with a baby? Don't hoard too-large sizes and too-grown-up buys just because they're cheap. Buy things for now and pass them back when you're finished.
Annabel, mum of Molly

I'd like to buy more baby clothes and accessories second-hand. A friend goes to car-boot sales, which is meant to be a great place for picking up things.
Abs, mum of Mae

If you're prepared to pay a little more than your average charity shop for designer baby labels, then there are a number of independent shops that specialise in buying and selling second-hand kids' clothes. This is where you can find your posh labels like Boden, Osh Kosh, DKNY, Monsoon, Petit Bateau and the rest. It's probably a good place to go to buy a christening outfit or a party dress. This isn't where you're going to find a 50p outfit, but a destination to buy something special at half its original price. The clothes will all be in mint condition, as they will have been carefully scrutinised before they were placed on sale.

There's a shop called Loopkids in Ealing, London, which I've visited. There'll be something similar where you live too. The clothes are all in beautiful condition, and you wouldn't realise you were browsing in a second-hand store if you didn't know better. These shops are also well worth using yourself to sell unwanted gifts or expensive clothes that have rarely been worn, but more of this later.

Scarlett has a wardrobe full of expensive unworn clothes. Get some of them second-hand – especially things like party dresses, which are only worn once or twice.
Yvonne, mum of Scarlett

Yes, don't be too snobbish to do it first time round (which I was for the most part)! NCT sales are supposed to be brilliant. I have bought and sold lots through the Friday Ad paper, and I have also bought and sold a lot from a shop that deals in new and used clothes – always in great condition. A few people I know buy and sell bundles of clothes on eBay – this seems particularly good for designer gear.
Ali, mum of Louis and Eddie

eBay is a wonderful source of second-hand baby clothes. You can also use it like a barometer to gauge the value of nearly new things. There's no fairer marketplace to pinpoint value than an auction, after all. Use similar rules on eBay as you would when buying second-hand elsewhere. Scrutinise the picture of the clothing for stains and missing buttons and if you need clarification email the seller and ask them; they're normally an honest bunch.

The best way of nabbing a bargain on eBay is to bid at the last minute – don't leave it too late, though, or you'll miss out. It's very easy to get over-excited by the thrill of the auction, so don't get trigger-happy. I've ended up with two almost identical raincoats for Rosie because I didn't expect to win both auctions.

I've also ended up paying over the odds for items, just because I got carried away as another buyer bid against me. So, hold your nerve. Set a maximum price in your head and stop as soon as you step over the mark. If you're not sure how much something is worth, search on eBay for similar items and see what they've gone for. Also, do include the postage price in your idea of the final value. Placing a large postage fee on a relatively inexpensive item is just one way professional eBay sellers boost their margins.

Bundles of clothes are especially popular on eBay. I've always gone out of my way to avoid them as I didn't like the element of surprise, but I know other people have bought them happily. You need to be clear that a bundle contains the items you're looking for and isn't just one dress and one outfit bolstered up with cheaper items like vests. Again, email the seller for a more detailed description if you want one.

Don't restrict yourself to eBay for online bargain hunting. Freecycle, Gumtree and the selling boards on social networks like Mumsnet are all good sources for second-hand clothing.

When you're shopping for clothes on eBay, watch out for brands that you know and like. Be wary of bundles; make sure they're not padded out with cheap extras like vests and socks. It is not worth buying the cheap labels on eBay. They're just as cheap new. Instead, look for good condition labels that would be expensive new.

Annabel, mum of Molly

Hand-me-downs

If you're lucky enough to have friends with older children, then swallow your pride and accept their hand-me-downs. Remember, they wouldn't lend or give you items that they didn't want to. I'd imagine there's nothing nicer than seeing your child's gorgeous little stripy dungarees on your friend's new baby.

I'm miffed to say I didn't benefit from any at all, aside from some lovely little heirlooms from my mum. But if any friends had offered me some second-hand clothes I would have bitten their hands off.

When you return one lot of clothes, ask if you can have the next size up to take away with you.
Lynsey, mum of Amber

Don't feel as if you have to accept clothing you don't really like. Just take the stuff you love; good friends won't be offended. That way you won't have to make excuses about why your baby isn't wearing a particular outfit. Also, you'll have so much stuff that you just won't have the room for unwanted clothing.

Obviously, if your friends haven't completed their families yet, they will expect the clothes returned. Return the clothing washed, ironed and in a good condition with a little gift to say thank you. And if you're worried about spoiling something really precious, don't borrow it.

Other friends may be quite happy for you to pass on the clothes to someone else when you're done, or donate them to a charity shop. If you decide to sell them on eBay or in a second-hand shop, pass on the proceeds to them; they'll probably be happy to go 50/50 anyway.

I didn't buy anything second-hand, but I had lots of donations from friends second time round. You have to make sure you take/refuse stuff from friends who won't take it personally if you turn them down . . .
Shonagh, mum of Daniel and Caitlin

The etiquette of hand-me-downs

- Establish when the clothes are given to you whether this is a gift or a loan
- If it's a loan, put a coloured dot on the label so you remember what belongs to who
- When returning clothes to a friend, wash and iron and return with a small gift
- Even if the clothing is a gift, see if your friend would like you

to pass on to another of their friends, or perhaps donate to their favourite charity shop

✂ Share any proceeds with your friend if you sell their clothes on eBay

I am lucky to have mates with older kids and my brother has an older boy so we inherited lots of clothes from them, which has saved us a fortune, because you can go mad in the shops with so much gorgeous stuff.

Rachel, mum of Josh

Making the most of gifts

You will be bombarded by generous gifts of clothing from your friends and neighbours. It's unbelievable how much will be bought for you and your baby. I think it's because people just love buying baby clothes; they can't seem to stop themselves and any excuse to buy a tiny pair of socks or a frilly dress will be snapped up.

Beware, some of these gifts will be hideous, some will be completely impractical, others will be duplicates of what you already have, or may already be too small for your baby. But there will be some stuff that you love and could have chosen yourself.

Before the baby is born, some friends and family may ask you what you need as a gift. This is a brilliant opportunity to actually get something you need, so don't fall into the trap of politely saying they can buy whatever takes their fancy. Give them some strict guidance; they'd much rather buy you something you need.

If you're not sure, it's always worth asking for slightly larger baby clothing. So many clothing gifts are just the tiny, tiny sizes, meaning your baby goes from having a huge wardrobe to having nothing to wear by the time they're three months old. It's always handy to get some clothes in 3–6, 6–9 and 9–12 months sizes.

Most high-street shops like Mothercare, John Lewis, Next and

Marks & Spencer are very happy for you to return and exchange baby clothing with them, even if you don't have the receipt. For example, as Rosie was a 'Christmas' baby, we must have been given about five or six 'My first Xmas' babygros, reindeer booties, Santa hats and so on.

Carefully pack away any items you don't like with labels and packaging intact and then when you've got the energy and inclination to venture out on a shopping expedition with your baby, swap them for something more useful instead.

Designer baby outfits from boutiques can be harder to exchange if you don't live close to the shop. And again, providing you can get away without offending the person who bought you the gift, it's worth considering selling the items on eBay. Designer baby items sell very well on eBay. Especially if you've kept the hanger, labels and posh packaging for the outfit.

We were given some very generous designer gifts for Rosie, but she didn't get to wear many of them before she'd outgrown them. I sold them on eBay and used the money to buy some larger second-hand eBay clothing for her. And I did the same with good quality clothing she'd worn once or twice too.

Make a note of who buys what pieces of clothing for you. The givers would be thrilled to have a little photo of your baby in their outfit popped in the thank-you card. And although it's sometimes easier said than done, if you can remember to dress your baby in the outfit they bought when they come to visit, it will be well appreciated.

Luckily, I realised not to buy too many clothes/toys when pregnant because you always get so much stuff bought as pressies when your baby is born. I find it unbelievable how quickly Josh grew too – he only wore some things once!

Rachel, mum of Josh

Growing pains

One of the reasons why it's important not to get carried away when buying clothing for your baby is because they grow so fast. Sometimes, they'll only get a chance to wear something once or twice before they outgrow it. Other times, you'll dig out a new outfit from the depths of their drawers and it will already be too small.

All the advice for buying second-hand and recycling gifts holds true as your baby grows older. By the time they're six months old, you may want to dress them in trousers and tops, dungarees or dresses and tights sometimes during the day, but this doesn't mean they need lots of clothes. Keep dressing them in terms of comfort. Once they start crawling, skirts and dresses can restrict little girls and make them trip over.

I think one of the reasons parents spend so much money on babies' clothing is because the clothing manufacturers cleverly market these mini-me outfits for baby. Just last week I saw a six-week-old baby in jeans, tiny Converse trainers, a check shirt, leather jacket and baseball cap. He looked like a surreal, shrunken version of his dad. He also looked extremely uncomfortable.

One of the simplest ways to save money on baby clothing is to not buy things before their time. So, don't buy shoes before your baby can walk, don't buy hardwearing trousers like jeans before they can crawl, don't buy hairbands before they have hair.

You can prolong the life of some baby outfits by altering them slightly. I chopped the feet off sleepsuits and babygros when they seemed a bit tight. Sleepsuits can also be transformed into romper suits, which are essentially a short-trousered babygro, nice and cool for summer.

The all-in-one nightdresses are also a resourceful pyjama option. They normally fall long below the baby's toes and have an elasticated bottom. It makes it really easy to change night-time nappies and babies won't outgrow them as quickly as a traditional babygro with legs and feet.

It was a waste of time to buy bigger clothes for Oli before he was born. I ended up with summer shorts that were too big for him and a winter jacket which now, when I need it, is too small for him. You can't predict how big your child is going to be so don't buy loads of stuff in advance.

Monika, mum of Oli

Make your own

You don't have to be a whizz with the sewing machine or a knitting-needle genius to make your own clothes. It's easy to feel intimidated about making clothes, especially if you've never done it before, but just make things at a level you're happy with.

More than any other resourceful thing you do, making your own baby clothes is so satisfying. It just seems right for our times to be stitching and recycling, rather than buying lots of cheap clothes that will then be thrown away. Moreover, not only is your baby wearing something unique, it's been made with love by you.

Sometimes sewing or knitting your own clothes doesn't end up being cheaper than buying things new, but it does mean you have some beautiful, original, high-quality outfits for your baby. Also, you can keep the costs down by recycling material from old dresses or shirts of your own, or from second-hand clothes in charity shops.

So whether you're making a whole new outfit from scratch, or just customising a bought outfit to make it original, making your own can be really satisfying. An easy first project might be to stitch some pretty ribbon around the top of a pair of socks. Then, as you grow in confidence, stitch some contrasting fabric or ribbon around the bottoms of trousers or around the neck-lines of dresses.

A simple way of hiding stains or disguising logos you hate is to sew a patch onto your baby's clothing. This might be cut in the shape of an animal or letter, a star or a heart, it might be a simple pocket or a pretty pattern from some material you love. It really doesn't matter, all you need to do is hand-stitch it on. This can work well to jazz up plain T-shirts, trousers or sleepsuits too.

Make your own pantaloons

This pattern will fit a baby 0–3 months, but could easily be adapted for a toddler by using more robust material and having a straight leg rather than an elasticated bottom.

Piece of material 45cm x 30cm (Use a second-hand silk scarf from a charity shop for very glam party pants!)
Shearing elastic
Cotton

1. Cut a paper pattern using the diagram as a guide. It should be six-sided like a hexagon with the top and bottom lines measuring 22cm and the four sides on the RH and LH sides measuring 15cm each. The length and longest width of the pattern should be 30cm x 30cm.
2. An easy way to cut the pattern is to rip the middle pages out of an A4 magazine, which roughly fits these measurements. Fold the magazine double pages into two along its centrefold, mark 11cm along the top and bottom with a pencil then cut the sides into a triangle ensuring the longest width measures 15cm.
3. Pin the paper pattern onto your material and cut the material. You will need to cut two identical fabric shapes – one to form each leg.

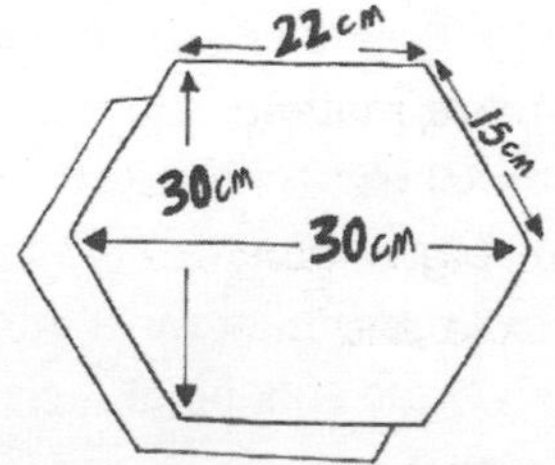

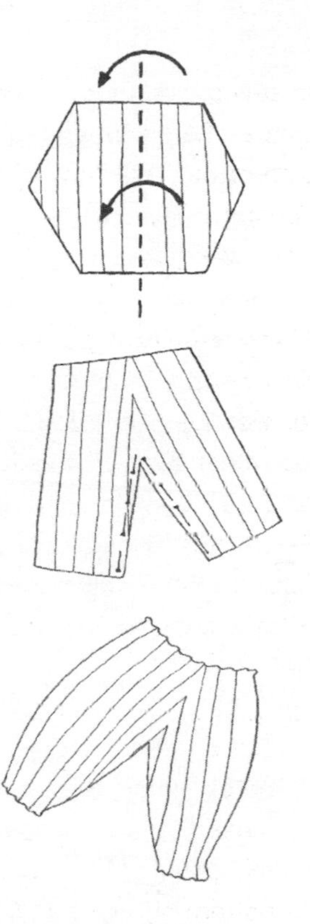

4. Fold each piece of material into two lengthwise, you'll now see that each piece will make one trouser leg – the inner pointed side foming the crotch of the pantaloons.
5. Sew the inside leg of each trouser leg. Attach the two leg pieces together at the crotch and sew the front and back seams of the trousers.
6. Iron the seams of the trousers, fold under the waistband and tack with shearing elastic by hand, or you may be able to thread the elastic onto your sewing machine.
7. Fold under the bottom edge of the trouser leg and tack round twice with shearing elastic.

Make your own sundress (3–6 months and 12–18 months)
Crawling babies and dresses or skirts don't work, they just trip your speedy baby up and get in the way. Best to keep dresses for younger baby girls or walking toddlers.

1 metre material (less for a smaller baby – any leftover material can be used for a matching sunhat – see pattern below)
Two big buttons
Needle and thread

1. Either use a favourite dress or pinafore as a template or use the pattern below.

2. For a 3–6-month-old, cut out a triangle-ish shape (with the pointy top lopped off). It should be 34cm wide at the bottom, 17cm wide at the top and 32cm long. For a 12–18-month-old the measurements should be 42cm wide at the bottom, 22cm wide at the top and 50cm long.
3. Use newspaper to cut a paper pattern and double the material up to cut two identical pieces of material – the front and back of the dress.
4. Using a cereal bowl, trace a semi-circle in the middle of the top of one piece of fabric. It should be around 10cm in diameter, leaving an even space on each side. This is your neck hole.
5. For the arm holes, mark a curve 3cm from the edge of the top of the material to fall 11cm down. Use a bowl or a compass to help trace the line.

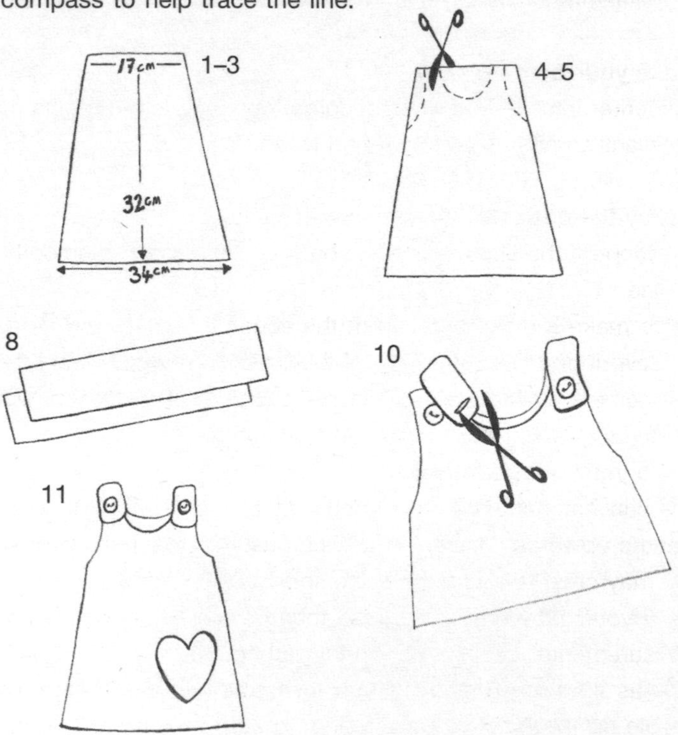

6. Ensuring the material is inside-out, pin the two pieces of material together and sew down each of the long sides, leaving 2cm at the bottom of the dress to hem.
7. Fold in your neckline, arm holes and bottom, hem with an iron for easy hemming.
8. For the straps, cut out two pieces of material 11cm x 20cm; this leaves enough for the hem. Fold the material inside-out and hem. Leave one seam open to turn the right way out.
9. Attach the straps to the inside back of the dress and sew several times to strengthen the seam.
10. Sew chunky button onto each front strap parallel to neckline. Cut and sew a button hole in the front of the dress.
11. Finish off with a heart-shaped pocket, double up the material for strength and sew onto front RH side of dress

Make your own apron

Favourite dresses that have become too small for little girls make excellent aprons for painting and messy play.

1. Lay the dress flat on the floor or table.
2. Chop off the sleeves and the back of the dress in a smooth line.
3. To make it look neater, hem the edges.
4. Sew ribbon ties to the top of the dress to secure around the neck and to the waist of the dress to secure around the waist.

Make your own sun hat

The sun hat pattern below should fit a baby from around three months upwards. Babies' heads can vary dramatically in size, so you may need to make the circle smaller once it's been cut. If you know your baby has a big head then be more generous with the measurements. Cushion or curtain fabric works well for hats as long as it's not scratchy. If you love soft cotton, you'll need to double up the material on the brim to stop it being too floppy.

Semi-stiff material 60cm x 60cm
Shearing elastic
Needle and thread
Compass and pencil
Old newspaper for template
Iron

1. Using a compass draw a circle on an old sheet of newspaper to make your pattern. The circle should have a diameter or width of 42cm.
2. Using the newspaper circle as a template cut out the shape in your material.

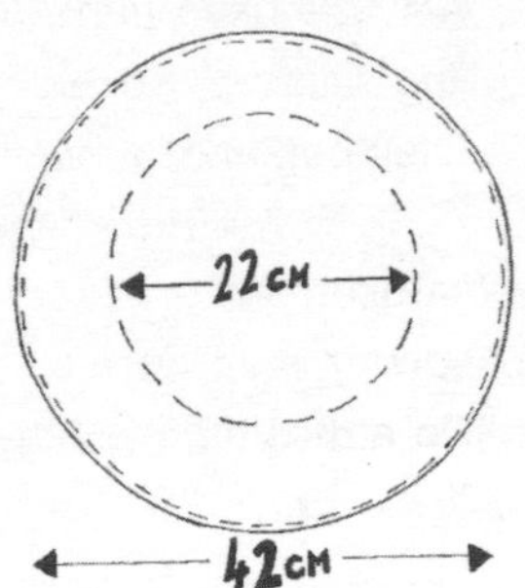

3. Hold the circle over your baby's head to roughly check the hat's going to fit.
4. Iron a small hem around the outer edges of your circle and sew by hand or using a sewing machine.
5. With your compass again, measure and draw a smaller circle onto your hat material, around 10cm from the brim. This circle would have a diameter or width of around 22cm.
6. Leaving a length of shearing elastic loose at the beginning and end, hand sew shearing elastic around the inner circle in neat stitches.

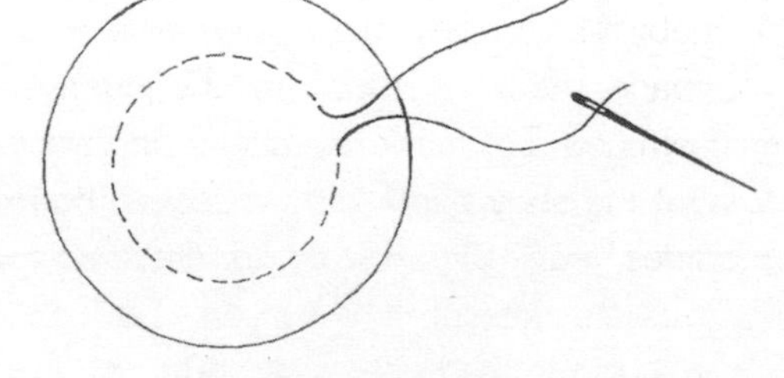

7. Gently pull on the two loose threads to gather the shearing elastic and test the fit on your baby's head. Once you're happy the hat fits snugly but is not too tight, tie the two threads together with a couple of firm knots.

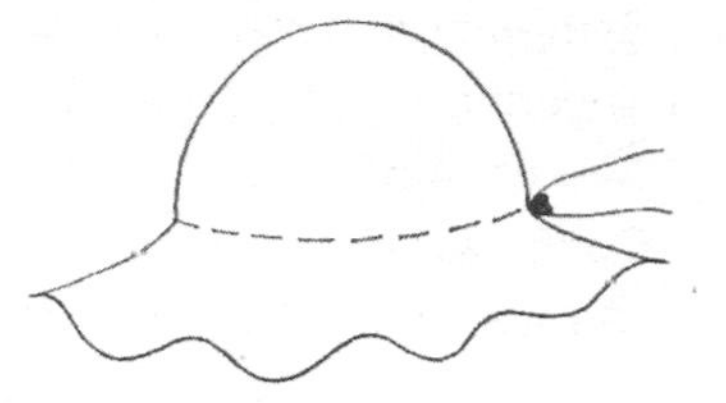

Make your own recycled mittens and booties

This is an easy pattern to make the most of accidentally boil-washed jumpers that have transformed into felt. If you don't already have anything suitable, put an old jumper in a hot wash and tumble dry at a high temperature for around thirty minutes. You may need to repeat.

Old woollen jumper
Scissors
Needle and thread
Chalk

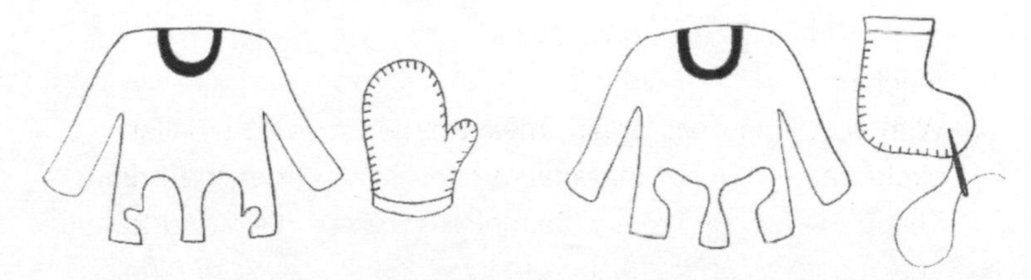

1. Using a piece of chalk, draw an outline of mittens and booties on to your jumper. Taking a measurement of your baby's hands and feet, leave an extra 2cm. If there's enough space, the bottom edge of the jumper makes an already-hemmed cuff for your mittens and the top of your booties.
2. Cut the shapes out both sides of the jumper and sew up the sides, leaving the top open. Once sewn, turn inside out.

CHAPTER NINE

Washing

Being a new mum is challenging enough without saddling yourself with too many moral dilemmas as well. I like the fact that at home by using re-usable nappies, I can do my bit for reducing landfill, but can have the flexibility of disposables (and there are a few brands that offer a bit more in terms of degradable materials) when we're out and about – and it also means not carrying a soggy nappy around with you.
Allison, mum of Lauren

There's something about having a baby that brings out everyone's domestic goddess. From scrubbing floors when heavily pregnant to washing new, doll-like, baby clothes before your baby is born, suddenly making things sparkling clean becomes more appealing than ever before.

Washing essentials

Must-haves

Trustworthy washing machine
Lemon juice
Bicarbonate of soda
White vinegar
Olive oil
Soft cloths and/or cotton wool
Elbow grease!

Naughty but nice

Eco cloths
Eco laundry balls
Gentle baby wipes (when out and about)
Yellow rubber duck

What you and baby can live without

Baby bath
Lotions and potions
Expensive branded disposable nappies
Nappy bin
Fabric conditioner

Cleaning the house

Even if you weren't environmentally conscious before, using too many toxic chemicals around your baby just seems wrong. Some of the home-made cleaning products that our grandmas used are resourceful because they're not only natural but also cheaper than buying branded cleaning products.

There are three household cupboard ingredients that seem to do just about everything when it comes to cleaning – distilled white wine vinegar, lemon juice and bicarbonate of soda. Vinegar is good for cleaning windows, tiles and baths and for removing limescale; bicarbonate of soda is good for scouring stains and lemon juice is a natural bleaching agent and disinfectant – good for removing stains too.

Invest in a set of micro-fibre eco cloths. They seem pricey at around £15 from John Lewis but will save you a fortune on cleaning products in the long run – with washable eco cloths all you need to keep the kitchen and bathroom spick and span is hot water and elbow grease.

Recipes for household cleaning products

- Scrubbing surfaces – make a paste with bicarbonate of soda and water
- Cleaning windows – fill your own spray bottle with water and either one-quarter cup white vinegar or one tablespoon lemon juice to cut grease
- Polish furniture – with a mixture of one teaspoon olive oil and one-half cup white vinegar
- Polishing ornaments (does anyone have ornaments these days?) – toothpaste for silver, a cloth dipped in white vinegar or lemon juice with salt dissolved in it for copper, then rinse with water when you're done. A paste made from one teaspoon salt, one cup white vinegar, and one cup flour for polishing brass

- Hot soapy water also seems to clean just about everything from dirty plastic toys to food on the walls and stains on the carpet
- Rip up old towels for instant free cleaning rags

Stain removal

You can clean anything with a baby wet wipe.
Maida, mum of Dino

Before Rosie, stain removal mainly consisted of sprinkling salt or pouring white wine on crimson red-wine stains on the carpet. With a baby, stain removal becomes a much more frequent and pressing concern.

Before weaning, baby stains are restricted to sick, pooh and wee. Hot soapy water seems to get rid of most of these stains. They're normally quite innocuous because your baby is only drinking milk anyway. The stains get fiercer and more stubborn as your baby's eating repertoire expands.

If you have baby sick on a carpet and can't get rid of the smell, mix bicarbonate of soda with a small amount of water until it is a paste. Spread it on the sicky patch and leave to dry. Hoover up and the smell will disappear as if by magic!
Mary, mum of Jack, Martha and Rosa

The trick with all stains on carpets is to deal with them as quickly as possible, and soak up the residue by blotting. Sometimes pouring a little soda water over a spill and trying to remove any marks using soapy water can help.

I haven't yet (touch wood) had to deal with a carpet pooh stain. While 'nappy off' time is a pastime full of pleasure for Rosie, it's a tense time for me. I try to keep her away from carpets and soft furnishings when she hasn't got a nappy on. Again, I think lemon juice, as a natural bleaching agent, would be a good thing to use on a pooh stain.

As they get older, toddlers can wreak havoc with crayon. If it gets on the carpet use a similar approach to candle wax. Try to scrape off as much as possible with a knife, then put layers of paper towels over the mark and press lightly with a warm iron. If there's crayon on the radiator, rub with a paper towel soaked in cold milk.

Cleaning toys

Keeping toys free from germs is important, especially with younger babies. Plastic toys can be washed in warm, soapy water or can go in the dishwasher on normal cycle. Wet wipes can clean toys if you're in a rush.

Soft toys can go in a washing machine inside a pillowcase on a delicate wash cycle. More delicate toys can be wiped with a damp, soapy cloth, followed by a clean cloth and dried with a hairdryer.

There are a few other ways to get rid of germs on soft toys that can't be put into the washing machine or hand-washed. A brilliant tip given to me by my health visitor is to put the toy in a brown paper bag and place it in the freezer overnight. This will get rid of all germs. Alternatively, you can freshen soft toys by putting them in a paper bag with little bit of bicarb of soda and shaking gently. Leave for a few hours, and hoover the powder gently away.

Washing clothes

They may be small, but goodness, babies create a lot of washing. It's not only the three babygros that they might be sick on or pooh over, or the sheets, it's your own clothes, too, that get soiled. It's made me realise that a good, reliable washing machine should be on the 'essential' baby list, alongside buggy and cot.

A tumble dryer would help dry baby clothes in the winter, but it's not essential and very energy-inefficient. Instead, if you have the space, consider getting an old-fashioned clothes pulley that dries washing from the ceiling, see pulleymaid.com. Or you could carefully hang washing on a clothes dryer in front of one of your hottest radiators and turn it around so each side gets close to the warmth. In the summer, if you have outside space, nothing beats hanging clothes out to dry on the line. The sunlight acts as a natural bleaching agent and can help to remove stains.

Soak any stained clothes in cold water with a few spoonfuls of bicarbonate of soda before washing. If you've got time, it's worth trying to scrub out tough stains with soapy water before you wash them. Lemon juice is a natural bleach on tough stains too: apply before you pop stained clothes in the washing machine. To remove odours use a cup of white vinegar in the rinse tray as an alternative to fabric conditioner.

Consider investing in a set of eco laundry balls, which work on a similar premise to the eco cloths. They replace the need for traditional washing powder and fabric conditioner and therefore cut out the need for a long rinse cycle so can save energy and money. Three eco laundry balls cost around £30 online but can be used in around 1,000 washes. However, they're not so effective for heavily stained washing.

Nappy endings

Everyone remembers the first nappy they ever changed on their baby. It feels like such a complicated procedure and your newborn seems so fragile. However, by the time your precious bundle is about two and a half years old you will have changed around 6,000 nappies. By then you'll be able to change them in the dark, change them standing up, sitting with your baby on your lap and even when they're running away from you.

Nappies can be a significant expense. You're likely to be changing your baby at least six times a day, more in the beginning, so you get through a lot. There are ways to save money, though. First, there's the choice between disposal nappies and re-usable ones. While disposable nappies are clearly more convenient, they're also more expensive. The average parent spends around £1,200 on disposable nappies until their child is potty trained. As a rough estimate, disposables will cost around £900 over two and a half years, whereas re-usables will cost just £400, so they're half as expensive.

Then there's the environmental impact of disposable nappies. The Women's Environmental Network points out that nearly eight million disposable nappies are thrown into landfill sites in the UK daily, that's 2.9bn a year. And they take hundreds of years to disintegrate. The disposable nappy companies argue that the energy used by regularly washing re-usable nappies can be damaging to the environment too.

The disposable/re-usable debate doesn't have to be a black and white, either/or argument. Many new mothers are overwhelmed by the idea of re-usable nappies and don't even consider it as an option. How about doing a bit of both? Using re-usables when you can and disposables when you're out and about or away from home? There are a number of environmentally friendly disposables on the market like Moltex, Bambo Nature and Tushies.

Cheaper disposables

The big nappy brands like Pampers and Huggies are expensive. They normally retail at around £6.00 for 30 nappies. For example, Pampers Active Fit for babies of around 5–10 months costs £5.88 for 26 nappies, that's 22p each. The supermarket own-brand equivalent at Tesco costs £3.97 for 32, the equivalent of 12p each. And the well-known brands aren't always the best. Interestingly, Tesco own-brand nappies score well in Mumsnet product reviews, where a panel of mothers tests different brands.

I haven't seen any difference between Tesco-own nappies and brands like Pampers.
Hazel, mum of Leo

The best way of seeing which nappies suit your baby is to try out a few different brands. The supermarkets are always running special offers, so if you don't mind switching and changing brands, that's another way of saving money. Then there's bulk buying. If your favourite brand is on special offer, buy as many nappies as you can carry. (But don't get too carried away; you don't want a cupboard full of nappies that don't fit your growing baby any more.)

Nappy changing equipment

The bare-bottom essentials
Nappies
Cotton wool or soft cloth or wipes
Bowl of warm water
A cheap and cheerful changing mat (or a towel or muslin)
A bin with a lid
Nappy cream (ask your doctor to prescribe a cream like Sudocrem, then you'll get it for free)
A stash of recyclable plastic bags for toxic nappies

There're so many things you don't need to buy but feel like you should. Here's some definite no-nos. First, a nappy-changing table – these can be so expensive and are just not necessary. I changed Rosie on top of a chest of drawers. As she grew older and more wriggly I changed her on the floor.

I found I didn't use the cot-top changing mat (I sold it). I always ended up changing them on the floor on a padded mat. I guess it depends on where you keep your nappies . . .
Ali, mum of Louis and Eddie

Second, do not worry about a special hi-tech nappy bucket, especially if you opt for disposables. These fancy bins, sometimes called 'Nappy Wrappers', look like they should live in a chemistry lab rather than a baby's nursery. They use so many different plastic bags to try to disguise the smell of dirty nappies that they must be bad for the environment.

I think the nappy bins are a waste of time; just chuck them straight in the normal bin.
Amy, mum of Seth and Agnes

Indeed, the super-duper, hi-tech, 'promise to disguise all smells' nappy bin is the most regretted purchase by mums I interviewed in my research. Although I never bought one, I was struck by how difficult they are to work when I visited a friend recently with a new baby. I hadn't got a clue how to open it up, never mind how to dispose of the nappy. We ended up wrestling with it, not ideal considering she'd just had a caesarean. I used to use a small bin with a lid in Rosie's nursery, then once she was weaned and her nappies became even smellier, I started putting them in a small bin outside instead.

Those nappy bins with the cartridge to supposedly stop smells escaping are a waste of time. I had one first time round, but couldn't always get the cartridges and it was more expensive. Much easier to get a small bin with a tight fitting lid and recycle carrier bags to line it instead.
Shonagh, mum of Daniel and Caitlin

The Nappy Wrapper – what an ugly, stinking waste of money that was! I can still remember the stench!
Ali, mum of Louis and Eddie

A plastic, padded nappy-changing mat is useful. It stops pooh and wee getting on the carpet and bed, and makes a softer lining for the baby to lie on, even if they're on the floor or hard surface. But again, it's not necessary. You could just use a special towel. When I was out and about, I'd use a muslin. (There's a pattern for a travel changing mat in Chapter 6.)

I bought a very expensive changing mat initially from Blooming Marvellous, it had a lovely red and white checked towelling cover – far more comfy than plastic and I thought there'd be no problems washing it on a regular basis! It obviously needed washing the first time it was used and was then never used again.
Abi, mum of Mae

Although disposable wipes can be handy when you're not home, you don't necessarily need them. It's much better to clean the delicate skin of newborn babies with cotton wool and warm water. Instead of cotton wool you could use a flannel, terry square or muslin cloth.

Baby wipes are more expensive and less environmentally friendly and not so good for your baby's skin as cotton wool and water.
Lynsey, mum of Amber

Again, some baby companies cleverly market special bowls for you to put water in to wash the baby. You don't need them. I just use a bowl from the kitchen. You'll want to wash it once a day anyway. Some mums swear by dunking washable wipes in a cup of chamomile tea if your baby has a sore bottom. You could also try sprinkling a drop of lavender oil into the water. Make your own wipes by chopping up fleece or facecloths into squares and soaking them in a cup of chamomile tea and a splash of olive oil in a Tupperware box.

Cloth nappies explained

Re-usable nappies have come a long way since we were babies. I've got vivid memories of my own mum soaking and stirring nappy buckets full of terry squares for my little sister. There was the complex folding, not to mention the nifty skill of securing the nappy without spearing the baby's tummy with the pin.

Today, although traditional terry nappies are still available, there are so many different kinds of new pre-folded or shaped nappies, attached with poppers or Velcro. There are stripy ones, spotty ones, organic ones, fleecy ones, pink ones, blue ones, even rainbow ones.

There are basically two kinds of re-usables: all-in-one nappies and two-part nappies. All-in-one nappies combine the inner nappy and the outer waterproof. They often look like disposables and fasten with Velcro. They're less fiddly but they do take longer to dry because they're bulkier and sometimes can't be tumble dried.

Two-part nappies are made from a nappy part and a waterproof wrap part, which may be pull-up or wraparound, and comes in three basic varieties. First, pocket nappies, which have a waterproof cover lined with fleece which forms a pocket. This pocket is then stuffed with extra absorbent material such as terry squares or special inserts, or even cut-up bath towels. Second, shaped nappies, which can vary in terms of sophistication but all require a separate waterproof wrap. And third, the most basic flat nappies, which will always require folding. They can also be used to stuff pocket nappies.

We used a mixture of Kissaluvs for daytime and Tots Bots for night. The Kissaluvs were less bulky and worked on a popper system – there was also a little popper so you could fold down the front when the umbilical cord was still healing. Tots Bots used a Velcro wrap, and were really lovely and snug. Both of these brands had the separate waterproof outer to go over them – Imse Vimse were our favourite – beautiful soft cotton with great designs if you wanted them or just plain white.

Allison, mum of Lauren

Real nappies are a huge saving – you can even buy the nappies second-hand for about £100 all in – check the classifieds on www.thenappylady.co.uk or ebay. Motherease are the best as they are birth to potty.

Lynsey, mum of Amber

How to fold a terry nappy

Even if you use mainly shaped nappies, pocket nappies or all-in-ones, having a few terry squares will mean you've got an economical, quick-drying option . . . and what's more they're incredibly versatile right through from newborn to toddler. It's always worth having a few in your bag for emergencies. Today, they're easier to secure thanks to a new product called the Nappi Nippa, a nappy pin for the twenty-first century.

Here are a few of the different folds you can use:

The pad fold

This is the simplest fold, but can just be used to slot the terry nappy into a Velcro wrapper.

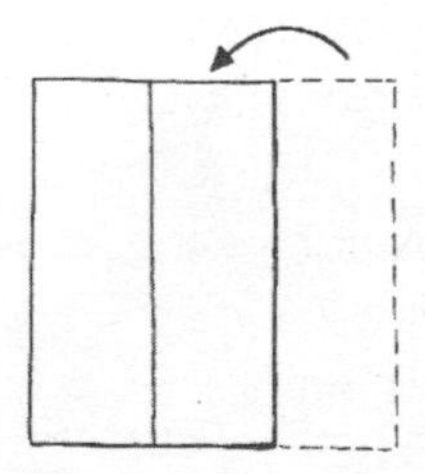

1. Spread the nappy. Fold one third of the width from the left edge towards the centre.

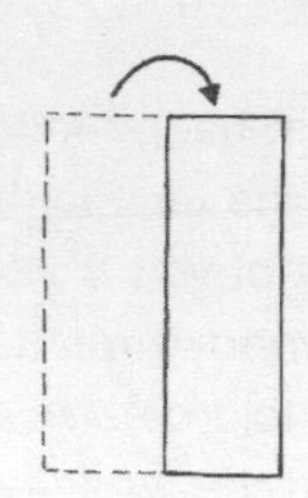

2. Now do the same from the right edge, leaving a strip one third of the width of the original cloth. The nappy should now be three layers thick.

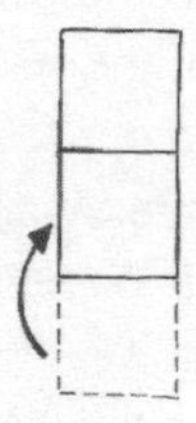

3. Fold one third up from the bottom so you have a six-ply thickness. Position this area in the front for a boy; for a girl, place it under her rear.

The kite fold

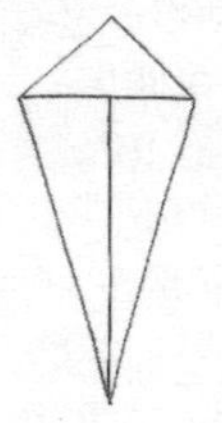

1. Lay the terry flat, and imagine a diagonal line running from top-left to bottom-right corner.
2. Fold bottom-left and top-right corners in to meet on your imaginary line.
3. Fold top-left corner down towards bottom-right.
4. Fold bottom-right corner up as far as needed, adjust to suit baby's size.

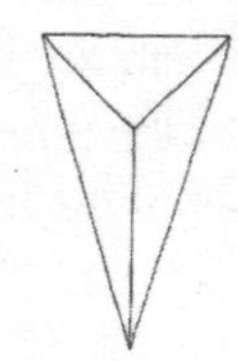

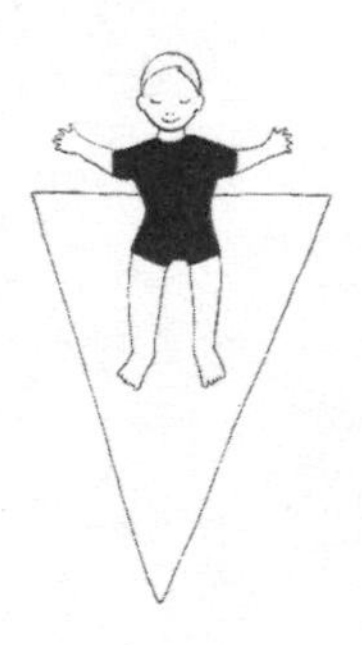

The neat nappy fold

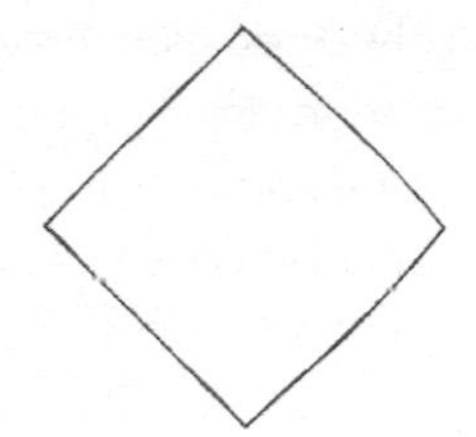

1. Lay the terry flat like a diamond in front of you. Fold the top corner down towards the centre. How much you fold depends on how wide you need the waist to be. The further in you fold the corner, the larger the waist of the nappy will be.

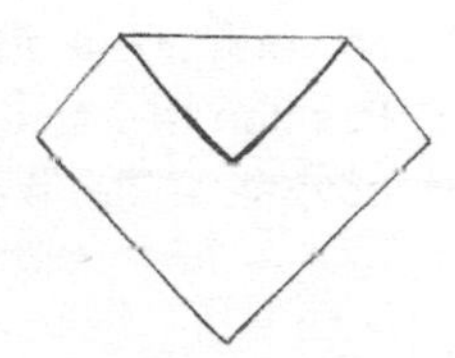

2. Fold the opposite corner up towards the centre. Again, how far to fold depends on how long you need the nappy to be and how narrow the point between the legs will end up being. You may need to spend a while experimenting with these first two folds.

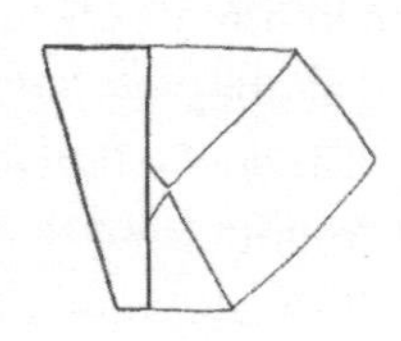

3. Now pull the left-side corner across and up to the middle of the flat edge at the top of the nappy. Do the same with the right-side corner.

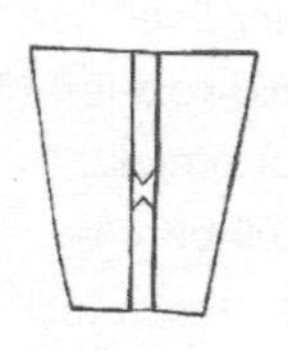

4. Place a liner in the centre of the nappy if required. Lay your baby on the nappy with the waist level with the top edge of the nappy. Pull the nappy up between the baby's legs and the wings around the baby's waist before fastening with a pin or Nappi Nippa.

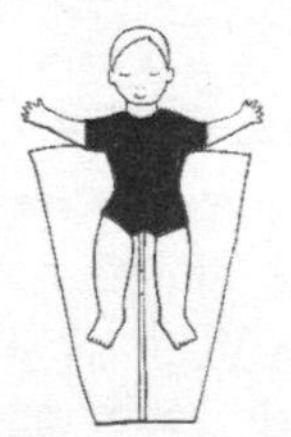

Cloth nappies essentials

Here's a list of what you'll need for starters:

1. Sixteen to twenty-four nappies depending on how frequently you want to wash them and how you're planning on drying them. For example, if you have just sixteen nappies that will probably end up being two day's worth if you change your baby about six to eight times a day. This will mean washing every day, and if you don't use a tumble dryer you'll need an extra day's supply to give you a chance to dry a batch properly.
2. Four to five wraps, if you opt for two-part nappies. They don't need washing as regularly as nappies.
3. A stash of nappy liners; these will catch the pooh, which you can then flush down the toilet. They also act as a barrier between the baby and the nappy. You can buy either disposable ones or re-usable fleecy ones.
4. Booster pads are recommended by some nappy manufacturers. They can offer extra absorbency at night.
5. Plastic nappy grips are the twenty-first-century alternative to nappy pins. Nappi Nippas seem to be one of the most popular brands.
6. A nappy bucket with a tight-fitting lid to put the dirty nappies into.

The initial set-up cost of cloth nappies can feel expensive, but you will save money in the long-term. As a rough guide, a basic two-part nappy system costs around £16 for six nappies. The outer wraps are around £10 each. All-in-one nappies cost around £8 each, and booster pads cost around £10 for ten. Remember, you can use all these nappies again if you have another baby.

And, there's no reason why you can't buy the nappies second-hand. They're often advertised on eBay or parenting websites like Mumsnet or nappy websites like The Used Nappy Company, and look out in local NCT sales. Some retailers will supply you with a trial pack of all their different makes to see which you prefer, which is a huge help as the last thing you want to do is shell out and then decide you don't like the system you've invested in.

Optional extras

If you're washing nappies anyway, you might not mind washable wipes too. Buy special ones or just use terry squares, flannels or muslin squares. You could also buy a drawstring mesh bag to place inside your nappy bucket, which makes the transfer of laundry to the washing machine easier. If you open the drawstring before you put the wash on, the nappies will come out of the bag as they wash. A waterproof, sealable bag is handy for dirty nappies when you're away from home.

Cloth nappies can be bulkier than disposables, making it hard for some babies to fit into their vests. Most cloth nappy retailers also sell something called the 'vest extender', which ensures your eco-friendly baby can still snugly fit into their vest despite a more padded bottom.

Washing nappies

Before you even wash your nappies, you need to decide how to store the dirty ones. Do you soak them in a bin of cold water with a nappy-soak product? (Watch out for products containing bleach; they may shorten the lifecycle of your nappies.) Or do you just contain them in a dry bin? A dry bin can be kept from smelling with a few drops of lavender oil each time you empty it. Once your baby is six months old, you could add a few drops of tea tree oil too. Soaking in cold water will help to remove smells and stains, especially if you include a spoonful of bicarbonate of soda, but makes it messier when transferring the laundry into the washing machine.

You'll be relieved to hear that the days of boiling nappies on the stove are long gone. Most modern nappies can be cleaned well when machine washed at relatively low temperatures. Obviously each manufacturer will make its own recommendations in terms of wash cycle, so read the labels. A general rule is to wash nappies at around 60 degrees, even lower if there are not too many stains. Following the recommendation of my health visitor I use a very gentle washing powder called Surcare for all Rosie's nappies and clothes. It's highly recommended if your baby has sensitive skin or is prone to eczema.

When Lauren was a newborn I just put a wash on every day as her nappy needed changing more often (or maybe I just checked it more often). All the nappies and outer wraps went in together at 40 degrees. As most of the big nappy action was caught by the liner (which was a biodegradable sheet that could just be flushed down the loo) then even if you didn't wash every day the used nappies were fine in the bucket (a little drop of tea tree oil kept it all fresh).

Allison, mum of Lauren

Washing tips for cloth nappies

1. Don't use fabric conditioner; it will reduce the absorbency of your nappies.
2. Add a slosh of distilled white vinegar to the conditioner drawer of your machine if you live in a hard water area. This will keep the nappies soft.
3. Make sure your nappies are rinsed well. If they're not they won't smell fresh.
4. Try a cold rinse cycle before your hot main wash to get rid of lingering smells and stains. If this isn't possible, add a spoon of soda crystals to the pre-wash drawer to break down stains.

Drying nappies

The best way to dry nappies is out in the sunshine on the washing line, but this isn't always possible. The sun acts as a natural bleaching agent so will help to keep nappies looking even fresher. The next best option is a clothes dryer, either on the ceiling or next to a radiator. If you need to drape the nappies over a radiator they can become a bit crispy, but shaking them while still a little damp can help. Tumble dryers can be helpful in the bad weather, but try not to rely on them too much as they can shorten a nappy's life span and will increase your electricity bills.

I will say that one of the things that made it easy was that we had a tumble dryer. The nappies are fairly thick so do take a while to dry on either a line or the radiator – in the summer I'd line dry them 70 per cent and finish them off in the dryer. In bad weather I just used the dryer. This enforces my point about not having my desire to do the right thing environmentally causing me lots of extra work – without a tumble dryer you'd probably also have to buy even more nappies to begin with to allow for the additional drying time.

Allison, mum to Lauren

Using a nappy laundry service

An even easier way of dealing with the palaver of washing and drying nappies is to use a nappy laundering service. They will provide you with a batch of modern, cloth nappies and wraps in return for a weekly fee of about £9–£10. They collect your dirty nappies weekly in exchange for a pile of washed nappies. It probably ends up costing around the same as disposables, but it is a little easier on the conscience. As they wash the nappies in bulk, they use less energy and water than washing at home.

Local council incentives

Almost all local councils offer some kind of incentive to encourage their residents to consider re-usable, rather than disposable nappies. In my borough, Richmond Council gives a lump sum of £50 to help set you up. Other councils offer money-off vouchers, a free trial period, a local nappy laundering service or a starter pack. It's always worth contacting them for local contacts and advice regardless. (The directory in Chapter 15 lists all the local council initiatives.)

Bath-time

Essentials:

Warm water
Olive oil
A firm grip
Some bath-time songs

I have wasted so much money on bath time. I bought a baby bath (which was good when small) then I bought a chair he could lie in, then one where the baby can sit upright. I think I used them both about five times each because Josh would never sit still and once sitting up he was arching his back to get out! Now he just lies totally in water loving it on a £3 bath mat with ducks on – a second sponge is great to have for Josh to suck too – he stays still then!

Rachel, mum of Josh

First, let's shatter some bath-time myths. You don't need a baby bath. Use a washing-up bowl or a sink when the baby is tiny, or bathe with them if you have someone else to help. Baby baths take up a lot of room. And babies grow so fast that you probably won't use it after six months anyway. By the time they can sit on their own, you can run a shallow bath and place them on a bath mat so they don't slip.

In the bath we used a simple frame with towelling cover that was very cheap. I never felt the need to have a fancier baby bath or more expensive support. Seth just loves playing with empty shampoo bottles.
Amy, mum of Seth and Agnes

Incidentally, if you can't resist buying a baby bath, then you can find a new use for it when your baby is a bit older. First, you can line it with some thick towels and cushions and prop your baby in there with some toys, like an impromptu play pen. Then, when they're toddlers, a baby bath can become a mini-sized paddling pool in the garden.

Pound shops often sell cheap baby baths (mine was a fiver).
Lynsey, mum of Amber

You don't need baby bath products. They can often irritate a baby's skin, especially a tiny baby. This sensible advice came from my midwife and health visitor: it's far better to just use plain water. Then when they are out of the bath moisturise their skin with olive oil. Some baby bath products, unless they're organic, include nasty chemicals like Parabens and SLS (Sodium Lauryl Sulfate), so check all labels.

Today's health professionals suggest it's probably best not to bath a baby daily anyway; it will dry out their skin. I found a nightly bath helpful when establishing a bed-time routine, but it's not necessary. With a newborn just top and tail them, which means gently wiping their face, neck, hands and bottom with cotton wool or a soft cloth soaked in plain, warm water.

Müller Corner yogurt pots make an ideal topping and tailing bowl for daytime nappy changes.
Mary, mum of Jack, Martha and Rosa

Don't bother buying expensive bath-time toys. Toy manufacturers have created a whole range of bath-time toys for parents to spend money on – from waterproof books to washable crayons and waterproof musical instruments. It's just not necessary.

However, your baby will enjoy playing with the water. Rosie's favourite 'toys' are an empty shampoo bottle, a sponge and a small, plastic watering can. She's also got a few yellow ducks. Sometimes I put some of her other toys in the bath for a change, like her tea set. Her stacking cups have got holes in the bottom so they're good fun and a plastic ping-pong ball was a great success. Other everyday items that would work well as bath toys include pots and pans, sieves, funnels and a tea strainer.

An empty shower gel bottle with a rubbery one-way opening makes a great bath toy. When full of water and squeezed it makes a fantastic raspberry and gives a hearty squirt.
Tilly, mum of James

Make your own

Make your own fish flannel puppet

Three different coloured flannels (or you could use an old towel)
Needle and thread (my sewing machine didn't like sewing flannel so it may be best to hand sew instead. Placing a piece of paper in between the sewing machine needle and flannel may make machine sewing easier)

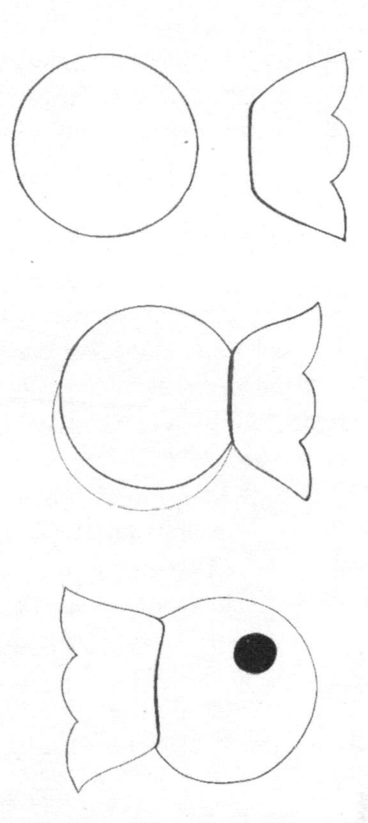

1. On a piece of newspaper, trace a circle using a bowl. Trace out the shape a fish's tail on the newspaper. Cut out the shapes – these will be your pattern.
2. Cut out the material around the pattern. You'll need two circles and one fish tail.
3. Turning the material inside out, sew the fish's body, leaving a gap at its tail, this is for your or your baby's hand.
4. Attach the fish's tail to the front piece of the fish's body, either by hand or with the machine.
5. Cut out a small circle using pinking shears for the eye. Sew on the fish's eye by hand.

Make your own hooded bath towel
Bath towel
Needle and thread

1. Taking a large bath towel (I bought a £4 one from Primark), cut around one fifth off the length into a separate piece to make the hood. For a bath towel measuring 160cm in length, I cut a piece 32cm in length for the hood.
2. Hem both the hood and the bath towel along the cut edge to neaten.
3. Fold the large piece of bath towel in two. Cut along the fold

from the centre to make an opening for the head. The opening should be approximately 30cm in width.

4. Stitch the hood piece to the edge of bath towel opening.

Bath-time songs

Singing special songs during bath-time can help to enhance your bath and bed routine. The songs are especially good for tiny babies who are too small to play with toys in the bath. They can also help to soothe babies and toddlers who don't enjoy being in the water.

Five Little Ducks
Five little ducks went swimming one day
Over the pond and far away
Mummy duck said quack, quack, quack, quack
And only four little ducks came back.

Four little ducks went swimming one day . . .
Three little ducks, two little ducks . . .
One little duck went swimming one day
Over the pond and far away
Mummy duck said quack, quack, quack, quack
And five little ducks came swimming back

Five Little Speckled Frogs
Five little speckled frogs
Sat on a speckled log
Eating some most delicious grubs
Glub, glub
One jumped into the pool,
Where it was nice and cool
Then there were
Four green speckled frogs
Glub glub

Baby massage

One of the best times of day to massage your baby is after bath-time. Baby massage can help reduce crying and colic and encourage better sleeping. It can also help you and your baby to bond if you're suffering from post-natal depression. It only needs to take five to ten minutes but if your baby isn't enjoying it, just stop.

Make sure the room is warm and draw the curtains or dim the lights to make it more relaxing. Lay your naked baby on a towel with a clean nappy tucked under their bottom to catch any accidents. Alternatively, lie your naked baby, tummy down, onto your own naked chest and tummy for some skin-to-skin contact and stroke their back and legs.

Pour olive oil into your hands and rub them together to warm the oil up. Be careful about using nut-based oils like almond oil, as some babies can be allergic to nut products. Similarly, be very careful about using essential oils: lavender is one of the few that is suitable for babies and it's ideal because it promotes restful sleep. However, it needs to be well diluted in your base oil (around one drop per two and a half tablespoons) and avoid using lavender on newborns, as it can irritate the skin.

Getting the right pressure for your massage strokes is important: too light and it will tickle your baby; too hard and he'll feel uncomfortable. Place your finger on your closed eyelid and press lightly, that's the kind of pressure you should be aiming for. Don't massage your baby's tummy before he's four weeks old and avoid his spine.

There are a number of different strokes you can do. Try doing each major stroke five times.

- Massage his tummy with clockwise strokes; this is good for wind
- Place your hands on his shoulders and stroke down to his feet

- Place hands flat on top of his chest and stroke upwards and outwards over collar bone, shoulders and down arms
- Milking – start at top of his limbs and squeeze gently, like milking a cow, moving down to wrist or ankle. As one hand reaches bottom, start with other hand at the top
- Open book – place hands together as if in prayer. Your hands are like a closed book, thumbs the spine and little fingers the pages. Place little fingers against his skin and 'open book' by spreading fingers until touching thumbs reach baby's skin. Separate hands and continue to move them outwards
- Rolling – place non-writing hand under the limb and main hand above. Roll the limb gently between the hands then move gradually down the limb
- If baby lets you roll him onto his tummy, stroke down his back and back of legs with alternate horizontal hands

CHAPTER TEN

Playing

I made a baby mobile from two coat-hangers crossed over each other, wrapped in ribbon to secure. Hang anything from it – shiny milk-bottle tops; colourful sweet wrappers; small toys and shapes; little bells, whatever you can find that will mesmerise baby. Hang it over the cot out of the reach of baby. Kate loved the one I made for her.

Nics, mum of Kate and Anna

Child's play is an expensive business. Before you know it, your tiny baby has filled your flat with the brightly coloured playthings. These toys are invariably plastic, cumbersome, noisy and expensive and won't always entertain your baby for very long. For all the new toys you do buy, your baby will be most fascinated with the box and wrapping paper.

Playing essentials

Must-haves
Treasure basket
Books
Set of keys!

Naughty but nice
Wooden truck and bricks
Tea set

What you and baby can live without
Baby walker (unless you live in a ballroom)
Baby bouncer

Forget about Whoozits, Lamaze and Baby Einstein, what babies really love is everyday objects. Your keys will always be your baby's favourite. In a room full of toys, your baby will gravitate towards anything and everything that isn't an official plaything – from pot plants to mobile phones, remote controls to hairbrushes. Baby toy manufacturers often market their products as educational, so it's easy to fall into the trap of buying them. But don't.

Baby developmental stages and suitable toys by age

Age	Developmental stage	Suitable toys
0–3 months	Can't focus on details or see colours yet, watches hands	Mobiles, mirrors, black-and-white patterns
3–6 months	Grab hold of toys in reach and puts everything in mouth, learn to roll. Has learnt to distinguish colours	Baby gym, ball, soft toys to chew, rattle
6–9 months	Learning to crawl, sit well, babble	Musical instruments
9–12 months	Cruising around furniture, pincer grasp, more communication	Walker, balls, bath toys
12–18 months	Standing without support and beginning to walk	Puzzles, shape sorters, stacking towers, sit-on riding toys, dolls or animals for imaginary play, crayons

Things to see

Small babies are mesmerised by the world around them. Until they're around three months, because of their inability to focus on far-away objects or distinguish colours, playing for them will be all about watching mobiles, looking at black-and-white pictures and watching you potter around the house. Often, all you need to do is put them in an interesting observation point – under the washing blowing on the line, in front of an open fire, near a bottle of water in the sun, a washing machine, a fizzy drink in a glass. At some point during this time they'll suddenly notice their hands and feet. Just pulling off their socks can keep them happy for a while. Then tying a balloon around their ankle or wrist can provide almost enough amusement to have a quick cup of tea and a read.

Use an old-fashioned clothes dryer to hang different items from and lay the baby underneath, a bit like an impromptu 'baby gym'. Use the same principles as the mobile on page 80 and hang anything that might be of interest, from little toys to kitchen utensils. This is a sustainable idea because you can keep varying the items to keep the baby's interest. Obviously make sure the dryer is secure and keep items out of the baby's reach. Try using:

Old sets of keys
Wooden spoons
Whisks
Spatulas
Crinkly paper
Ribbons
Milk-bottle tops
Tea spoons
Jar lids

We just had a pine cone on a piece of string instead of a mobile.
Rebecca, mum of George

If your baby has a toy arch or baby gym, for a change of scenery, colour and texture, hang wooden spoons, small metal whisks, spatulas (nothing sharp or dangerous obviously). It makes a refreshing change from the bright rainbow colours that dominate most babies' toys.
Lynsey, mum of Amber

Monochrome world

Small babies love black-and-white patterns. There's a heap of black-and-white books and cot bumpers on the market, but it's really simple to make your own. The artist Bridget Riley paints monochrome pictures that mesmerise babies. If you've got some of her prints already, get them down to baby level.

We printed out a range of bold black-and-white patterns from the internet: there were zebra stripes and swirls and checks. If you can't find anything suitable online, make them yourself with a thick black felt-tip and some white card. Bold, simple patterns and smiley faces are the most popular.

Stick the black-and-white art in spots around the house where the baby might be gazing – above her changing mat, against a coffee table, against the bath while you're having a shower. Small babies can't see long distance so you need to stick it close to them.

I also bought a black-and-white spotty T-shirt from a charity shop for 50p and it became essential. We could tie it to the side of her buggy, drape it over a table at home or drape it over the back seat when we were in the car.

Sensory bottles

Sensory bottles are a resourceful toy. While older babies like to shake and rattle them, younger babies love to watch and chew them. They're very easy to make yourself. All you need is an empty plastic bottle and the filling. They're a good way of showing baby everyday objects that they can't play with but they can see. Select the size of the bottle, depending on how old your baby is and the filling you've chosen. While a really large bottle might make a satisfying noisy rattle for a one-year-old, or a fascinating spectacle for a three-month-old, it's going to be too unwieldy for a six-month-old to shake and explore themselves.

Choose an empty plastic bottle. And your sensory filling and tape the lid on. Older babies from around one year old would enjoy helping you decorate the bottle with stickers. Here are some ideas for fillings:

Drinking straws
Paper clips
Stones
Feathers
Toothpicks
Glitter
Marbles
Milk-bottle tops
Dried pasta
Dried rice
Dried lentils
Cooking oil and water
Beads
Glitter, food colouring and water

It's best not to overfill the bottles or they become too heavy. (Especially liquid fillings.) You can colour dried rice or pasta by sprinkling food colouring into a plastic bag full of the dried pasta and then (removing the bag) baking on a very low heat in oven for twenty minutes.

We made rattles from an empty bottle and uncooked rice. Charlie likes that more than his other bought rattles.

Emma, mum of Charlie

Eat lots of pistachio nuts, save the shells, wash them, add to redundant baby bottle or plastic drinks bottle, secure lid and shake!

Nics, mum of Kate and Anna

Fill unused baby bottles (I tried so many different brands!) with dried beans or pasta and seal on the tops with tape. Seth loves

shaking them and also they are good for crawling practice as they chase after them as they roll across the floor.
Amy, mum of Seth and Agnes

Mirror, mirror on the wall

Babies love gazing at their own reflections. Many baby gyms come with a mirror attachment, but if you don't have one, find a safe plastic mirror that you can prop on the floor for your baby to gaze in. If you've got a big mirror in your bedroom or bathroom it can provide valuable entertainment time while you shower and get dressed in the morning.

Baby bookworm

Even little babies love books. When they're small it's easy to make your own books for them. Secure the pages with a ribbon tied through punched holes or, if you're feeling particularly crafty, you could even sew the pages to bind.

- Black-and-white patterns. Staple some of your monochrome pages of art together to make a book for a small baby
- Family photos. Collect a series of favourite photographs of your baby, and you as well as grandparents, uncles, aunties, friends and favourite pets. It will become your baby's favourite book. (If you've got access to a laminator in someone's office, even better.)
- Material textures. A book that needs sewing. Young babies love feeling the different texture of materials. Using remnants of materials make a book and sew different scraps onto each page. Include ribbon, velvet, fur, silk, buttons, zips – anything with an interesting texture
- Scrap book. Cut out pictures of animals, toys, food, babies from magazines and catalogues and paste them into a little scrap book to read. Once your baby is around fifteen months old, they could help you

Baby booklist

There are so many baby books to choose from the library that it can seem overwhelming. The books below are some of Rosie's favourites. I've also listed them because she enjoys them as much today at eighteen months old as she did when she was five months old.

The Hungry Caterpillar by Eric Carle or *Brown Bear, Brown Bear, What do you see?* (Bill Martin and Eric Carle)
Any books by Janet Ahlberg and Allan Ahlberg, they've written *The Baby's Catalogue*, *Peepo!*, *Each Peach Pear Plum*
Dear Zoo by Rod Campbell
There Was an Old Lady who Swallowed a Fly by Pam Adams
Where's Spot? by Eric Hill
Goodnight Moon by Margaret Wise Brown and Clement Hurd

Things to hear

Wind chimes fascinate small babies. If you already own some, move them to a place where your baby can enjoy them. If not, you could easily make your own using the cot mobile instructions, but stringing bells or pieces of copper piping onto them instead to chime together. There're some instructions on making a bamboo wind chime for the garden later on in the chapter.

Make your own bell mittens

From around six weeks, your baby will be fascinated by their hands. Sew a little bell securely onto a pair of scratch mittens. They'll look to see where the sound is coming from and may associate it with the movement of their hands.

I suspect I've sung more in the past eighteen months, than I ever did before Rosie was born. Singing is one of the best impromptu sources of entertainment you have at your disposal. There are so many nursery rhymes and action rhymes to keep you both entertained, and if you can't remember the words, humming a pop tune or a piece of classical music will make your baby smile.

From around six months old babies will enjoy playing instruments to accompany the music and from around one year old, toddlers will enjoy trying to learn the actions to accompany the rhymes. All babies love songs that involve them being thrown around, tickled, bounced and so on. If you don't know the tunes to any of the songs below, just make them up.

Songs to sing

Row, Row, Row Your Boat

Row, row, row your boat
Gently down the stream
Merrily, merrily, merrily, merrily
Life is but a dream.
Row, row, row your boat
Gently down the river
But if you see a polar bear
Don't forget to shiver.
Row, row, row your boat
Gently to the shore
But if you see a lion
Don't forget to roar.
(Once your baby is sturdy enough you can put them on your knee facing you, hold their hands and row them back and forth.)

The Wheels On The Bus

The wheels on the bus go round and round,
Round and round; round and round
The wheels on the bus go round and round,
All day long.
The doors on the bus go open, close,

Open close; open close
The doors on the bus go open close
All day long.
The wipers on the bus go swish, swish, swish,
Swish, swish, swish; swish, swish, swish
The wipers on the bus go swish, swish, swish
All day long.
The mummies on the bus go chatter, chatter, chatter
Chatter, chatter, chatter; chatter, chatter, chatter
The mummies on the bus go chatter, chatter, chatter
All day long.
The babies on the bus go waaa, waaa, waaaa
Waaa, waaaa, waaaaa; waaa, waaaa, waaaaa
The babies on the bus go waa, waa, waaaa
All day long.
(This song can go on for hours, just make up your
own verses. Grannies knitting, toddlers bouncing,
driver asking for tickets please . . .)

The Grand Old Duke Of York
The Grand Old Duke of York
He had ten thousand men
He marched them up to the top of the hill (hold baby high)
And he marched them down again
And when they were up, they were up (hold baby high)
And when they were down, they were down
And when they were only halfway up
They were neither up nor down.

Wind The Bobbin Up
Wind the bobbin up, wind the bobbin up
Pull, pull, clap, clap, clap
Wind it back again, wind it back again
Pull, pull, clap, clap, clap.

Point to the ceiling.
Point to the floor.
Point to the window.
Point to the door.
Clap your hands together, one, two, three.
Put your hands upon your knee!
(This song's actions are self-explanatory.)

Two Little Dickie Birds
Two little dickie birds,
Sitting on a wall
One named Peter, one named Paul
Fly away Peter, fly away Paul
Come back Peter, come back Paul.
(Use two fingers for the birds. Place 'paper hats' on each finger, or make a bird finger puppet with an old glove.)

One, Two, Three, Four, Five
One, two, three, four, five,
Once I caught a fish alive.
Six, seven, eight, nine, ten,
Then I let it go again.
Why did you let it go?
Because it bit my finger so.
Which finger did it bite?
This little finger on my right.

Eeny, Meeny, Miny Mo
Eeny, meeny, miny mo
Catch a baby by the toe (wiggle toe).
If he chuckles, let him go.
Eeny, meeny, miny mo!

Round And Round The Garden

Round and round the garden
Like a teddy bear (finger goes round child's palm)
One step, two step (move up his arm with your fingers)
Tickle you under there! (Tickle under arm.)

This Little Piggy Went To Market

This little piggy went to market (grab baby's big toe)
This little piggy stayed at home (second toe)
This little piggy had roast beef (third tow)
This little piggy had none (fourth)
And this little piggy (little toe)
Went wee, wee, wee, wee (tickle up to chin)
All the way home!

Tommy Thumb

Tommy thumb, Tommy thumb
Where are you?
Here I am, here I am.
How do you do? (Wiggle thumbs)
(Replace first line of rhyme and wiggle different finger)
Peter pointer, Peter pointer . . .
Toby tall, Toby tall . . .
Ruby ring, Ruby ring . . .
Baby small, Baby small . . .
Fingers all, fingers all . . .

My Little Piano

My little piano
You're my little piano,
Ting, ting, ting! (play piano on child's back)
You're my little banjo
Pinch, pinch, pinch! (pinch baby's back)
You're my little drum kit,

Bang, bang, bang! (tap gently)
You're my little trumpet
Blow, blow, blow! (blow a raspberry)
You're my little baby,
Kiss, kiss, kiss! (kiss baby)

Slowly, Slowly
Slowly, slowly, very slowly
Creeps the garden snail.
Slowly, slowly, very slowly
Up the wooden rail (fingers creep up child's body).
Quickly, quickly, very quickly
Runs the little mouse.
Quickly, quickly, very quickly,
Round about the house (fingers run all over child's body).

Heads And Shoulders
Heads and shoulders, knees and toes, knees and toes
Heads and shoulders, knees and toes, knees and toes
And eyes and ears and mouth and nose
Heads and shoulders, knees and toes, knees and toes.
(When a baby is little you can point or tickle each body part, once they are around fourteen months old, they'll learn to point themselves. This song works well at nappy-changing time.)

Hickory Dickory Dock
Hickory dickory dock
The mouse ran up the clock (fingers run up the child's arm)
The clock struck one
The mouse ran down (fingers run down)
Hickory dickory dock

Incy Wincy Spider
Incy wincy spider
climbed up the water spout,
Down came the rain
and washed poor Incy out,

Out came the sunshine
and dried up all the rain,
And Incy Wincy spider
climbed up the spout again.

Musical instruments

It's easy to make your own musical instruments for your baby. They'll enjoy these from around six months. The sensory bottles filled with dried pasta, rice or lentils make very satisfying maracas. A camera film case with dried rice or lentils is a good, hand-sized rattle; just make sure the lid is glued on securely. A wooden spoon with a saucepan pot a lid and a colander make a noisy drum kit. A one-year-old might enjoy a 'stringed' instrument from half an egg box with strong rubber bands stretched around it to pluck, but this will need to be supervised. The 'crinkly' layers from a box of chocolates makes noisy percussion too.

Make your own jingle bells

Simon made this musical instrument for Rosie and it was her favourite toy for weeks. It also makes quite a nice noise compared to other headache-inducing musical toys.

A pine stick, small enough in diameter for a child to grip, but large enough to drill through. Buy from a DIY or builders merchant.
Strong fishing line
12 small bells
Sand paper
2mm drill

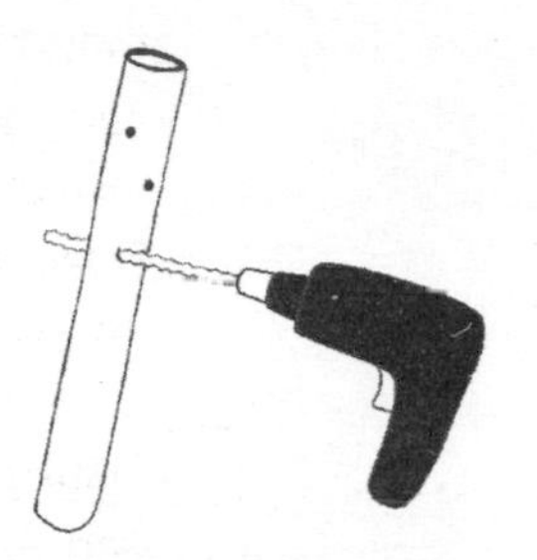

1. Cut 15cm off the pine stick.
2. Drill six small, 2mm holes on opposite sides at 1cm increments from the top of the stick.
3. Thoroughly sand all holes and top and bottom of the stick, ensuring that your remove any splinters of wood from inside the holes.
4. Tie a strong knot in one end of the fishing line and thread a bell on.

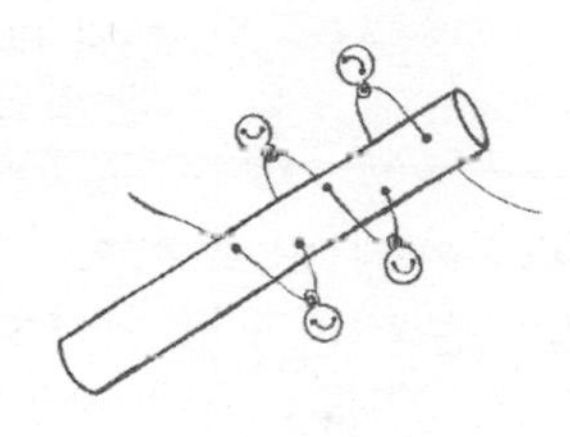

5. Pass the line through the holes starting from the bottom, adding a new bell each time you exit a hole.
6. Tie the line off by passing through the final hole several times.

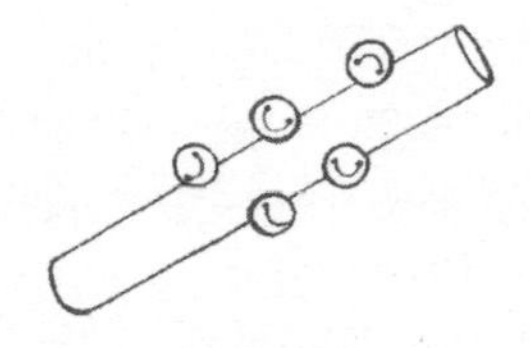

7. Have a good, hard tug at each bell to ensure that there is no possibility that the line could break or come loose.

Make your own milk spoon rattle

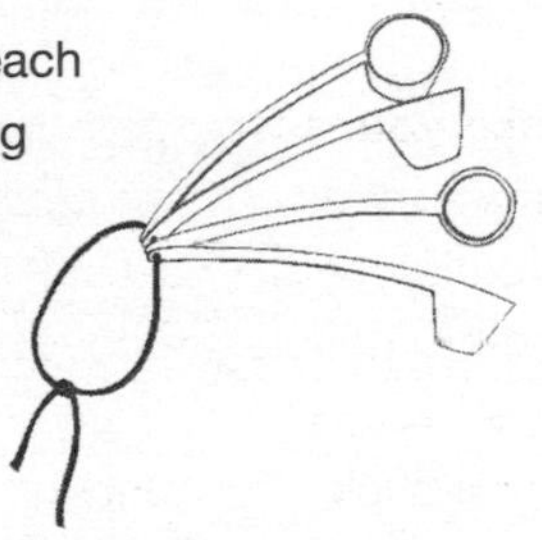

If you're using formula milk, you'll find each container comes with a plastic measuring spoon. Collect them, and once you've got around five, drill a little hole in the top of the handle and thread some string through. Tie securely and you've got a rattle.

Make your own music session

There are many specially tailored music classes for babies. They're great fun, but there's no reason why you can't create them at home. Just invite some friends and babies over. Put a box of musical instruments in the middle of the circle. Put in anything that makes noise. Put on a nursery rhyme CD or just sing songs among yourselves. Choose a mixture of songs with plain singing and actions too. Younger babies love stuff that involves them being jiggled around. Songs like 'The Grand Old Duke of York' and 'Row, Row, Row Your Boat' let you throw them around a bit, while nursery rhymes like 'Old McDonald' let them bang their instruments. At the end of the session you could calm them down by blowing lots of bubbles around the room.

Seth has a million toys but is never happier than when he has a couple of wooden spoons to bang together, or any other kitchen utensil.
Amy, mum of Seth and Agnes

Things to touch

Even tiny babies are fascinated by new textures. From 0–3 months you could rub your baby's arms or legs with different fabrics like silk, velvet, wool and towelling. As they get older, they'll enjoy holding the fabric themselves.

From around five months old, as your baby becomes interested in everyday objects, playing becomes easy and economical. It's just a question of plundering your cupboards and drawers for safe household objects for your baby to play with. Many of these items will need supervision. One of the easiest household objects to transform into a toy is the wooden spoon. Using a thick black felt-tip pen, draw a simple awake face on one side, and a sleeping face on the other.

These days, Charlie has the most fun tearing up paper to be honest, so I sometimes give him a kitchen roll to play with. Four rolls for £1 in Iceland and it keeps him busy for a good half-hour! It's also very amusing to watch.
Emma, mum of Charlie

The treasure box

Treasure boxes are a simple and satisfying project that can keep even the most curious baby occupied for ages. You don't need to buy anything new. You don't even need to make anything. Just find a selection of household objects to entertain your baby.

Use a shallow container like an old shoe box or basket. It can be jazzed up instantly with some wrapping paper or wallpaper. I cut out Rosie's name in chunky letters in a contrasting colour and pasted them on the lid.

The best treasure boxes contain items with a mixture of materials, shapes, textures, noises and smells. It's all exciting new territory for a baby from around six months who will love exploring the fascinating world of everyday objects. Use your common sense, but don't be too precious. Just keep an eye on them when they're playing with their new things. And you might have to remove items once they can chew with their teeth. For example, a natural sponge may not be suitable for a baby with teeth who likes to chew things.

Whizz around each room in your house for inspiration. In the kitchen, plunder stuff like wooden spoons, tea strainers and plastic beakers and lids. Bedrooms hide treasure like bangles and hankies to suck – choose interesting material like velvet or silk. In the bathroom hunt out items like loofahs, sponges, eye masks. A bottle of vitamin tables makes a wonderfully noisy rattle and shaker – just make sure the lid is childproof. Living-room treasure might include an old remote control or a calculator.

Get your partner involved in the hunt too. They'll unearth treasure in unexpected places. My husband found a flashing bike light, an old remote control, a rubber shower head and some pipe lagging. Stuff I would never have considered.

Perch the box between your baby's legs if they're a sitter. If they're more of a tummy wriggler, pop it in front of them. Hey presto – you've got at least twenty minutes to have a cup of tea and read the paper.

You can either have one treasure box with a variety of different things inside or create a few different ones with different materials as a focus. Use the small drawstring bags that hold washing machine tablets to contain small objects. Here are some more ideas:

Wooden

Egg cup, bracelet, spoon, wooden toys, wooden massagers, hair-brush, pine cones, curtain rings, old-fashioned clothes pegs, wooden spools.

Metal

Bracelets, small tin of tuna or beans, toy car, teaspoon, baby-jar lids, whisks, coins, tea strainer, old set of keys, remote control (batteries removed), hand mirror.

Rough and smooth

Toothbrush, shells, sandpaper, scourer, pebble.

Shiny

Tin foil, mirror, bike light, milk-bottle tops, CDs, sparkly purse, shiny bracelet.

Brushes

Toothbrush, hairbrush, washing-up brush, nail brush, artist paint brush, decorating paint brush, blusher brush.

Paper

Wrapping paper, cardboard, bubble wrap, envelopes with junk mail inside, crinkly cellophane, sweet wrappers, newspaper, loo roll, cardboard tube, little cardboard box, coloured tissue paper.

Material

Ribbons, lace, leather glove, woollen glove, velvet, silk, fake fur, felt, ball of string, ball of wool, zip, Velcro, sponge, denim, suede, lavender bag, purse with crinkly paper inside, feather, cotton wool, cotton reels strung onto a shoelace.

Glove games

Similar, supervised fun can come by filling plastic gloves with different materials for your baby to handle and squeeze. Use plastic surgical gloves or food preparation gloves and tie a knot in the top to contain the substance. Try not to overfill them in case they burst. Here are some suggested fillings: dried or cooked pasta, jelly, coffee beans, water, shredded paper, tea bags, baked beans, ice cubes, sand, grass, shaving foam, Rice Krispies or Cornflakes.

Messy play

This is even more fun for a baby of six months and up, as they get to properly handle and explore the different textures, rather than feel them through a plastic bag. It's up to you how you let them play. On a warm day, if you had baby friends visiting, you could sit them all in a paddling pool to play with the different textures. If it's just you, contain the mess by placing a bowl on some plastic sheeting. Even tidier is putting it on their highchair tray.

You could use: shaving foam, jelly, cornflour, tinned spaghetti, tinned baked beans, cooked or dried spaghetti, cooked or dried rice, sand, water, playdough, Rice Krispies, Cornflakes, shredded paper, tea bags, mashed potato with food colouring.

Ruby played undisturbed with her tea set for nearly one hour when I placed it on a plastic sheet with lots of Rice Krispies. When she wasn't eating them, she was pouring them and spooning them into her tea cups. She was even rolling around in them.

Maria, mum of Ruby

Things to do

Sometimes it's worth organising activities for your baby. It might take a few minutes to set up but it will keep them happy for a while. Some activities are really easy to set up. Rosie will play for ages with a bowl of water and some cups and spoons from the kitchen outside. She'll play for even longer if I add some mild bubbles and make the water warm. Sand is another good activity for babies once they're old enough to know not to eat too much. Rather than buying an expensive water or sand pit, just use a kitchen bowl.

Baby Van Gogh

From around six months old your baby will enjoy crafts like painting and sticking. As each month passes, they'll enjoy it even more. These activities are perfect for rainy days when both you and your baby are bored and need some excitement. They do need to be supervised, though, as most babies enjoy eating paint, chalk, crayons, glue. I'm sure it's fine in moderation, but best to keep an eye on them. You'll be able to contain the mess if you sit them in their highchair.

Aside from being good fun for both of you, these craft activities make 'works of art' that are brilliant presents for grandparents, godparents and aunties and uncles. They also make perfect decorations for your fridge and walls.

Sometimes, you don't even need paint. On warm days, use a bowl of water and a paint brush to 'water paint' the patio or path. Chalk also easily washes off pavements and paths, so can be used in the garden. Chalk is cheap, but you can also make your own.

Make your own chalk
⅓ cup plaster of Paris
4 tablespoons of water
Food colouring

Combine the ingredients and stir until the consistency of toothpaste. Pour into a home-made mould from loo-roll tubes, cut and rolled tighter to make chubby-sized chalk. It should dry in around twenty minutes.

The most economical paint to buy is powder paint, because it will last for ages. Supermarkets, IKEA and high-street retailers like WH Smith tend to sell cheap paint and crayons for kids. IKEA sells big rolls of paper too. Keep an eye out in charity shops. Or you can make your own paints; that way you know exactly what's in it too.

Make your own finger paint
2 cups cold water
⅓ cup cornflour
2 tablespoons sugar
¼ cup washing-up liquid
Food colouring or powder paints

Mix two tablespoons of sugar and 1/3 cup of cornflour in a saucepan, then slowly add 2 cups of cold water. Cook over low heat for five minutes, stirring constantly until the mixture is a clear, smooth gel. When cool, stir in 1/4 cup of washing-up liquid. Scoop into plastic containers, and stir in food colouring drops or powder paints. Store leftover paint in airtight containers like leftover jars and lids.

If you really want to restrict mess, you could have finger painting at bath time. Once they're old enough to stand in the bath, they'll enjoy painting on the tiles. Just sponge off at the end.

Make your own bath-time finger paints
2 tablespoons liquid baby soap or shampoo
1 tablespoon cornflour
Food colouring

Pour all ingredients into plastic containers that can float in the bath, mix and you're ready to go.

Paintbrush ideas

Smaller babies will love finger painting, enjoying the feeling of the paint in their hands. From around one, babies will enjoy painting with a chunky brush. But don't restrict painting to brushes and fingers, you can use anything: vegetables – potatoes, carrots, beans; fingers, hands, feet; toothbrush; leaves and twigs; spoons; cars (make tracks through the paint); cotton reels; string.

Printing

Almost anything can be used to print with, see the list above. Potato prints can be very effective. Cut the potato in half and then cut different shapes into the flat surface. The key to good potato prints is making sure the cut surface is as flat as possible. For small prints like cotton reels, pour the paint onto a small saucer and place a thin piece of sponge on top of the paint. When you press down on the sponge with the reel, the paint seeps through giving you just the right amount of paint, rather than overloading and making a mess.

Hand-print pictures

Hand prints can create lots of different paintings. For a seasonal picture, paint a brown tree-trunk and using autumnal colours make lots of hand prints around the top of the trunk to make a tree shape. These hand prints could be interspersed with stuck-on leaves. A similar technique could be used to paint a Christmas tree, a caterpillar, even a sunflower. It just involves you painting some basic shapes before you add the hand prints. If your baby doesn't like hand prints, you could draw around their hand, cut out the shape and then let them paint that.

Marble painting
This technique works well with older toddlers, but they must be closely supervised as marbles are a choking hazard.

Circular washing-up bowl
Circular piece of paper to fit the base of the bowl
A few marbles
A few plastic spoons
Selection of different-coloured runny paint in small containers

Put the circle of paper in the bottom of the bowl. Drop a marble into a paint container and fish out with a plastic spoon. Drop the marble onto the paper and tilt the bowl around to leave a paint trail. When the marble runs out of paint, drop into another colour and repeat the process until you have a pattern of trails all over.

Butterfly painting
Butterfly or mirror-image painting is one of the best techniques to turn your baby's painting into beautiful butterflies. Fold a piece of paper into two and then open it out again. Help your baby drop some different colours of paint onto one side of the paper, particularly around the fold line. Fold the paper into two again, so that the blank side touches the painted side. Carefully open the paper to reveal your mirror-image painting. You can transform these paintings into butterflies by cutting the paper to a butterfly-wing shape and painting on a body and antennae afterwards.

Paper ideas
You don't always have to use paper for painting. It all depends on whether you want to make the painting a present or stick it on the wall or not. Have a look in your recycling box for good scraps of paper. Never throw away shoe boxes or good cardboard boxes – turn them into doll's houses or glue together to make robots or

other modern art structures! You could use: old newspaper, old envelopes, boxes, kitchen- or toilet-roll tubes, scraps of cardboard, paper plates, old bed sheets, curtains, shirts.

Sticking ideas

Babies love sticking. Buy some PVA glue or make your own and start collecting interesting bits and pieces for them to stick onto paper. Paper plates make a good base for sticking art. Help the baby dab the glue onto the page or plate and give them a selection of materials to stick down. Try: leaves, twigs, grass, flowers, hay; drinking straws; shiny sweet wrappers; scraps of wrapping paper; scraps of fabric; lollypop sticks; buttons and sequins; tinsel; cotton wool (they can paint on top of this too); old birthday or Christmas cards; pictures cut out of magazines and catalogues; shells and sand; different sorts of dried beans – kidney, black eye, butter or lentils.

Make your own glue

Flour

Water – add just enough to make paste to a thick, creamy consistency

Use to stick light objects only, like paper and glitter.

Make your own play dough

You can buy play dough in the shops, but it's much cheaper and more fun to make your own. Plus, as babies tend to like to eat a little, you know exactly what it's made of.

1 cup plain flour
½ cup salt
1 cup of water
1 teaspoon cooking oil
2 teaspoons cream of tartar
7–8 drops food colouring

Mix flour and salt, add cream of tartar, water and oil. Add some food colouring and mix well. Cook over medium heat until ingredients form a ball, which shouldn't take longer than one minute. Your toddler will enjoy playing with it while it's still warm. Store in zip-lock bags or Tupperware containers to keep pliable and fresh.

Make your own salt dough
350g plain flour
375g table salt
275ml water
1 tablespoon vegetable oil

1. Mix the plain flour, salt and vegetable oil in a mixing bowl.
2. Gradually add the water, stirring all the time.
3. The mixture will eventually become dough. If it's too sticky, add more flour, if it's too dry, add more water.
4. Knead the dough for around five minutes until it's nice and smooth.
5. Leave the dough to stand for about twenty minutes before play. (It can also be stored in the fridge wrapped in cling film or in an airtight container for up to a week.)
6. Make models and shapes with your baby. Angel and Christmas tree cookie cutters make beautiful Christmas decorations.
7. Bake your creations in an oven on a baking tray. The oven should be preheated to a low heat, around 50C. After thirty minutes increase the temperature to 100C.
8. Baking times are long so it's worth baking them on days when you're cooking a slow casserole. It will probably take around five hours, depending on the shape and thickness of your models.
9. The cooled models could be painted with poster paints. Or you could add glitter or food colouring to the dough once the mixture is ready.

Mummy's little helper

As your baby becomes a toddler, they can begin to help you around the house. This can be helpful, but is also another activity to keep them occupied. Babies are big observers and enjoy copying what's happening around them. This often means your baby starts wanting to help tidy and clean when you are.

In the kitchen, once you've childproofed the cupboards, it's worth letting them have one 'safe' drawer or cupboard they can open and play in. It could be your pots and pans cupboard or the place where you keep their Tupperware, as long as there's nothing breakable or dangerous in there. This will be a handy 'toy cupboard' when you're trying to cook or tidy in the kitchen.

From around one year old, Rosie has been obsessed with sweeping. She now has her own dustpan and brush (not a toy one, just one that's her own). She really enjoys sweeping the kitchen and patio outside, and I'm not going to complain! She also enjoys wiping the table and washing the floor with her own special cloth when I'm doing the same. It's an excellent way of combining housework with childcare!

Washing the windows can become a good game, especially if you've got big glass doors in the house. Soap up the lower part and your baby can rub patterns and paint onto the soap while you properly clean the windows.

Washing their toys and/or dolls can also become an absorbing game. It's best done outside on sunny days but could be done inside too. Get a bowl of warm, soapy water and a sponge or flannel and they can help you clean their grubby things. If you need to paint and decorate a room, your toddler could be kept busy with a pot of water and a paint brush. As they get older you could give them a little space of wall on which to 'help' paint.

From around twelve months old, toddlers can help you with baking, especially if there's some biscuits involved. They can stir with their own wooden spoon and play with/lick the bowl once you've spooned most of the mixture out.

Make your own oat biscuits
125g plain flour
125g brown sugar
125g unsalted butter
100g oats
50g desiccated coconut
1 tablespoon syrup
1 teaspoon bicarbonate of soda dissolved in 2 tablespoons of boiling water

Mix the dry ingredients together. Slowly melt the butter, add syrup and dissolved bicarb soda. Pour melted butter onto dry ingredients and mix well. Roll a spoonful of mixture into a ball, flatten with fork onto greased baking tray. Repeat. Put in oven, 160 degrees for fifteen to twenty minutes until biscuits golden brown around the edges.

Things to do in the garden

If you have a garden, or can walk to a park or a patch of grass, there are lots of outdoor activities you can do with your baby, especially once they're a toddler. When Rosie was a baby, less than six months old, we'd always spend the last hour before bedtime in the garden. This is normally the time of day when babies are grouchy and tired and the fresh air cheered her up. When she was tiny, I'd walk around with her in the sling and as she got older she'd wriggle on a blanket, nappy off, in the summer.

Make your own bamboo wind chimes

Young babies especially love the gentle sound of bamboo wind chimes. Cutting different lengths of bamboo will create different notes, whereas the same lengths will all make the same tone when they bang into each other.

One length of bamboo, 10–12 inches, for top of chime
Six further lengths of bamboo to hang down
Twine or string
Sharp serrated knife
Drill

Measure the first piece of bamboo around four inches long and then each of the next five lengths should be one inch longer than the previous. With a sharp serrated knife cut fine grooves – evenly spaced – into your long length of bamboo. Drill a hole through the top of each of the six shorter lengths of bamboo, thread the twine through the hole and tie onto the top bamboo so it falls neatly in the groove. Pull a length of twine through the top piece of bamboo, tie the ends together around six inches above the centre. If you tie the ends through a large button, this will keep the chime balanced. Hang from a tree or somewhere else high.

Make your own bird cake
Dripping or lard
Wild bird seed
Apple
Bread
Old yogurt pot or plastic cup
Piece of string, around 50cm long

Carefully pierce a hole in the bottom of the yogurt pot, and thread part of the string through, so there's enough left to tie into a big knot that won't disappear back up the hole when tugged. Chop up the apple and bread into small pieces. Melt the dripping or lard in a saucepan, as soon as it's liquid add the apple, bread and bird seed. Make sure there's enough fat to stop the mixture becoming too crumbly. Once the mixture is the right consistency, fill up the pot, keeping the string upright. If there's a pool of fat on the top once it's full, sprinkle on some extra seeds. To stop the fat dripping out through the hole in the bottom of the pot plunge it halfway up in cold water. This solidifies the fat. Once cold, hang the cake out in the garden and carefully cut and peel off the pot.

Make your own pine-cone bird feeder
Peanut butter
Bird seed
Pine cone
Piece of string

This is a bit quicker to make than bird cake. Smear the pine cone in peanut butter and then roll in birdseed. Tie a length of string around the top of the cone and attach to a tree.

Bug watching

Bug watching, like bird watching, is an activity to keep both babies and toddlers fascinated. Babies from six months old will be interested in watching big bumble-bees in flowers, if you point them out, or spiders weaving a web and a troop of busy ants. By twelve months old, they'll be able to spot them themselves. Snails, slugs and worms provide much amusement too. Keep an eye on smaller babies to ensure they don't pop the bugs in their mouths – I once 'rescued' a half-eaten, juicy slug from Rosie's mouth when she was about eighteen months old. Since then, unsurprisingly, she doesn't eat bugs any more. A matchbox would make the perfect container for toddlers who wanted to collect empty snail shells.

Gardening

Most toddlers love gardening. They might be a little over-enthusiastic with the watering, but it's another handy activity that enables you to get on with things while entertaining them too. Invest in a small watering can, so they can help you outside; these can also be used at bath time or in the paddling pool.

I made a sensory garden for Leo that was all herbs and vegetables, so it was safe to play in and fun to create. He really enjoyed smelling all the different plants from tomatoes to lavender and I didn't get too concerned if he nibbled any of the herb leaves! Top up the soil with big stones to stop them eating so much soil!

Hazel, mum of Leo

Make your own toddler rock garden

Go for a walk to collect some rocks the size of your fist. Your toddler can help choose them. If there's nowhere suitable for rock-collecting where you live, collect a bucketful of big pebbles at your next seaside trip. Bring them home and supervise your toddler washing them outside. Select a few pebbles to paint together. Once they're dry find a space in your garden for them and show your toddler how to stomp them into the earth to make them secure. Your toddler could wash his rocks and relocate them as often as you like.

Planting seeds

Toddlers can help to plant and nurture their own garden. Select fast-growing seeds like nasturtiums or sunflowers. Nasturtiums can be a good choice as the seeds are large and the flowers and leaves are edible. Either plant the seeds in a special spot in your own flower-beds or make or buy a solid planter that should be around toddler waist-height. When the planter is not in use, the compost can make an excellent surface for games with cars and animals and mud cakes.

If you don't have a garden, grow seeds with your toddler in pots or window boxes. Strawberries and lettuce grow well in window boxes. Your toddler could paint and decorate any flower pots you use.

Make your own egg cressmen
Eggs
Cotton wool
Cress seeds
Water

Boil an egg and enjoy it for breakfast. Place a wad of cotton wool in the bottom of the empty egg shell: it should fill it halfway. Place the egg shell in an egg cup and decorate the egg with felt-tip pens. Saturate the cotton wool with water. Sprinkle seeds on top. Water the seeds daily. Tepid or warm water seems to speed up the growing cress.

Make your own indoor rainbow
Small mirror
Glass of water
Sunny window sill

Place a small mirror in a clear glass of water. Put the glass on a sunny window sill. Position the mirror in a glass so that the sun hits it and causes a rainbow to shine on the wall.

Teddy bear picnics and dens
Make tea-time special by having a picnic in the garden. Spread a blanket on the grass. Sit your baby with a selection of their favourite teddy bears, dolls and soft toys. Serve tiny cream-cheese or

marmite sandwiches cut into shapes with cookie cutters, sticks of cucumber and a small slice of cake.

Toddler dens can be made easily. The more time and patience you have, the more sophisticated their playhouses can be. The quickest, easiest house to make is by hanging a large double sheet on the washing-line and pulling out and weighting down the ends to make a tent-shape with some pebbles or rocks from the garden. Alternatively, drape the sheet between two secure chairs or over a table.

Make your own table-top playhouse
A collection of pretty sheets and tablecloths
Sewing machine
A table

Sew a more sophisticated playhouse with windows and doors using pretty old sheets and tablecloths. Use an outdoor table as a base for the house. Measure the top and sew one piece of material to fit. Then measure, cut and sew four pieces of material so that they're big enough to hang to the ground once attached to the table-top material; they will be the walls of your playhouse. These four pieces of material should be sewn to the sides of the table-top material, to make a cross shape. There's no need to sew the sides/walls that hang down. Transform one of your walls into a pretty window by cutting a large square hole in the centre; you could sew a material cross inside to make four window panes. Transform another wall into the door by cutting the piece of material in

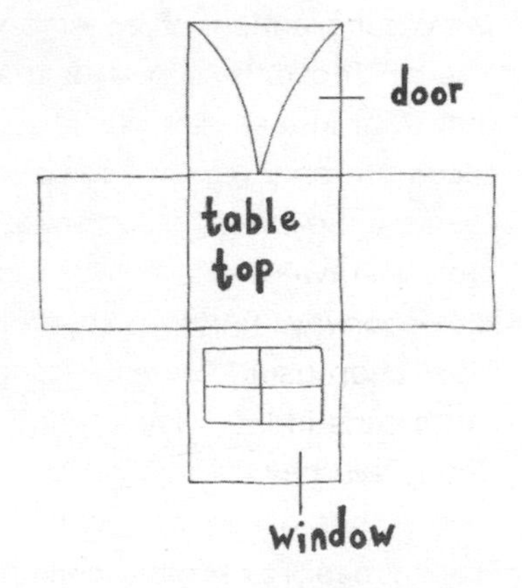

two, cutting from bottom to top. These two pieces can be tied to the table legs to make a fabric doorway.

Make your own bean teepee
7–9 long bamboo poles
Twine
String
Runner bean seeds and/or sweetpea seeds

A bean teepee makes the perfect toddler hideaway and support for green beans. Select a spot in the garden where your toddler can run in and out of their den without trampling on other plants and vegetables. Dig the earth over a circle around three to four feet in diameter. Add compost. Push the ends of the bamboo poles outside the circle. Leave a gap between two of the poles to make the doorway. Tie the poles firmly at the top using twine or string. Plant the beans in late May, or early June. Plant two bean seeds per pole about two inches deep into the soil inside the teepee. For a more colourful teepee you could plant some sweet-peas as well. Water well. Beans tend to take around seven to fourteen days to appear as seedlings. Make sure you protect them well from slugs and snails – be on guard when it's wet. When the beans are a few inches high tie them loosely to their poles. After seven to eight weeks they should reach the top of the poles.

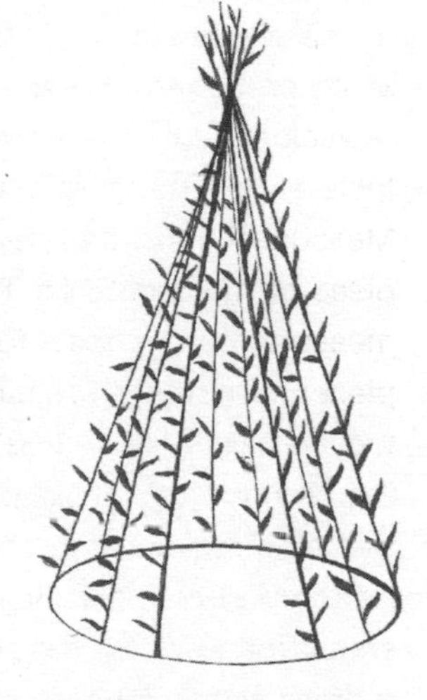

Make your own wind wheel

Piece of thick card, 30cm x 30cm
Coloured fabric remnants, 30cm x 30cm each
Dowelling
Drawing pin and map pin
Small bead
Water-based spray mount
Ruler
Scissors
Pen

Spray card with spray mount and place coloured fabric on top and smooth. Use contrasting fabric or other coloured card for other side. Fold the covered card in half diagonally and in half again and then unfold. Use a ruler to make a point three-quarters of the way to the centre of each of the four diagonal creases. Cut along the lines dividing each corner into two points. Bring every other point to the centre and hold with finger. Push drawing pin through all the layers. Remove and put the map pin through the hole. Slip bead onto the end of the map pin behind the wind wheel head and push the pin into the dowelling around 1–2cm from the top.

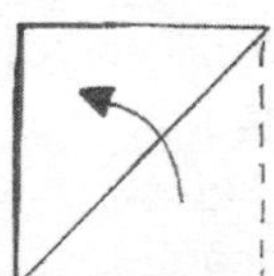

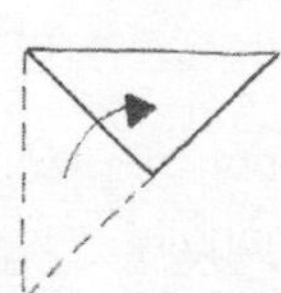

Toys to make

Before you get carried away in the toy shop, spend some time making a few simple toys yourself. For starters, toy boxes are easy to make. All you need to do is cover or paint some sturdy cardboard boxes or look out for an old pine chest at car-boot sales or second-hand furniture stores.

For Amber's toys we just covered two decent cardboard boxes with pretty wallpaper.
Lynsey, mum of Amber

Make your own bag of monsters
Squares of felt in three different colours
Needle and thread
Bells and squeakers (buy online or from haberdashery shop)
Pinking shears
Stuffing

To make four monsters, double up your felt fabric and cut out a circle, triangle, hexagon and oblong with pinking shears so that each shape is cut in two pieces to make the front and back of your monster. Each monster should be around the

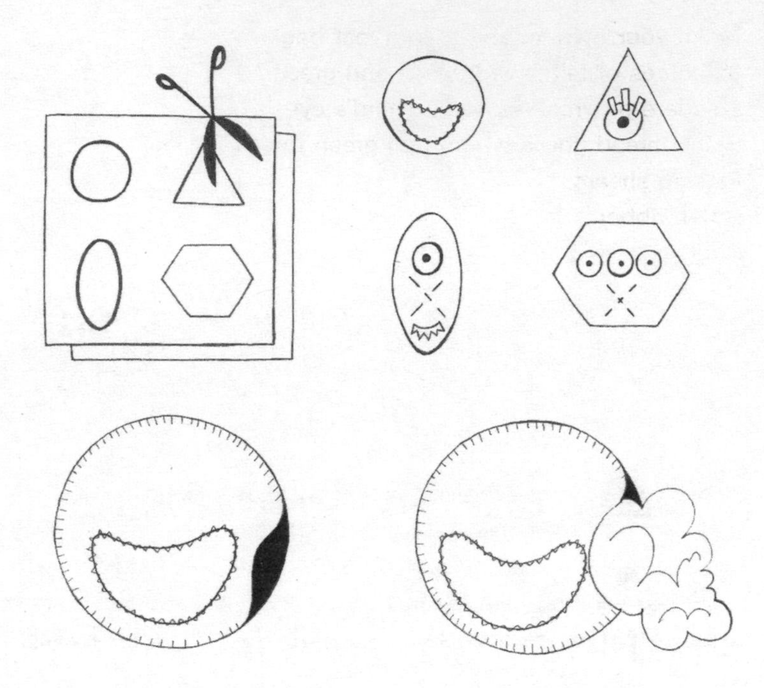

size of the palm of your hand. Sew different 'faces' onto the front of each monster in contrasting felts. Be inventive: monsters can have one eye, three eyes and a multitude of different expressions and colours. Embroider scraps of felt for facial features or embroider mouth or cross-shaped nose with thread alone.

Place the two pieces, front and back together, and use a zigzag stitch on machine to hem and join edges, leave a small gap for stuffing. Stuff and add bell or squeaker to each monster. Close up hem by hand.

Make your own ladybirds in a leaf bag
3 squares of felt in red, black and green
1 square of white felt for ladybird's eyes
Black thread (for ladybird) and green thread for leaf
Pinking shears
Green ribbon
Stuffing

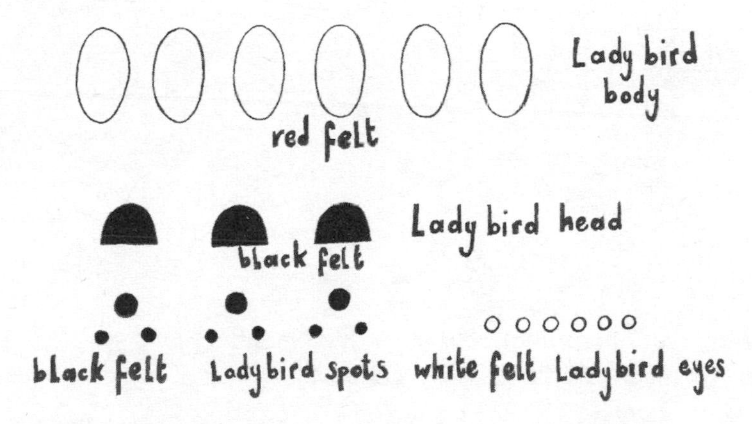

To make three ladybirds, cut out six oblongs in red felt, they should be the size of the palm of your hand. Cut out three semi-circles in black, they will make the ladybird's head and nine black circles for the ladybird's spots, these can be different sizes. Sew the spots and head onto three pieces of red fabric. Cut out six small circles in white felt for the eyes. Stitch the eyes on to top front of each ladybird. Holding two pieces of fabric right side together, hem the edges of the ladybirds, leaving a small gap for stuffing.

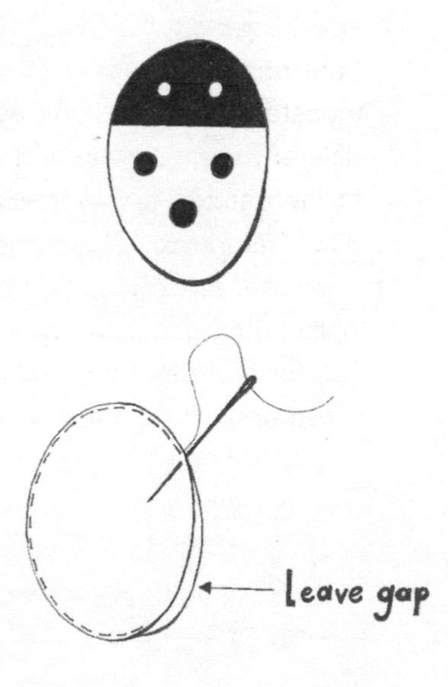

Turn them the right way round and stuff firmly, stitching up the gap by hand. For the ladybird bag cut out two identical leaf shapes in green felt, large enough to house the three ladybirds. Sew the two leaves together leaving a sizeable gap for the opening of the bag. Firmly stitch two pieces of green ribbon to the outer comers of the leaf bag to make handles so your toddler can carry the ladybirds around.

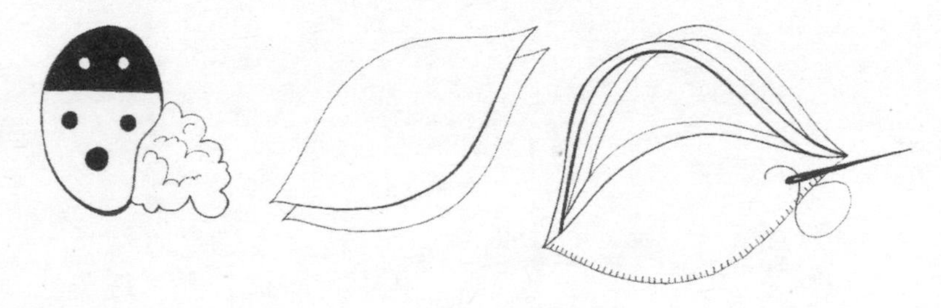

Make your own pom pom chick (two months plus)
Large piece of cardboard (cereal box)
Yellow wool
Orange felt
Scissors
Needle and thread

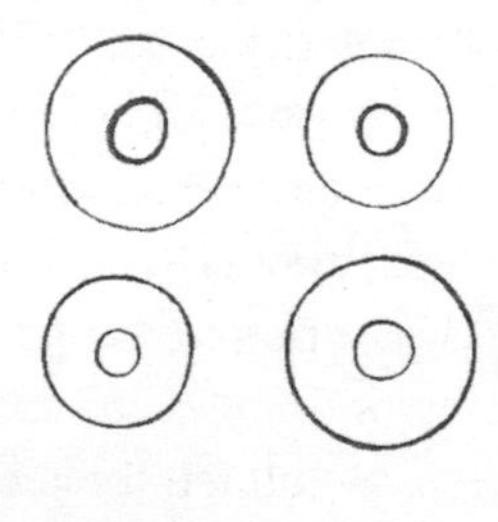

1. Cut out two large symmetrical circles (chick's body) and two smaller symmetrical circles (chick's head) from the cardboard. Use something to draw around – a coffee jar or CD for the body circle and a coffee mug for the smaller circle. Use something smaller again like a cotton reel to cut out another circle in the middle. (The size of the inside circle determines how much wool you can wrap around and how thick the pom pom will be.)

2. Place the two same-sized circles together and start winding the wool around the ring. Just keep wrapping and wrapping, tying on the end of each length of wool to an already attached length on the pom pom.

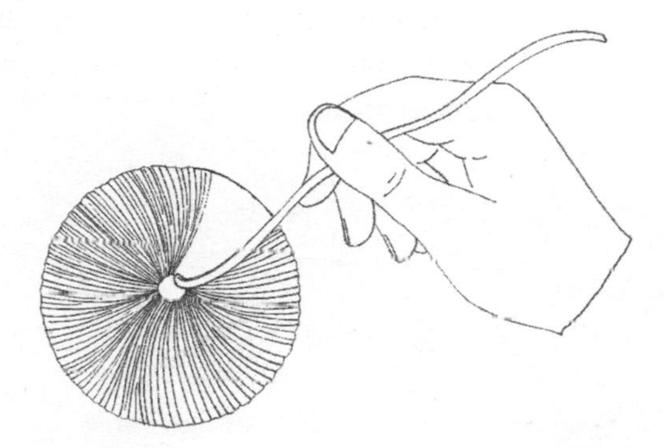

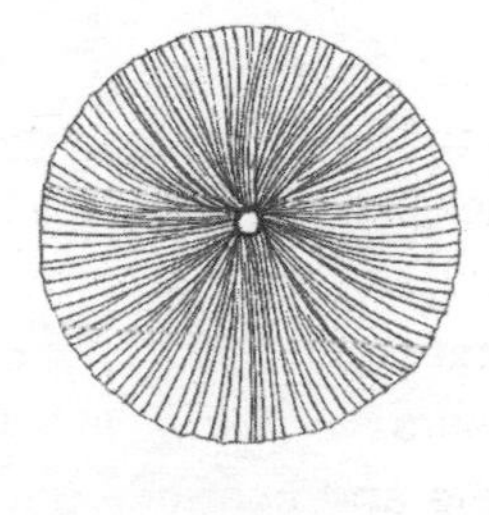

3. Once both circles are full of wool, create a gap to reveal the cardboard. Using scissors cut around the circle in-between the two pieces of cardboard.
4. Get a relatively long piece of wool and wrap this around the core of the pom pom, in-between the two pieces of cardboard and tie a knot. Plump up the pom pom to make a nice round.

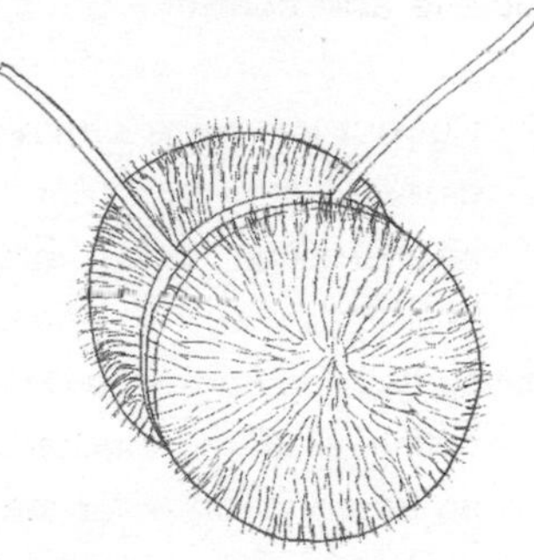

5. Now, attach the head to the body with a needle and thread.
6. Use a piece of paper and place the body on top, and roughly draw out where you would like the chick's feet to be

positioned. Then remove the body and draw out the length needed for the feet to be securely sewn on.

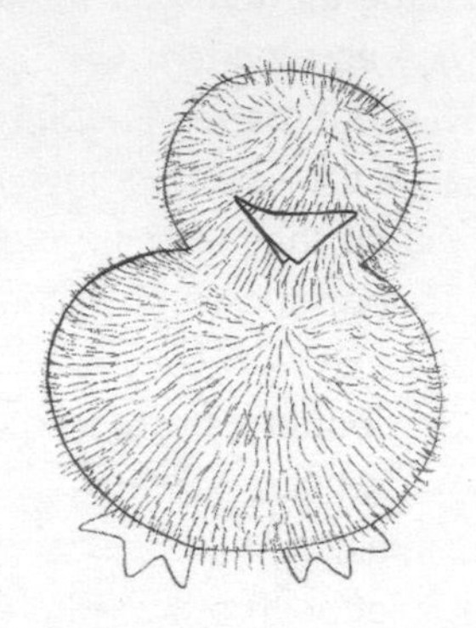

7. Cut two foot shapes out of the orange felt using the paper template, and sew to the base of the chick's body.
8. Lastly, cut out a small orange felt square for the beak. Fold this in half to form a triangle and sew onto the chick's head.

Make your own simple doll (three months plus)
A square of soft fabric
Scraps of spare wool or cotton wool
A short piece of wool or thread

1. Cut a square shape from a soft piece of fabric. The bigger the square, the bigger the dolly.
2. Fold the square into a triangle.
3. Find the centre of the folded edge and stuff with scraps of material, spare wool and cotton wool.
4. Tie a short piece of thread around the stuffing to make the dolly's head.
5. Sew or draw on two eyes and a mouth.

Make your own soft blocks

It's nice to use material with pictures on it. These three pieces of material will make three soft blocks of 10cm, 15cm and 20cm:

Three pieces of material, measuring 1 metre, 1.5 metres and 2 metres
Stuffing – cotton wool, material scraps or dried lentils or rice

1. Trace the three different-sized squares onto newspaper to use as a pattern.
2. Cut out the fabric squares, each cube will need six squares.
3. Sew the seams of four fabric squares in a row wrong side up, so that seams are neat on right side of fabric.
4. To form the sides of the block, right side of fabric facing you, lay out your row and pin two more squares onto the top and bottom sides of the second square along.
5. Wrong side out, sew up the remaining seams; soon you'll be left with a box with an open lid.
6. Leave half of the final seam open so you can turn the block the right way out and stuff.
7. It's surprising how much stuffing you need. Use cotton wool, remnants of material or dried lentils or rice for a more robust block.
8. Handstitch the final seam.

Make your own dog sock puppet (three months plus)
White sock
Circular white/red and pink craft foam
Black pom pom
Needle and thread
Piece of paper

1. Put the sock on your hand and pinch it in the middle to create a mouth. Keep hold of the mouth, turn the sock inside out and sew at each end to create a crease at either end of the mouth.

2. Take two pieces of red craft foam or red material and sew a smaller pink circle to one – that's the tongue.
3. Sew the red circle into the top of the sock mouth and the pink and red (tongue) into the bottom of the sock mouth.
4. Sew the black pom pom to the middle of the top of the puppet – that's the nose.
5. Use two white circular pieces of foam and sew on two smaller black pieces, to create the eyes, sewing them onto the sock.
6. Take two small, white, circular pieces of foam, pinch each at the bottom and sew them together securely, creating some ears and sew these onto the puppet.

Make your own pull-along caterpillar (twelve months plus)
Seven toilet rolls
One yogurt pot
String or ribbon
Acrylic paint
Masking tape
Short stick or twig

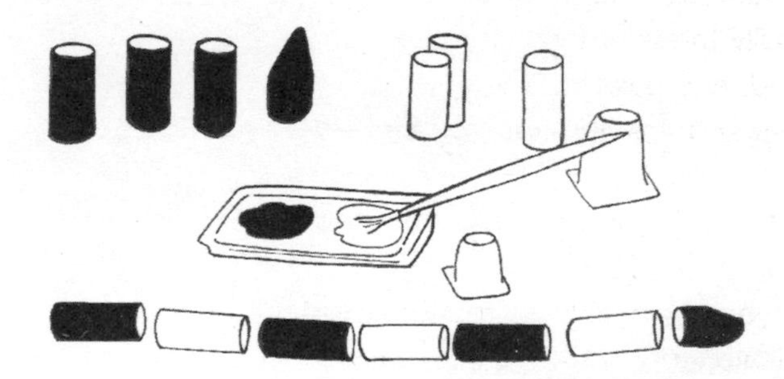

1. Cut out three triangles from the end of one of the rolls, so that it can be brought together to make a pointed end. This will be the tail.
2. Bring the pointed tail together and secure with masking tape.

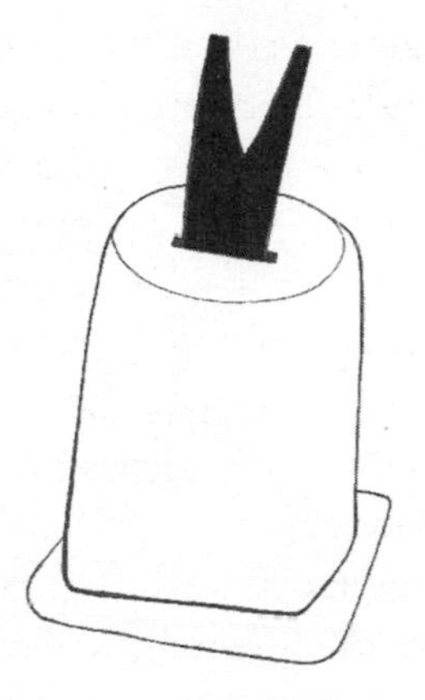

3. Then lay out the snake, with the yogurt pot as the head, six rolls as the body and finally the constructed tail tip.
4. Choose the colours for the snake and paint them – acrylic paint is good as it works on a broad number of surfaces.
5. Cut a slit in the yogurt pot for the snake's head, for a mouth, tongue and the pull-along ribbon that will be attached later.
6. Attach the end of some ribbon or string to the tail either with masking tape or glue, but make sure it's sturdy. Then thread it through each of the rolls.
7. Finally thread it through the head, and paint on some eyes and nostrils.

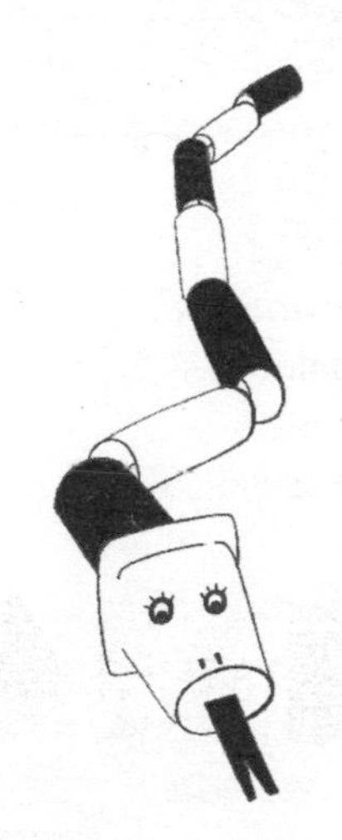

Make your own peg-doll people (twelve months plus)
Old-fashioned wooden clothes pegs
Scraps of fabric and ribbon

1. Draw facial features on the tops of the pegs with a thin permanent black marker. Smiles seem to work best, as my straightline mouth made a rather sinister-looking dolly.

2. Glue or sew scraps of fabrics and/ or ribbons onto the dollies to make clothing.
3. A toddler would prefer the clothing to be sewn together so they could take it on and off.

Make your own rubber ball
Three balloons
Bag of rice
Take two balloons and snip the stalks off with a pair of scissors. Stuff one balloon with rice until it is almost full. Stretch the other balloon over the open side of stuffed balloon to seal and secure. You could snip the stalk of a third balloon, then cut 'holes' all round it – stretch the third balloon over your ball to make a spotty coloured ball.

Things to buy

While your baby could probably happily play away with home-made toys, a set of keys and a wooden spoon, it's difficult to resist the temptation to buy toys. However, unless the toys are real bargains from the supermarket or IKEA, it's best to buy them second-hand online or in charity shops and second-hand sales.

I never bought items like a baby walker, baby bouncer or playpen. If you decide you want to, never buy them new; you won't use them for long enough. Buy second-hand and then sell again on eBay. You may find friends are desperate to give you these items, partly because they take up so much room. Incidentally, a travel cot makes an excellent playpen.

I like my ball pool idea that cost me £5: a cheap paddling pool and 100 balls from Tesco's.
Hazel, mum of Leo

If you do not have an abundance of toys, rotate a few toys at a time. Babies can get over stimulated anyway with lots of toys around them and they also get bored of seeing the same toys all the time. Rotating them in this way, baby gets more out of the toys he has. A toy your baby dislikes one week may be mesmerising the following week.

There are a number of classic toys that will last longer than an afternoon's entertainment. They also tend to be less irritating for adults, in terms of flashing lights and electronic noises. You don't have to have the latest 'all-singing, all-dancing' electronic baby toys – the classics have remained popular for good reason.

You'll find you and your baby use these classics differently as your baby grows. For example, stacking cups will be knocked over by a six-month-old, built by a toddler and used as an absorbing bath toy throughout. A trolley will be an indispensible walker for a nine-month-old and handy toddler transport for dolls and animals.

This can be a useful guide when investing in toys or making suggestions for gifts for your baby. Here's a list of Rosie's favourite toys:

Wooden trolley
Building bricks
Dolly

Tea set
Soft ball
Animals
Cars
Board books
A Brio wooden train set (look on eBay for second-hand ones)

Classic toys that are worth buying include: stacking cups – babies love these from five to six months and as they grow can learn to build towers. Put one inside the other and place other objects inside and shake them. They can also be used as a bath-time toy or in the sandpit. A trolley with wooden bricks will help them walk. Ball – find a soft one that a baby can grip. Duplo – babies love the bright colours and watching you building things then pulling them down. Later they can build themselves.

Amy (a nanny) and mum of Alfie

Things to borrow

Borrowing and swapping toys with friends is an effective way of boosting your baby's toy collection. There are toy libraries all over the UK, the National Association of Toy and Leisure Libraries (NATLL) can tell you where your nearest one is. My local one is open one afternoon a week. It's perfect for trying different products if you're thinking about buying something. They're also handy for all those annoying noisy, plastic toys that you don't want to buy, but your baby loves to play with.

Children's toy manufacturers would have us believe that we need to buy toys that are not only entertaining but help to make our babies clever too. Don't put this pressure on yourself and your baby. Everyday activities from passing a wooden spoon from one hand to another, to exploring the different textures in a treasure box, learning to crawl upstairs and pushing a block along the floor pretending it's a car are just some of the simple ways that child's play can be a serious business without the expensive help of children's toy brands.

CHAPTER ELEVEN

Pottering

Joining the library is free and M quite enjoys going there and looking at the books, and the other children in there. It's also quite a nice way to meet other people with babies, as most libraries will run some sort of baby/toddler group for free.

Susan, mum of Madeline

Pottering essentials

Must-haves

Comfortable shoes for long walks with pram
Bag packed with clean nappies and change of clothes
Bread for the ducks!
Plenty of fresh air
Friends (old or new) with babies to meet

Naughty but nice

One weekly paid-for activity, like swimming or Music Bugs
Latte, babycino and carrot cake in the local café

What you and baby can live without

Daily expensive classes like baby yoga, baby signing and
Monkey Music – be selective
Annual membership to the Baby Gym!

If you stay at home all day with your baby, you'll go stir crazy. Even a short walk to the end of the road to buy a pint of milk and a bar of chocolate will revive you. Admittedly, it can be difficult to get out of the house, especially in winter. By the time you've changed their nappy, fed them and winded them, dressed them in warm clothes, undressed them to change another dirty nappy, and start all over again, it's nearly feed-time again. A blast of fresh air always revives the soul, so it is worth making the effort.

My first trip out of the house on my own with Rosie felt like a big adventure. It took me all morning but I was so proud that I'd made it out. I can vividly remember drinking my latte out of a paper cup, standing up in my local café with Rosie in her sling. I was petrified that she would wake up if I sat down. I'm sure she wouldn't have done, but I wasn't quite ready to deal with a crying baby while out and about alone.

From the time your baby is around six months old, the pair of you will have a very hectic, very satisfying social life, if that's what you choose. From swimming on Monday to lunch with friends on Tuesday, to playgroup on Wednesday, Tiny Teddies at the library on Thursday and coffee morning and Music Bugs on Friday, the weeks will fly by and it doesn't have to cost the earth.

What to do when they're tiny

When your baby is really small, fresh air is important for both of you. This is the perfect time to go for long, long walks. The fresh air will send your baby into a lovely sleep, plus you'll get to stretch your legs, exercise and get out of the house. Take full advantage of their peaceful sleeping to nip into a café to read the papers and enjoy a quiet coffee.

LOTS of walking with the pram (which made me pretty fit and I lost weight quickly). It's amazing where you're willing to walk to give the baby a decent sleep and fill in your day . . .

Amy, mum of Seth and Agnes

These long strolls can end up taking all day. They're a lovely chance to get to know new friends that you've met with small babies too. Make sure you've packed lots of nappies, a spare pair of clothes, blankets, pram rain cover, muslins, formula if you need it. Stash a bottle of water, raincoat and some snacks for yourself, too.

Exercise

By the time your baby is a couple of months old, you may feel ready to do some exercise. It can be pretty difficult to get the time out to exercise when your baby is small, especially if you're breast-feeding. However, there are a number of things you can do to help get back into shape or baby-friendly exercise classes you can join.

Long, long walks are an excellent way to lose weight, get fit and get some fresh air. You could combine strenuous walks with friends with a few exercises like squats and sit-ups (if the grass is dry) in the park. A few companies, e.g., Buggy Fit, offer a version of this as an exercise class for new mums. It's a brilliant idea, but if the classes seem too pricey, why not create your own Buggy-cise class with some friends?

Buggy Fit in Bushy Park was good fun and I wish that I had done it a bit earlier – granted, it was £5 a session (although the first session is free), and just walking around the park on your own is free, but again it's a good way to meet people, feel a bit fitter and still cheaper than exercise classes, or gym classes. And it probably costs the same as going for a coffee!

Susan, mum of Madeline

I joined a post-natal exercise class in my local church hall with my friend Emma. It was reasonably priced, around £5 a class for a six-week course and that included a crèche for the babies and a cup of tea and biscuit afterwards. (My kind of exercise class.) A couple of lovely grandmas looked after the babies and jiggled them in their prams in the heated church porch as we did aerobics in the hall. It was also a great way of making new friends as we all had small babies.

An even cheaper option might have been going halves on a second-hand exercise DVD with a friend and doing it in each other's living rooms as the babies slept or watched bemused as we jumped around.

And of course, although it's not so much fun, there are ways you can exercise at home alone. You can do sit-ups while your baby's sleeping or sitting in their bouncy chair (it will make them laugh). You can do bicep curls using heavy books or baked-bean tins. And remember to do twenty pelvic floor exercises every time you stop at the traffic lights, watch TV, clean your teeth and eat breakfast.

Domestic goddess

This is a time in your life when you'll spend a large amount of time in cafés. It's always good to get out of the house, but it's so easy to spend as much as £10 a day on these outings, especially if you end up buying lunch or cakes as well. I think coffee-shop outings are essential for new mums, but there are ways of cutting down your visits.

Start taking turns to host coffee mornings or lunches with your friends. I have two circles of new friends that I've met since having Rosie. One set of girls are my NCT group, and the other I met at my ante-natal classes at my GP's surgery. Every Friday afternoon, someone from my NCT group hosts our meeting. And every Monday lunchtime, someone from my ante-natal class hosts a lunch at their house. They're my favourite days of the week. It's a lovely, relaxing way to catch up with new friends, exchange notes over the babies and share advice and tips.

As the babies get older and more mobile, from around five months, meeting in someone's home, rather than a coffee shop, is a much better option, especially if you all want to be out for longer than an hour. This means the babies can happily play with toys (and they love other babies' toys) in safe and comfortable surroundings, rather than wriggle impatiently on your lap.

How to be a Vegas Mama

Use your coffee mornings for poker sessions. Be inventive with chips – dummies, muslins, rattles will do. Trade in your winning hand for stuff you really want, like an hour's babysitting, a bottle of wine, home-made lasagne or the loan of a new DVD.

Cheap, cheerful, simple lunch for friends

Roasted vegetables and couscous
Either the night before or during your baby's morning nap, chop up a selection of vegetables into chunky pieces. Use vegetables like sweet potatoes, butternut squash, red onions, garlic, carrots, courgettes, aubergine, mushrooms and peppers. Toss them in olive oil, herbs and salt and pepper in a large baking tray. Put them in the oven for about forty minutes. Couscous only takes about ten minutes. Pour the couscous into a large bowl, dissolve some stock cubes in a pint of boiling water, depending on how much couscous you have. Cover the couscous in the stock, and cover with a plate for five minutes, then fluff with a fork, taste and add more water if needed. (You could blitz leftover roasted vegetables into a tasty baby purée if your baby is weaned, providing you haven't added salt.)

Bread and cheese
This is an even simpler lunch, though it may end up being a bit more expensive . . . Buy some lovely fresh bread from the baker, some nice hunks of cheese, dips like hummus and serve . . .

Chocolate Juliette
Big bar of good quality chocolate (200g)
Small packet of digestive biscuits
Handful of nuts (pecans and pistachios work well)
150g unsalted butter
Tablespoon golden syrup
Handful of dried fruit (optional)

Put the biscuits and nuts into a large plastic bag and bang with a rolling pin to crumble. Slowly melt the butter and chocolate in a pan. Line a container with cling film, it's best if it's square, and it can be plastic as this cake doesn't need baking. Mix the crushed biscuits into the chocolate mixture and add any extras like dried fruit or glacé cherries. Pour into the container and leave to cool and set in the fridge for two hours. When slicing, hold knife under hot water first; this will help stop it from crumbling. You could also melt your favourite chocolate bar instead – like Mars Bars – for a different taste.

Jean's Bakewell Tart

My mum's Bakewell tart is always a resounding success and it's surprisingly easy to make.

250g short-crust pastry
110g self-raising flour
110g white sugar
110g butter
2 medium eggs
Almond essence
Apricot jam
Flaked almonds

1. Grease a pie dish approximately 36cm x 24cm.
2. Roll out the pastry to fit, with two-thirds pressed up the sides.
3. Prick the pastry all over.
4. Spread jam smoothly all over the pastry, the same thickness as a jam sandwich. Apricot or raspberry taste best, but any flavour will do.
5. Put dish in fridge.
6. Preheat oven to 160 degrees.
7. Mix flour, sugar, butter, eggs and almond essence in a large

bowl until the mixture is light and fluffy. Taste to see if you need to add more almond essence.

8. Spread the sponge mix over the jam and pastry lightly with a knife and spoon, trying not to pick up any jam.
9. Sprinkle with flaked almonds and bake in oven for thirty minutes.

Don't feel as if you have to host an elaborate lunch for your friends. The stress of preparation while looking after your new baby will send you into a frenzy. My NCT group decided not to host lunches for each other, after a few months of doing so. Instead, we all turn up to the meeting with a sandwich. All the hostess needs to worry about is making the tea (and pouring the wine!).

More recently, as our babies are now all weaned and eat normal food, the hostess has started providing tea for the babies. It's best if it's picnic food, as there won't be enough highchairs to go around, so this is food they can shove in their mouths while they carry on playing.

Lauren's tea party

My friend Allison made lovely baby pizzas at our last NCT meeting. She spread whole-wheat muffins with some tinned tomatoes and grated cheese and placed them under the grill, before cutting them into baby-sized pieces. The babies loved them.

Rosie's tea party

I keep it really simple when making Rosie's friends some tea. I cook some fish fingers and sausages in the oven, which I cut into little pieces and serve alongside fingers of brown toast smeared in hummus. Then for pudding it's chopped grapes or blueberries in little, individual containers for them all.

Once the babies are around twelve months, it can be nice to provide a special activity for the babies on the weeks you're hosting, from rolling out a large piece of paper and giving them all some crayons to giving younger babies some old catalogues and magazines to rip up. This can keep them occupied for ages, giving the mums an even better chance to relax.

In the summer it gets even easier. You could get the paddling pool out, or put some sand in a big bowl for them all to play with. Pre-warn your friends if you've got a messy activity in mind, so they can bring a change of clothes.

The great outdoors

Babies love seeing other children play. Even when they're quite small, a trip to the playground to stare at the kids playing can keep them occupied. By the time they're around five months old, they'll really enjoy going on the swing at the playground. When Rosie was small I used to sit on the swing and cuddle her. She loved it.

You don't need to join expensive music/yoga/gym clubs unless the aim is to meet new mums – the best entertainment that Madeline gets is taking her to the local playground where she loves watching the other children play.

Susan, mum of Madeline

Parks and playgrounds are a great way of meeting other people and don't cost anything. As babies get older, even just putting them on a swing for ten minutes is a lovely activity.

Shonagh, mum of Daniel and Caitlin

As the weather improves, start meeting your friends for picnics in the park. Each bring a blanket for the babies to lie on and a handful of toys for them to play with. Then spread out in some dappled shade under a tree. Before Rosie was too much of a wriggler, I used to let her have nappy-off time as she lay on her back on the picnic blanket. She loved it.

Feeding the ducks and watching dogs in the park goes down a treat.
Yvonne, mum of Scarlett

Feeding the ducks is another cheap activity that will put a big smile on your baby's face. You can combine this with a walk, keeping them in their buggies. Once they're old enough they can help you feed the ducks, though they might enjoy eating the bread too.

Once your baby can walk, everything becomes a bit easier. It means you can let them out of their buggy to have a run around the park, without worrying about the ground being wet or dirty. And if you buy them a cheap pair of wellies, splashing in the puddles is a wonderful way to pass the time.

The simple life

As your baby becomes a toddler, you can feel under pressure to take them to lots of expensive classes and activity groups. However, there are so many simple outings you can do with them yourself that won't break the bank and will keep them just as happy. If you live in the country, trips to visit the horses, sheep or cows in the field or a trip to the local farm will be fascinating enough. Ditto a trip to the beach to watch the waves and play with the sand or pebbles.

All the parks are great. Charlie loves the little ferry that goes over to Ham. He also loves the giant chess board on Church Street and really silly things like watching the trains go by from Kneller Gardens. He's obsessed with the geese down by the river.
Emma, mum of Charlie

Start looking at your local area through the eyes of your toddler. Everything is so new and exciting for them. I remember Rosie being mesmerised by a big yellow digger digging up the road outside our house when she was about nine months old. All morning, I held her on the window sill as she pressed her nose to the glass, fascinated for ages.

On empty days when you're desperate to think of ways to entertain them take simple trips like watching the trains rush by, visiting the local pet shop or whizzing them around the supermarket in the trolley. My nanny friend Amy used to take her young toddlers to visit Heathrow airport to watch the planes take off. Our local garden centre is wonderful. Aside from a few cages of bunnies, it's also got fish, and a safe area for Rosie to run outside. There's even a small play area inside for toddlers.

Freeloader

If money was no consideration you could book a different activity for your baby for every day of the week. From swimming lessons to baby massage, baby yoga, baby signing, baby singing and dancing, there's even baby gymnastics! While I'm sure some of these activities are wonderful for mother and baby, they also cleverly tap in to the anxieties of new mothers that you must be 'stimulating' your baby.

We do activities like Tumble Tots, Monkey Music, etc., but they are definitely NOT cheap!
Yvonne, mum of Scarlett

I decided to pay for just one class for Rosie – Music Bugs. It lasts one hour on a Friday and involves singing, dancing and lots of musical instruments and puppets for her to play with. She really likes it, as do I because some of my friends go too. It costs me £5.50 a week, which I rationalise by thinking that I could easily spend that amount on a latte and a cake in a coffee shop.

However, there's no reason why you couldn't create a musical session for your baby at home with some friends. Just pop a nursery rhyme CD on, sing loudly and let the babies bang on some pots and pans with wooden spoons. (For nursery rhyme and baby song lyrics see Chapter 10 on **Playing**.) Similarly, most libraries do a free weekly sing-song and rhyme-time for mums and babies.

Nearly all of these expensive mother-and-baby classes offer a free trial session so you can see what they're like before you commit to paying for a course. There's no reason why you can't take full advantage of these sample classes, even if you've got no intention of committing to the course. So far, Rosie and I have been to Tumble Tots, The Baby Gym, Gymboree, Monkey Music, Jo Jingles and Baby Signing! In fact, that was how I was seduced by Music Bugs.

I'm not sure that swimming classes do offer special sample trials. If you've got your heart set on taking your baby to a proper swimming class visit your local swimming pool, rather than expensive classes like Baby Aqua. Lots of new parents are taken in by the idea of these special baby swimming classes because of the opportunity to have a great underwater shot of their waterbabies. If you really want the picture, you can always take it yourself with a disposable underwater camera. it will work out cheaper than a course of classes.

The cheapest option is to take them swimming yourself. Save money for classes when they're a bit older and will actually be taught how to swim. It's worth getting babies used to the water when they're very young. Local swimming pools sometimes have floats and toys you can play with. If not, it might be worth investing in a little watering can to take with you. Encouraging them to stretch out their arms and legs while whizzing them around the water on their tummy is great fun. Young babies seem less keen to lie on their backs in the water. They'll be happiest being jiggled up and down. You can sing and play action songs to them like 'Hokey Cokey' or 'Five Little Ducks' if you want to recreate activities from expensive swimming classes.

I take Josh swimming every week now – it's cheaper than joining a class but if you want to meet people it is worth going to a class.
Rachel, mum of Josh

Bookworms

Local libraries are wonderful places for new mums and their babies. Join for both you and your baby, if you're not a member already. You'll save a fortune on new books and, contrary to popular belief, you will still want and be able to read once your baby is born. For a nominal fee you can order and reserve books from the library. Last year, I spent around £2 ordering all the books on the Booker shortlist: before I would have spent a fortune buying them all new.

And it's not just about borrowing your favourite book of fiction. You can also use the library to order baby books like Gina Ford (for routines) and Annabel Karmel (for weaning), which can be expensive when you buy them new. Aside from the obvious benefits of being able to read good books for free, libraries offer a really valuable service for young families too.

Many libraries run a free rhyme-time/story-time – in line with the National Bookstart programme – pop in and ask or ask your health visitor.
Lynsey, mum of Amber

Since Rosie was around twelve weeks old, I have taken her to a singing session at the local library called Tiny Teddies. It's lovely way of meeting local mums and we often end up in the café round the corner afterwards. You can always tell when it's Tiny Teddies day because the local cafés are heaving with buggies and babies.

From as early as a few months old, babies love the relaxing routine of being read to and looking at books before a nap or bedtime. When they're young, books with bold, black-and-white, geometric patterns work best. From around four to five months they'll like fabric books with crinkly bits and different textures they can touch and feel. Once they're about nine months they'll love simple board books with bright pictures and flaps to look behind. Every week Rosie gets about eight books out of the library. When we get home they keep her busy for ages, it's like buying new toys.

Local libraries have lots of activities and story telling and also our central one in Reading had some great 'hands-on' gadgets to play with in the kiddy corner. I'm a great advocate of reading to your baby too so we always borrowed loads of board books.
Catrin, mum of Theo and Cerys

Don't forget that libraries can be a fantastic rainy-day destination. They're a safe place for your baby to crawl/ run around. And they sometimes have toys as well as lots of books for your baby to play with. Rosie's favourite library game is to take all the books off the shelves. I follow her around, putting them away again. It can keep her happy for nearly an hour!

Let's play

If you live in a Sure Start area there are loads of classes and groups that are totally free.
Ali, mum of Louis and Eddie

Baby and toddler groups are a cheap way to get out of the house and entertain your baby. You'll even get a cup of tea and a chance to make some new friends. Once your baby is crawling around, they'll probably be old enough for toddler groups, but you'll have to keep a close eye on them when they're young. These playgroups come into their own once your baby is a toddler and running around.

Toddler groups are normally run by local church groups in church halls or community centres. For the nominal fee of around £1 you can come with your babies and while they play with all the different toys, you can relax with a cup of tea and a biscuit.

These drop-in mother-and-baby groups which are all over the place in church halls, etc., are so cheap. £1 and you can have a couple of hours with new toys, a cuppa and a chance to meet other mums.

Emma, mum of Charlie

Look out for parent-and-baby/toddler groups, usually at church halls or community centres. Isleworth has an excellent centre for under 5s, which costs about £2 for a morning or afternoon session (they usually give you a discount if you arrive in middle of session) and 50p for a cup of tea. Nice way of meeting new people or going along with other parent friends.

Nics, mum of Kate and Anna

Toddler groups do seem to vary dramatically, but the good ones are wonderful. Some in my area even have a waiting list. Others might seem a bit dirty or won't have very nice toys. The only way to find out is to sample them and ask friends for advice. Ask your health visitor or local library for a list of local groups and look out for ads outside church halls or in local coffee shops.

You don't have to be a particular religion to go to these groups, even though they're often held in a church hall. However, you might find the kindly old lady who gives you your tea asks you a few questions about your faith! Some of the groups just let the babies play, others might organise a little sing-song during the session. If you play your cards right, you could easily visit a different baby and toddler group every day of the week.

One o'clock clubs are free and a brilliant place to spend an hour or two and meet other mums. You can see a list of toddler groups on www.netmums.co.uk. Often you only have to pay a pound or so.

Lynsey, mum of Amber

One o'clock clubs are also normally free or very reasonably priced drop-in centres for parents with babies and toddlers. They tend to be situated in parks and may close in winter. Similarly, look out for soft play centres in your area. Again, these seem to vary quite dramatically in terms of general griminess and noise, so ask advice from other local mums.

We go to a great soft play centre at the Peckham Pulse – costs £1.35 for an hour.

Yvonne, mum of Scarlett

CHAPTER TWELVE

Juggling

Leo has been with his childminder since he was about six months old. When you're choosing a childminder, have a look at how clean the place is; a pristine house is not necessarily a fun house. I found that of all the people I went to see, I felt the most confident with the person who automatically took Leo to play and didn't just focus on talking to me. After all, I'm not the important one in the equation.

Hazel, mum of Leo

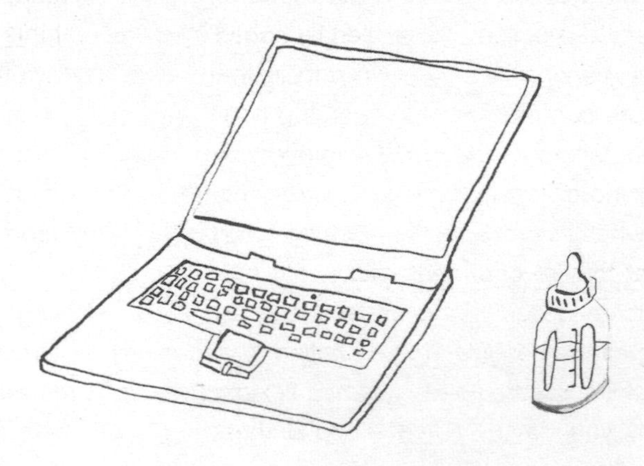

Returning to work is a peculiar time. You don't want to leave your baby, but the thought of being able to sip a coffee while reading the paper on the commuting train sounds like bliss. There are ways to be resourceful about returning to work, although this obviously depends on your own financial circumstances and the nature of your job.

As a freelance writer I never really had the whole momentous 'returning to work' malarkey after six months, like many do. It was something I sort of kept up with, although admittedly it meant working in the evenings, weekends or during Rosie's sleep times. Sometimes, I felt this was worse, because it was pretty exhausting. But on balance, I think I'm lucky that on good days I can almost juggle both things.

If you're in the sort of work that can be done from home or in your own time, then now is the perfect moment to become freelance or talk to your employer about reducing hours in the office. However, there's only so much you can do during a baby's naptimes and inevitably at some point you're going to need some extra help.

A lot of my friends have found maternity leave a time to reflect and consider their future career. Some of them move into completely different fields, because they feel their job just isn't compatible with being a mother. Some investigate those entrepreneurial ideas they've always had but never had time to indulge. Indeed, many successful businesses have been launched by women at this stage in their lives who've spotted a gap in the market and wanted to have more control over their working hours.

Others talk to their current employer about reducing their hours, working more flexibly or working from home. I've also got many friends who have returned to work full time happily with good childcare that they're confident with.

Childcare doesn't have to cost the earth. By ensuring you're claiming all the benefits you're entitled to and mixing and matching resourceful childcare (friends, family, flexible working) with traditional childcare, you may be able to keep all those juggling balls in the air.

Childcare options

There are three choices for conventional childcare for babies and toddlers: nanny, childminder and nursery. A childminder is probably the cheapest option, followed by nursery and then nanny. However, the costs all depend on individual circumstances. While an au pair may be suitable to help out once your baby is at school, they are not allowed to be in sole charge of children under the age of two.

Money-saving childcare options might include using family and friends, experimenting with flexi-working so you and your partner can juggle childcare between you, sharing childcare with a friend so you look after their baby one day and they look after yours another. These alternatives can be combined with conventional options to reduce costs. So if you need to work a three-day week – perhaps your mum can help out one day, your partner another and then use a childminder for just one day.

Baby swap shop

My friend Emma has been resourceful about childcare, which has enabled her to keep the costs down to work part time rather than full time. Charlie is looked after by his grandma one day a week, looked after by a friend Alison with a baby called Ellie on one day and attends a local nursery on the other day. Then, on one of Emma's days off she returns the favour to Alison by looking after Ellie too.

Looking after two babies is not easy. But both Alison and Emma are happy with the trade-off, it's saved them both nearly £60 a week in potential nursery fees and it means Charlie and Ellie have become great friends. Alison and Emma are lucky that they're next-door neighbours, so it's relatively easy to drop off a baby and a highchair to each other's houses. They went half-each on a cheap double buggy from Mothercare to ensure the babies get out and about and they plan to sell it on eBay when the arrangement ends. Incidentally, there are lots of great, cheap double buggies for sale on eBay.

But in order for this arrangement to work well, you need to set up some ground rules. Emma and Alison agreed on a trial period of a month to see if it worked, before they committed to a longer relationship. It can be an exhausting day looking after two babies, so it's a big undertaking. Emma copes by making sure she's really organised. Lunch, milk and snacks are prepared the night before, the double buggy is laid out ready to go, as are the toys.

She often takes the babies to a toddler group in the morning to make things easier and also finds a trip to the swings works wonders. Swings are great because you can push two babies at the same time. Other activities that work well with two young babies include feeding the ducks.

Lunchtimes are tricky, as are milk times, but this is something that gets easier as the babies get older. From about eight months they're more confident with finger food, so you can always distract one with a toasted soldier while you spoon-feed the other. Similarly, from around nine months they're able to hold the milk bottle themselves.

Nappy-changing is challenging, but if you have your wipes and clean nappies in the living room you can change one on the floors while the other is playing. All this is probably a piece of cake for mothers of twins.

Have finger foods on hand at lunch so while you're feeding one, the other isn't screaming the place down. I set up a nappy-changing station downstairs. I also had two play areas set up so each baby had their own play mat with their own toys. Make sure you've got everything you need in the house because you don't want to be running out to the shops in the rain with two babies. Arrange to see a friend on the days you've got two when you're out and about, it means you can do a lot more. We would all have got cabin fever if we hadn't bought a double buggy. Agree boundaries with your friend beforehand so you don't take each other for granted. Try and make sure you see your friend socially every few weeks or it can become too much like a business relationship.

Emma, mum of Charlie

Grandmaternity

Grandmothers and other family make wonderful and cheap child-minders. Although my mum lives about 300 miles away she still comes and stays once a month to look after Rosie for me for a few days. It's such a tremendous help but it also means they get to spend time together, which they both love. Some people are able to use their parents as regular childminders. According to the charity Grandparents Plus, more than a third of grandparents spend the equivalent of three days a week looking after their grandchildren, the equivalent of around £1bn a year!

And this is a modern phenomenon: in the early 1970s the proportion of children cared for by grandparents was 33 per cent, today it's more like 82 per cent. In November 2007, the Australian government suggested that grandparents could take a year of unpaid leave when a grandchild is born. Practical or not, the sugges-tion does address a genuine social issue.

My mum looks after Kayla five days a week. Make it formal, agree conditions in advance. We sat down and really talked about it when I was still pregnant and we kept on talking. You need to make it formalised and treat it like a business relationship. They are your childminder. It can be difficult though. Sometimes Mum will give Kayla an afternoon bottle even though I don't want her to. So I have to remind her and tell her, 'I know you're her grandma but I'm her mum.'

Nicky, mum of Kayla

You also might want to speak to your mum about what they're going to do with your baby during the day. I have one friend who feels her mother-in-law doesn't take her son outside enough, which means he's still got lots of energy in the evenings when he should be exhausted. Another friend of a friend felt her mother-in-law put her son in front of the TV far too much. So it's worth setting out some ground rules in terms of activities. Let them know that you want your baby to have fresh air every day.

If your mother-in-law offers to help, lay out the childcare arrangement as if she's a professional childminder. Agree on days and times each week. It will give you peace of mind and mean you don't constantly feel as if you're asking for favours. Most grandmas help out for free so make it as easy as possible for them. I don't expect her to do loads. I measure out the formula, the bottles are ready and I prepare his bag as if he was going to nursery. I also suggest activities for them to fill their day, from local toddler groups to trips to the library and leaving some old bread to feed the ducks.

Emma, mum of Charlie

Childcare benefits

Before you dismiss conventional childcare out-of-hand as something you can't possibly afford, understand what benefits and extra help you might be entitled to. It's well worth doing your homework. According to the government, nine out of ten familes are eligible for tax credits and there are three different kinds:

1. Child Tax Credit (CTC) is worth over £42 weekly for one child and it increases for more children. And you can be eligible even on a high salary. In general, families with incomes up to £58,000 (or £66,000 if there is at least one child under one year old) are eligible. There's also extra help if you have a

child with a disability. CTC is paid directly into your bank account, in addition to Child Benefit.

2. Working Tax Credit (WTC) is a top-up for your wages if you're on a low to middle income.
3. Childcare Element of the Working Tax Credit is designed to help working parents cover childcare costs. You can claim up to 80p for every £1 you pay for registered or approved childcare. The limit is £175 a week for one child and £300 for two or more. To be eligible you have to work sixteen hours or more a week.

You may also be able to get extra help from your employer through the voucher scheme. Some employers offer childcare vouchers in return for a reduction in part of your cash salary. It may seem like you're earning less money, but it's certainly worth it in terms of tax, and will mean you're better off in the long term. Basically, you 'sacrifice' up to £55 a week from pre-tax salary to be redeemed from official childcare providers. However, do your research, as accepting childcare vouchers may affect your entitlement to tax credits, so do your sums and see which one saves you most money. HMRC, the government department, has lots of information including a calculator on their website www.hmrc.gov.uk/taxcredits as well as a helpline. (Details in **The Directory** in Chapter 15.)

Childcare vouchers can only be paid to registered childcare providers. Ask your employer to see if they'll provide any help or support for childcare. Apparently around one in ten do help their employees with childcare vouchers, subsidised workplace crèches and nurseries. It's worth asking. However, if you get any kind of childcare support from your employer then you can't claim tax credits yourself.

Flexible working

If you've worked for your employer for over six months you can ask them about flexible working, which might include flexible hours as well as the opportunity to work from home as a new parent. The government has now made this a law so your company has to listen to your request and can only refuse when there is a clear business reason. To make sure you word your request correctly you can download a form from www.dti.gov.uk/workingparents or call the working families free legal helpline on 0800 0130313.

There are lots of different options with flexible working. From part time to flexi-working – where you agree to work certain hours and dip in and out to clock up your agreed working hours – or job sharing – where you split your job into two and share it with another person. Working from home may not sound like it would make a big difference to family life but it does. It means you can take a long commute out of the day so your baby won't have to be in childcare for as long. It also means you can start work earlier and finish earlier. I get much more done when I'm working from home as there are no interruptions.

Or perhaps staggered hours would work for you and your family – for example, instead of 9–5, you could work 7–3 or 11–7. Then there's compressed hours when you work more hours, fewer days of the week. So, for example, you might work ten-hour days, four days a week. My friend Marcela's husband Reinhardt works in this way. He's a project manager and his organisation let him work two really long days and two normal days in exchange for Fridays off when he can look after their daughter Ellie. It's a perfect arrangement because it means he gets to spend quality time with his daughter and also that Ellie only has to go to a childminder two days a week.

Childminders

Childminders are often one of the most affordable options for childcare. Rates vary from area to area but probably cost from £5 to £8 an hour. A childminder won't look after your baby exclusively but will have a small group of kids to care for, normally in their own family home. However, childminders are only allowed to look after one baby under the age of one, so make sure yours is the only small baby in her care. Having said that, they might also be looking after a toddler, who needs a lot of attention too. All childminders who care for children under eight years old must be registered and inspected by Ofsted.

The advantages of childminders, aside from cost, include the fact they're likely to be more flexible than nurseries in terms of your hours and holidays. You may also like the fact that your child is being cared for in a family home by one carer.

Do your homework. Call your local children's service for a list of childminders in your area and set up appointments with those you like the sound of that have vacancies. It's probably worth meeting at least three. You can also carry out some background checks by reading their Ofsted reports and speaking to other parents who use them.

When you arrive, walk around the house and make sure it's clean and comfortable. Are there any good toys for your baby to play with? If the childminder looks after older children you want to make sure your little one won't spend the day in the car ferrying them to and from school or back and forth to clubs. Similarly, find out simple things about the childminder's own routine – when do they do banking, shopping chores? You might want to know if they take the children to the park, toddler groups and the library; all activities that you would do together if you were at home.

Questions to ask childminders

How long have you been childminding?

What extra training have you done?
What other children will be with my child and how old are they?
Have you joined any quality assurance schemes?
Do you belong to a childminder network?
Do you charge for sick days?
How do you spend the day and how do the other children's schedules fit in with my child?
Do you go out on day trips?
What kind of meals and drinks do you give the children? (Be firm about what you do not want your child to have – no fizzy drinks, Haribo and fast food, for example.)
Do you keep a file about a child's progress?

Like all childcare options it often comes down to a gut reaction. Do you like them? Are they the right person to look after your baby? Do you like the other kids they look after? But do bear in mind that compared to your little baby, toddlers are going to seem messy and noisy and bouncy. Once you've chosen your childminder ask for a trial run of a couple of mornings just to make sure it suits you all. Make sure you agree on feeding, learning, TV-watching and discipline and ensure your contract includes hours, pay, sickness and holiday pay. You can ask them for up-to-date certificates for registration, public liability insurance and first aid. (Check all rooms and the garden is insured. If not, your child will be excluded from these areas.) For more information call the National Childminding Association 0800 1694486 or www.ncma.org.uk.

Some of the things I looked out for with my childminder were: what happens if she is too ill to look after my child? Does she have emergency cover or people she uses? What are her emergency procedures? Check her flexibility on picking up ten minutes earlier or later and if she charges for ten minutes above contracted hours. Are there any behaviour issues with the other children and how does she deal with them? What illnesses prevent your child attending and for how long? For example, if they've all had chicken pox bar your child, can they still attend after two days of high temperature? What events does she do to bring the other parents together so that you all know who each other are – after all, your children are spending an intense amount of time together.

Hazel, mum of Leo

Molly goes to a childminder who lives across the road from me. We met when we both had babies and she then decided to retrain as a childminder. Having someone nearby makes it easier. It means you don't have to get in the car or get the buggy. I also think it's easier to have a childrinder close to home rather than close to work. The fact I knew Emily already helped my decision. If someone's house is clean and pristine, that's probably not a good sign. Check and see if they're smokers.

Annabel, mum of Molly

Nannies

Nannies are probably the most expensive options for childcare, but there are ways to make it affordable. Nannies normally look after your baby in your own home and can help to fit in with more unusual working hours. Nanny wages can range from £132 to £400 a week, depending on where you live and their experience, according to government literature. However, my friend Amy, who is a nanny, says in London the day rate is around £90, and that doesn't include tax and National Insurance. However, costs could be cut if they lived in your home. But you'll also have to pay their National Insurance and tax contributions. And you may want to put them on your insurance if you want them to drive the family car. Other costs include holiday and sick pay.

Unlike childminders, nannies don't have to be registered by

Ofsted but they can register voluntarily. However, it's worth employing a registered carer as you will then be able to claim tax credits. Nannies are a great solution if you want to have a big say in how your baby is looked after and you want them to be cared for in your own home.

But nannies don't have to be a preserve of the rich. Nannies are more cost-effective if you've got more than one child or twins. My friend Yvonne shares a nanny with her big sister who has two young boys and lives nearby. It's an ideal arrangement because it means they can split the costs of the nanny between them while the cousins get to grow up together.

Similarly, my friend Allison employs our friend Amy as nanny for her little girl Lauren. They met in our NCT classes. Amy has a little boy Alfie, a few weeks older than Lauren. And she looks after both of them together. The fact that Amy cares for her own child too, means she's not as expensive as a nanny without a small child.

Nanny shares are one way of cutting costs. This means you share a nanny with another family, and can split the costs of wages, holiday pay, tax and National Insurance between you. Look out for nanny shares on local websites like Gumtree, Mumsnet, simply-childcare.com or in local newspapers. Your local NCT branch may have a nanny share register. This enables you to use a nanny part time by sharing her days with another local parent.

Aside from word-of-mouth, nannies are normally found through nanny agencies. However, this can be expensive, as the agency will expect a fee of hundreds of pounds to find your nanny and then additional commission during their first six weeks of employment. You could cut these costs by using the websites listed above instead.

It's important to get at least two recent references when you're interviewing potential nannies. Don't just rely on written references but call the parents up and speak to them. Ask about the nanny's attendance, sick days, activities with the kids and make sure the nanny has baby experience.

A nanny is one-to-one childcare and they are solely there for your child. Your baby is able to be in their home environment and nap in their own cot. It means there's not such a disruption when Mum goes back to work. It will be the next best thing to having Mum around. It means you have more control over what your child does during the day and can stick to their routine.

Amy, mum of Alfie and a nanny

Questions to ask a nanny:
What kind of experience do you have?
How would you organise my child's day?
Would you keep a food and day diary?
Where would you take my child out?
How do you feel about early starts/late finishes?
Can you babysit in the evenings?
What qualifications and training do you have?
Are you registered?

Nurseries

Nurseries seem to fall into the middle ground of childcare as far as price is concerned. They're more expensive than childminders but probably less so than nannies. In London, nurseries can be as much as £68 a day but they're considerably less outside the capital. However, government literature says nurseries should cost £205 a week for inner London, £182 for outer London and £152 elsewhere. The price can include nappies, food, milk, as well as activities like music classes. In a nursery your baby will get to spend time with more children and be involved in lots of different activities.

It's worth looking around a few before you make your decision. When I was choosing a nursery for Rosie I visited ten, which may have been excessive but they vary enormously. One was horrendous and fulfilled all my worst nightmares. It seemed dirty and chaotic, there were lots of crying babies with snotty noses and it smelt of nappies. But some were wonderful, calm environments with happy, busy children pottering around with caring staff. And there were lots that fell in-between.

The law requires nurseries to have a set ratio of carers to children. Babies under two years old should have one carer between three children, the ratio increases to one carer and four children once your baby is two years old. The reason I chose Rosie's nursery was because of its calm environment and also the age and experience of staff. Some nurseries seem to be run by teenagers, which shouldn't really matter, as they've got loads of energy, but I was personally reassured by the attitude of older staff who had their own children.

Questions to ask a nursery:
What is the staff turnover?
Talk me through an average day?
What will the babies eat and drink?
How often do you change nappies?
How often do they go outside?
Is the food organic?
Will they have a key worker?
What's your policy when a baby is ill or has an accident?

Things to look out for:
- Do you like the staff?
- How clean is it?
- How calm?
- Does it smell of nappies?
- How happy do the children seem?
- Is the food freshly cooked at the nursery?

My friends Abs and Nics have slightly older babies, Kate is four and Mae is three, and they've both been in nurseries since they were about one. I valued both of their advice when I was trying to find a nursery for Rosie.

It's worth asking around if you know people in the neighbourhood or hanging outside nurseries and talking to parents. Word-of-mouth is best. When I was first looking for Kate I was wooed by a state-of-the-art nursery with a brilliant Ofsted report. After a year or so I realised it was too big and didn't have a cosy, homey feel. The turnover of staff was unbelievable. Check the notice periods of nurseries. I had to give sixty days notice when I wanted to drop a day or change a day permanently or even go on holiday. I was looking at toys and activities but it's about the staff, that's what's important.

Nics, mum of Kate and Anna

The nursery staff are so important. When your babies are little you just want them to care. Make sure you ask about the turnover of staff, that's a key indicator of happiness. I liked my nursery because the staff took real pride in the room. Actually, expensive toys are not important, it's about the thoughtful play activities that really matter. Smaller nurseries will be more flexible and might be able to swap days.

Abs, mum of Mae

Make your own nursery bag

When your baby starts at nursery you'll need a bag to cart all their stuff in and out. It might include a change of clothes, their favourite soft toys (we have to take mummy and baby giraffe), a pair of wellies for toddlers, warm cardigan and nappies and wipes. Often there's lots of different bags hung on hooks in the hallways, so it's worth making your own nursery bag distinctive so it's easy to find.

1 metre of strong cotton material
Scrap of contrasting material for pattern
Needle and thread and/or sewing machine

1. Double over the piece of material to make a bag measuring around 50cm x 50cm.
2. Cut out a newspaper template of the first letter of your child's name; make it chunky and big enough to fill the front of the bag. Cut the shape out in contrasting material.
3. Pin and then neatly sew the letter onto the front of the bag.
4. With the inside of the material facing outwards pin and stitch the two seams on either side.
5. Pin a 2cm hem on both sides at the top of the bag, where the opening is. Stitch.
6. For the straps cut out two pieces of material 50cm x 20cm. Fold them into a tube and sew so no inside material can be seen.

CHAPTER THIRTEEN

Healing

After giving birth, if you have stitches or are even just feeling a bit bruised, get some super strength Arnica. Also for at least a fortnight after giving birth have a bath every day with lavender oil in it. It's great for healing and preventing infection, plus the lavender is really soothing.

Tilly, mum of James

Remedies for pregnancy and new mothers

When you're pregnant and then looking after your baby, the thought of getting close to unnecessary chemicals and drugs seems alien. Even if you weren't interested before, now is a time when you may investigate old-fashioned home remedies for common minor complaints. Here are some suggestions.

Morning sickness

Keep a stash of dry biscuits like Jacob's cream crackers by the side of your bed and try to eat some before you get up. Ginger is a natural remedy for nausea, try ginger biscuits or make yourself some ginger tea – peel and slice a thumb-sized piece of fresh ginger and add hot water. The smell of fresh lemon can help with waves of nausea. Slice a lemon in half and sniff.

Acupressure, which is often used for travel sickness (remember those wristbands?), can work with morning sickness, too. Using the tip of the thumb, press on the inside of your arm about three fingers width from your wrist crease. If it feels tender you've found the right spot. Hold pressure for a count of ten and rest for ten. Repeat six times until the nausea subsides.

Stretchmarks

As well as daily moisturising your expanding bump and bust with cocoa butter creams, wheatgerm, almond or vitamin E oil, drink lots of water, cut back on caffeine and ensure your diet is rich in vitamins C and A along with proteins from eggs, nuts and fish.

Insomnia

Eat well before bedtime to ease night-time indigestion. Replace stimulants like chocolate, coffee or tea with a cup of chamomile tea. Get plenty of fresh air and exercise in the daytime so you feel more physically tired. Have a warm lavender bath to relax before bed. Homeopathic remedies are best prescribed by a professional.

If your mind refuses to 'shut off', try one 30c tablet of the homeopathic remedy Coffea under your tongue before going to bed or if you wake in the night.

Healthy labour

Regular cups of raspberry leaf tea from your thirty-second week of pregnancy will strengthen and tone your uterus muscles, helping them to contract more effectively during labour, which may help to shorten the second stage of labour.

Late babies

It is unusual for a baby to be born on their due date. Rosie was two and a half weeks late, which I found very frustrating. I tried all the old-fashioned remedies listed below and nothing happened for me, but it may work for you. My best advice is to keep busy, rest as much as possible and enjoy some last-minute dates with your partner, meals out, cinema trips, that sort of thing. Once your due date has passed try eating a hot curry, having sex, eating pineapple and going for a long walk – they're all supposed to help induce labour! Depending on your own individual circumstances you may be offered the choice of induction from around forty-one weeks.

After labour

If you've had stitches or are feeling bruised after the birth, start taking super-strength arnica tablets as soon as possible. It's worth buying them and stashing them away while you're still pregnant. A bath with a few drops of lavender oil will also soothe any tenderness.

Constipation and piles

Constipation and piles are very common when pregnant and just after giving birth. One of the best ways to avoid piles is to avoid constipation. Drink lots of water, eat high-fibre foods like brown rice and pulses. Add prunes and dry figs to a breakfast cereal like All-Bran. Half of all women get piles during pregnancy or post-natally. If you do suffer, try soaking three dry figs in water overnight and eating them every morning along with their soaking water. Daily pelvic floor exercises can help, as will regular exercise, even if it's just a short walk. To relieve pain and itching have a warm bath with a sprinkle of salt. An icepack could also help relieve painful piles.

Remedies for newborn babies

Dry skin

Common culprits for newborn babies' dry skin include harsh washing powder, fabric conditioner and bath soap or shampoo, so it's best to avoid these for starters. Don't bathe newborn babies daily, top and tail them instead, using cotton wool and warm water. Avoid using any baby-bath products. Moisturise and massage their skin daily with olive oil. From six weeks old, dry skin could also be treated with an oatmeal bath. Put two tablespoons of oatmeal in some muslin and hang under the running bath taps. (This soothes itchy chicken pox too.)

Cradle cap

Massage scalp firmly with olive oil daily. If baby has hair, brush with baby brush. Don't pick the scabs! If an area looks red or feels warm it may be infected so take baby to health visitor or GP.

Nappy rash

Keep the baby's skin as dry as possible by changing nappy regularly. Change immediately if the nappy is soiled. Wash baby's bottom with cotton wool and warm water, avoiding any products or scented baby wipes. Pat dry with a towel. If their bottom is really sore, use a hairdryer instead. Let your baby have nappy-off time as much as possible; fresh air really does work! Protect your floor from accidents by laying baby on a changing mat or towel. A calendula cream or organic product like the Green Baby Nappy Balm may help as a barrier cream; apply each time you change nappy while bottom is sore.

Colic

Carry your baby in a sling. Try a dummy. If you're breast-feeding watch your own diet and avoid things like spicy food, alcohol and caffeine, making a note of what food seems to then irritate your baby. Breast-feeding mothers could also try drinking soothing herbal teas like fennel or lemon balm. Try gently massaging baby's tummy in a clockwise direction. Rhythmic motion settles babies, whether it's a trip in the car or a walk in the pram. Cranial osteopathy may relieve symptoms, especially if you had a difficult birth. If this doesn't work colic drops, gripe water or Infacol from your chemist may help.

Constipation

Constipation can be painful for babies, but tends to be unusual among breast-fed babies. There seems to be no rhyme or reason to babies' bowel movements – varying from nothing for days to seven dirty nappies within six hours. Lying your baby on their back and moving their legs gently in a cycling motion can help. Massage his tummy in long strokes clockwise and alternate this with the cycling exercise. Breast-fed and formula-fed babies can be offered one ounce of cooled, boiled water once or twice a day. From six months old, once a baby is eating solids, constipation is more common, especially during the early days of weaning. Diluted prune juice may help.

Common cold

Your baby's first common cold is a painful experience for both of you. He may be irritable, unable to sleep soundly and struggle feeding because of a blocked nose. Bear in mind that the average baby has eight to ten colds before their second birthday, so it is something you'll both get used to. Make a steam room in your bathroom by running the shower hot. Sit in the room with your baby for ten to fifteen minutes, several times a day. Keep the door shut to keep the steam in. This should help to loosen any congestion. Have lots of tissues to hand!

If he has a blocked nose, you can relieve the stuffiness by gently placing your mouth around his nose and sucking the mucus. If you'd rather not do it yourself you can buy rubber bulb syringes from the chemist, but I always thought they looked painful. These can be combined with saline drops also from the chemist.

At night-time add a few drops of eucalyptus oil to a bowl of warm water and place in your baby's room, not too close to his cot. If he also has a cough you may want to prop up his cot a little by stuffing a pillow or some blankets **underneath** his mattress.

Fever

Babies have higher temperatures than older children, and everyone's temperature tends to go up during the day and down after midnight. In general, a baby isn't considered feverish unless her temperature is over 100 degrees F / 37.7 degrees C in the morning or over 101 degrees F / 38.2 degrees C in the evening.

If your baby is under twelve weeks old, it's always best to consult a doctor if they have a fever. Use your instincts: if a baby over twelve weeks old has a temperature of 101 degrees but seems cheerful, there may be less reason to worry than if they have a temperature of 100 degrees but are lethargic or floppy. If you're ever concerned call and visit the doctor; they're always happy to see babies.

There are natural ways to cool babies down simply by removing clothing and blankets, keeping his room cool and sponging down with a cool flannel. Make sure he's getting as much fluids as possible.

If your baby is over eight weeks old you can give them a dose of paracetamol like Calpol to lower their temperature. From twelve weeks old you can use ibuprofen like Nurofen for children.

Teething

Gently rub a cooled chamomile tea bag on your baby's gums. Don't use this remedy if allergies run in the family as some people can be allergic to herbal teas. Don't leave the baby alone with the tea bag as it may rip. Give your baby a frozen banana, peel the banana before you place it in the freezer or it's difficult to get the skin off. Or give your baby a cold piece of cucumber or carrot to gnaw on. Once your baby has cut his first tooth be careful of giving him a cold carrot just incase he bites off a piece and chokes. Rub some ice on baby's gums. Make an effective teether by wetting and freezing a face cloth. Some homeopathic teething granules from chemists may help, but read the ingredients carefully; lactose or other ingredients ending with 'ose' may be sugar and should be avoided.

Bumps and bruises

Once your baby starts crawling, pulling themselves up to stand and then trying to walk there will be lots of tumbles. From nine to twelve months old, it felt like Rosie had a permanent bruise on her forehead from falling over. If they've had a big bump, a cold compress with a wet flannel or frozen pack of peas wrapped in a towel may relieve swelling. Special homeopathic remedies like arnica cream can help bruises too, provided the skin isn't broken.

CHAPTER FOURTEEN

Giving

We sent out birth announcements by text and family jungle drums. When everyone sends presents and cards (as they inevitably will) send (cheap) postcards in an envelope with a photo enclosed to say thank-you.

Annabel, mum of Molly

Giving essentials

Must-haves

Digital cameras are worth splashing out on
Card or thick paper from somewhere like Paperchase
Glue
Scissors
Stash your baby's 'artwork' for wrapping paper

Naughty but nice

Word stamp kit

What you and baby can live without

Professional portraits

Suddenly, giving gifts and sending cards featuring your baby become a compulsive habit. It's addictive. Nearly every card I've sent over the last year or so, and I like to send a few, has starred my daughter in one form or another. From footprints to handprints, grumpy-face postcards to happy, messy-face greeting cards, I don't think I'll ever get bored of posting her.

It's the same with presents. From the moment your baby is born, scrabbling around for inspiration for birthday and Christmas gifts becomes effortless. A photo in a frame, a footprint on a coaster, a handprint on a canvas all become thoughtful, unique presents.

There are lots of craft professionals and kits around that help parents make gifts like these, but it's relatively easy (and much cheaper) to make them yourself. Or at least make some of them yourself.

Birth announcement cards

This is an ideal project to start while you're pregnant. When your maternity leave begins, you're itching to get ready for the arrival of your baby. This is the sort of thing you can do in front of a black-and-white film one afternoon. It's well worth being prepared and even addressing and stamping the envelopes before the baby's born. Then all you've got to do is fill in the 'vital statistics' like date, sex, weight and name once the baby arrives. I still vividly remember writing them when Rosie was just a few days old, sleeping in her Moses basket next to me.

There are lots of variations on home-made cards, and also degrees of creativity and involvement. You may be happy cutting cards from a big sheet of cardboard, or you may prefer to buy some blank cards and envelopes that you can then decorate.

The wordy card

I decided to avoid the fluffy pink or blue style and chose card that reminded me of brown wrapping paper. I've got a word stamp kit and I used that to stamp some words on the front. (Pedlars.com sells nice letter-printing kits, as do lots of independent gift shops.) And that was it. Once I'd chosen my words, each card took about two seconds to make and was very satisfying. It's probably best to keep the message short as the choice of words make the design.

A baby daughter
A baby son
Hello, my name is Rosie
Hello, I'm here
He's arrived
She's arrived
We'd like to introduce
Here I am
Rosie Grace Paynter
New Baby

The photo card

The disadvantage with these cards is that you can't make them while you're pregnant, as they obviously feature a photo of your beautiful newborn. However, you can stamp and address your envelopes and also research the photo development company. We print our photo postcards through photobox.com but there're lots of other similar websites. If you've got a digital camera, all you've got to do is upload your photos onto their website and request they're made into postcards. They make lovely birth announcement cards and you can scribble the vital statistics on the back.

The arty card

The easiest way to make an arty card is to buy some stickers or embellishments from a crafty website like www.cardmakingcrafts.co.uk. Then all you've got to do is stick your chosen motif onto the front of the card. Or make your own. Trace the shape of a sleepsuit or a pram or a stork onto some newspaper and cut out of paper or material to stick on the card.

The digital card

Nowadays, of course, a lot of our announcements are made digitally. While I'm a big fan of old-fashioned post and love the days when a handwritten envelope falls on the doormat, it makes sense to send some birth announcements by mobile and email. Again, this is something to get organised as you beat time in the final days of pregnancy.

I did our birth announcements in Word with clipart and some nice card. I prepared it all in advance plus envelopes so I only had to insert 'the who, when, how heavy' bits, then print and cut. (I've now got a mini guillotine which would have made the cutting even easier!) I also prepared an email round robin in advance with addresses all set up so my husband could add a photo and details and send it off to all those online.

Catrin, mum of Theo and Cerys

Thank-you cards

Your baby will receive loads of gifts from friends, families and well-wishers. Writing so many thank-you cards can feel overwhelming with a newborn to care for, so take your time and don't feel you have to send them immediately. People understand how busy you are. The formula for make-your-own thank-you cards can be the same as the birth announcement cards above. However, one thing you'll certainly have to include is a picture of your baby. Sometimes it can make sense to send a digital birth announcement by text and email and then post thank-you cards with pictures and details of the baby a little after the baby is born. Otherwise it feels as if you're permanently writing cards.

Or, paint some liquid paint on your baby's tiny foot and print the shape on some card to make a precious thank-you note. I found footprints were easiest to do when Rosie was asleep. Don't overload the foot with paint, it will lead to smudges. Pastel colours are too faint, so be bold with your choice of paint. Brown paint, surprisingly, works really well. They look like chocolate footprints. Aside from cards, baby footprints make beautiful framed pictures. Once your baby develops their own artistic streak and starts painting, you can cut their artwork into squares and stick it onto cards for a stylish personalised thank-you note.

Christmas cards

It's so nice to be able to send personalised Christmas cards. It's a bit like being the Prime Minister or a member of the royal family. Plus, if you keep up the tradition of making and sending cards featuring your children, they'll become a wonderful portrayal and timeline of family life. I think photocards work really well as Christmas cards. You may not want to feature so make your baby the star of the show. Photo Christmas cards also mean you don't have to worry about including a new photo in your cards. They're the best of both worlds.

Easy Christmas cards

The cutest, easiest ones to make just involve you dressing up your baby in some sort of Christmas-themed outfit. It could be a Christmas babygro, or you might be able to pop a Santa's hat, or some reindeer antlers on their head. Or drape them in tinsel. There's a danger that you might fall into the smug happy family bracket, I know some of my single friends can get quite sickened by cutesy, cutesy Christmas cards featuring a baby dressed as an angel, but Granny and Great Aunty Doris will love it. I think the best ones are those with a little sense of humour. In a way, with tiny babies it's quite easy. You can pop a Santa's hat on their head and prop a little sign in their hands saying 'Happy Christmas', while they're asleep and there you have it. As they get older it's much harder to keep them still and also to make sure they don't eat the props. From about six months, you may just need to rely on a comedy Christmas hat.

Slightly harder Christmas cards

This year I got my husband involved in making our Christmas card. It's our first proper family Christmas card so I've been a bit overexcited about it all. Rosie was born on 20 December, so last Christmas passed in a daze. Much to my dismay after harbouring dreams of sending cards featuring a tiny baby in a red babygro, I'd had to send cards before she was born signing her as the bump. Last year we used Photoshop to make a collage-style card. We chose ten of our favourite pictures of Rosie, with one or two including us too, and laid them out like a patchwork quilt interspersed with pictures of letters to spell HAPPY XMAS. I really like letters and take pictures of my favourite ones, which we then used. However, you can also find pictures of letters online – just search for them in Google images. I think pictures of Scrabble letters would work well too.

Photos

It is astonishing how many pictures you can take of a small baby. Be prepared to be amazed. They are so cute and adorable and cuddly that when you're not staring or kissing them, you're taking pictures: pictures while they sleep, pictures while they sit, pictures while they feed, pictures while they're bathed. Pictures of their hands and feet. As I write this, Rosie is ten months old and already we have thousands of pictures of her.

This may be the first time you've become interested in photography so here are a few tips on how to take the best pictures of babies. Indeed, spend some of the money you save from the tips in this book to buy a digital camera. You won't regret it.

1. Make sure you get someone to take a picture of the three of you when the baby is still tiny.
2. Black and white is more flattering. It's especially effective if you're in the photo too, as you won't be looking your best when the baby is first born.
3. Close-ups on a baby's face can make lovely pictures. They work well blown onto canvas too.
4. Try not to get too flash-happy with small babies. If the room's too dark, move towards natural light or switch some lights on.

Fortunately, this new-found creativity and passion for photography doesn't have to be wasted. There're lots of resourceful ways of using these wonderful photos for gifts.

Photo albums

You'll want to keep a photo album for yourself, but they also make wonderful presents for grandparents. I think they're best if they're focused on a short timescale or event. For example, when Rosie was twelve weeks old, we went on holiday to Italy with my family to celebrate my mum's sixtieth. As a present I made a small photo album with pictures from the holiday.

Similarly, Simon made me an amazing album when Rosie was two months old. I think it's the captions that can make home-made photo albums such wonderful presents. A picture of Rosie in her tiny furry snowsuit with ears said, 'Why have you dressed me like a bear?' And the picture of her out of the bath in her hooded towel simply said, 'Gandalf.'

If you want to splash out, websites like photobox.com can make professional albums that look like picture books and you can write the captions online. Look out for their two-for-one offers on albums. Then they begin to be more affordable.

Photos on canvas

If you're sick of your home looking like everyone else's with the same IKEA prints of Georgia O-Keeffe orchids and black-and-white photographs of San Francisco Bridge, then a painting of your baby can make a cool alternative. Some (rich) people get specially commissioned paintings or use a professional photographer to capture their baby, but there's no reason why you can't do some of the work yourself. Close-ups of baby faces always look good on canvas, as do more abstract angles, so just feature their eyes or their mouth, or zoom in on small hands or feet. Your local photo shop can put them on canvas for you, or you can do it online.

Simon made a beautiful anniversary present by making a mosaic of Rosie with thousands of tiny pictures from our past. Some of her, some of our wedding, of friends and families. If you're close to the picture you can see all these amazing little photos, but from a distance it just looks like a mosaic baby. It was time-consuming and difficult, but made such a wonderful present. If you want to have a go download the photo mosaic software online: there are a few free versions.

Mounting and framing photos

There's an easy trick to mounting and framing photos so they look more professional and finished. Choose the colour of the card depending on the tone of your photo and also the colour of your frame. If in doubt, you can't go wrong with cream or white. Photos always look best if you leave more space beneath them, than above them.

Mounting and framing your own photos professionally
Stanley knife
Enlarged A5 photo
Two pieces of thick A4 card
Pencil
Ruler
One A4 frame
Spraymount adhesive
Flat, smooth bread board, or other large surface you can safely cut on

1. Enlarge your favourite photo to A5, which will mean it measures around 15cm x 21cm.
2. Take both pieces of card and mark in pencil on the back where the frame should be cut and the picture should be placed.
3. For a portrait picture, using a ruler and pencil draw a horizontal line 6cm from the bottom and 4cm from the top of the card. Then draw two vertical lines 4cm from either side.

4. For a landscape picture draw a horizontal line 5cm from the bottom and 3cm from the top. Then draw two vertical lines 3cm from either side.
5. Positioning the card on a safe surface to cut, firmly hold the ruler against your penciled lines and score the card with the Stanley knife. If you do it firmly and smoothly the card should cut easily to make a frame.
6. Put your photo upside down and spray the back with your spraymount adhesive, making sure the edges and corners are well covered with glue.
7. Carefully stick the photo onto the whole piece of card using your pencil marks as guidelines.
8. Spray the inside of the card frame with spraymount and carefully stick the frame onto the photo and card.
9. Your mounted picture is now ready to be placed in its frame.

Happy Birthday to you, Happy Birthday to you

There's something magical about a first birthday party and it's a lovely occasion to celebrate. It's easy to get over-excited and spend lots of money, when there's really no need, so try to contain yourself. The Future Foundation estimates that an average one-year-old will have up to £150 spent on a party, and up to £70 on a present, which just seems silly. Similar research by American Express suggested that parents in the UK are spending £1.4bn on first birthday parties (£450 per family). Party bag presents for the child's guests cost an average of £49.

Keep it small and keep it short: So close friends and relatives only and just invite them for a couple of hours. An afternoon tea party from, say, 3–5 p.m. works well. It means you don't have to provide much food for adults and it shouldn't clash with too many babies' sleep-time.

If you want to provide nibbles, keep it simple. Bread sticks, carrot, cucumber and celery sticks to dip into home-made hummus will work well, as will a cheese board and French bread.

Make a birthday cake yourself. That way you'll know exactly what's in it and can offer a little slice to the birthday boy or girl. I made a banana cake, as it felt healthy and Rosie loves bananas. You can keep the cost down by only offering alcohol to adult guests when the cake comes out. Then you can give everyone a glass of Cava. A frozen raspberry or strawberry in the glass, makes it seem very glamorous.

Healthy banana birthday cake

This birthday cake is a healthy alternative for toddlers who haven't yet been introduced to the joys of sugar. It's also a good option for one-year olds who haven't yet eaten eggs, as they're not an ingredient in this recipe.

85g All-Bran breakfast cereal
125g self-raising flour
150g of dried fruit or sultanas
Three large mashed bananas
One tablespoon of soft brown sugar
275ml milk

Soak the All-Bran in the milk for a few minutes.
Add the other ingredients and mix well.
Pour the mixture into a well-greased 1lb loaf tin and bake in the oven for one and a quarter hours at 180 degrees C until a sharp knife comes out clean.

Make your own robot cupcakes or a cupcake farm

A batch of cupcakes can be transformed for a toddler's party into a troop of robots or an animal farm. Carefully placed pink marshmallows on pink-iced cupcakes make good pig faces. Piped white icing makes sheepish cupcakes.

Robot cupcakes can be a stylish alternative or addition to birthday cake, especially for older toddlers. Group the cupcakes in threes, so one is the robot's head, one the body and the other the legs. Decorate the plain-white iced cakes by cutting out shapes in brightly coloured roll-on icing. Children will have fun mixing up the body parts for the robots. Nine cup cakes make three robots.

Make your own Robot Cupcakes

2 large eggs
125g caster sugar
125g margarine
125g self-raising flour
1 tablespoon vanilla essence
Cupcake tin
Paper cupcake cases
Ready to roll coloured icing

1. Preheat the oven to 180 degrees C. Place all the ingredients in a bowl and beat together until smooth.
2. Line a cupcake tin with cupcake cases and half-fill each case with the cake mixture.
3. Cook the cakes for 18–20 minutes. They are done when they have risen, golden-coloured and spring back into shape when lightly pressed.

4. While the cakes are in the oven, roll out the coloured icing on a surface dusted with icing sugar or flour to around 5mm thickness. Using a sharp knife cut out your robot shapes in different colours.

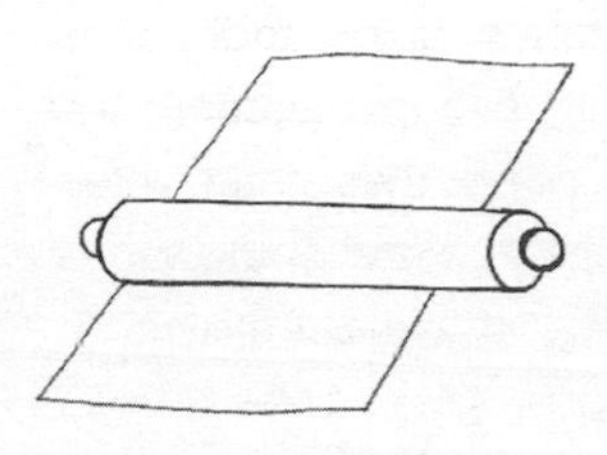

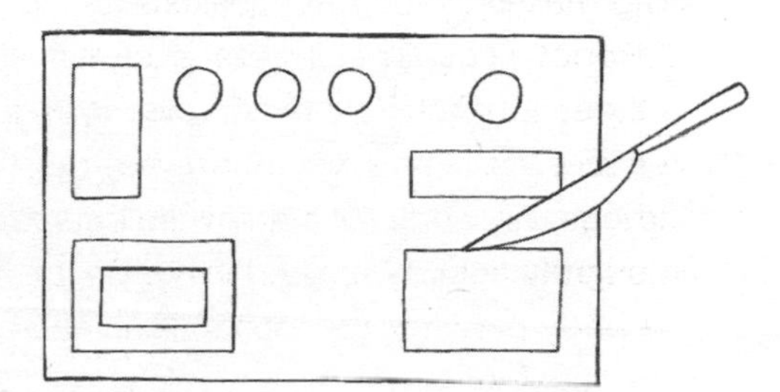

5. Once the cakes are cooked and cool, carefully place your icing robot shapes – one cake should be the robot head, one the body and the other the legs. Display the cakes in groups of three.

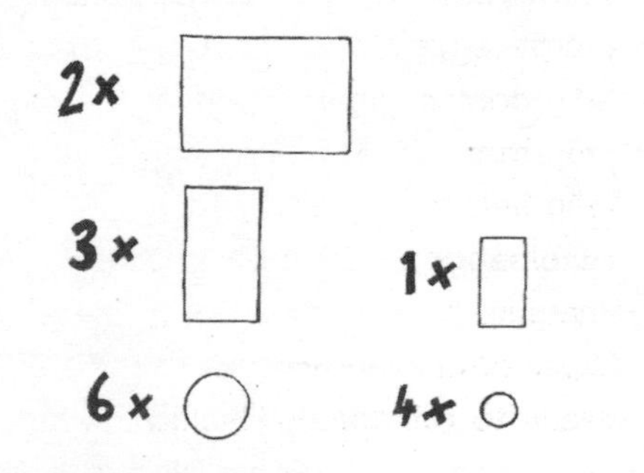

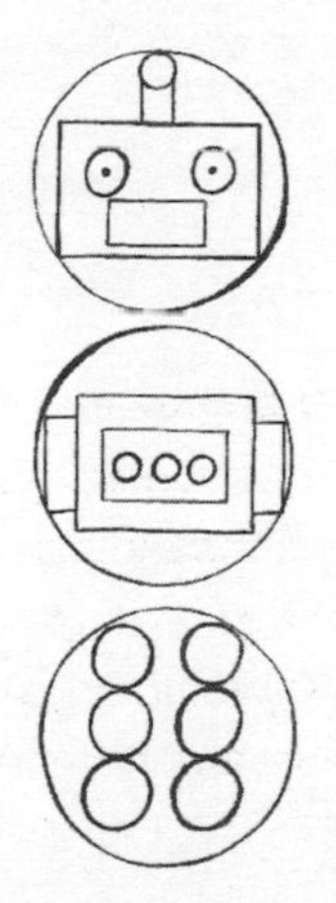

Get adults to slip their shoes off as they enter the house, then there's no chance baby's fingers can get squashed. You might want to have a space where the baby's toys are spread out for their friends. This is probably the last chance you'll have to have a grown-up party in lieu of celebrating your baby's birthday. So make the most of it. There's no need to worry about balloons or nursery rhymes. Play music you and your baby like instead. You can always play a nursery rhyme CD if the babies need entertainment. A bottle of bubbles will make the day extra special for your birthday boy or girl.

Wrapping paper

Use your child's own paintings to make versatile wrapping paper; potato prints always work well. Or buy colourful comics like Beano; the bright pages are perfect for wrapping presents or you could use them to make party bags.

Party bags

There really is no need to do this. But like me, you may get over-excited and want to make some stuff. Don't go overboard. Rosie's party bags contained a slice of birthday cake, a tub of bubbles and a packet of raisins. With older toddlers, look out for job lots of toy animals and dinosaurs at car-boot sales and stash away for party bags.

If you had lots of time on your hands you could make the bags yourself. Toddlers love carrying their own little bags around, so they could become a present in their own right. I used brown paper bags instead. If you had the time and the inclination you could also put a home-made toy in there. Or include a home-made biscuit or gingerbread man in the party bag. Decorate with white icing or write the initial of the child's name on it in icing. At Rosie's first birthday, all guests left with a white-iced biscuit in the shape of number one.

Make your own party bag

1. Cut two squares of 10cm x 15cm.
2. For straps, cut two strips of 10cm x 3cm.
3. Place the two squares on top of each other with the inside of the material facing outwards.
4. Sew a seam 1.5cm inside the edges.
5. Fold the straps in two and sew along edge and attach to top of bag.
6. Turn the bag the right way round.

Keep the party short and keep the food simple. Two of my friends made pudding and Ruby's birthday cake, which was a big help.

Maria, mum of Ruby

Don't have any food that might be unsuitable for your baby and their friends. Just in case. That means no nuts in bowls.

Emma, mum of Charlie

The most important ingredient at your baby's first birthday party is a large glass of champagne for you and your partner. You've all survived and thrived the first year of your baby's life. You've re-cycled and mended, knitted and sewn, baked, crafted and made your own. It's time to celebrate.

CHAPTER FIFTEEN

The Directory

Chapter One: Planning

Managing money

www.babycentre.co.uk/baby/familyfinance/

Practical, common-sense financial guide to managing your money with a baby.

www.babycentre.co.uk/baby/familyfinance/parentsmoneysavingtips/

Money-saving ideas and tips from fellow parents and parents-to-be, plus more general support and advice.

www.babycentre.co.uk/baby/buyingforbaby/knowhow/budget/

Advice on the essential things you need for your newborn; what you can live without, money-saving tips and the golden rules when buying on a budget.

www.moneysavingexpert.com

Sound money-saving advice and tips from financial expert Martin Lewis.

www.moneysavingexpert.com/banking/Budget-planning
Download this excellent budget planner.

www.bbc.co.uk/consumer/your_money
Advice and guidance on managing your finances.

Price checking
www.kelkoo.co.uk
www10.uk.shopping.com
www.pricerunner.co.uk
www.dealtime.co.uk
These shopping comparison sites will scour retailers for you and search for the cheapest price.

www.fixtureferrets.co.uk
Gives details of which supermarkets are running special offers on what products.

Parenting clubs
www.bounty.com
Join the Bounty Club to receive a pack of samples when your baby is born. The club continues to give new parents free packs during the baby's first year.

www.bootsparentingclub.com
Exclusive offers, pregnancy and baby advice and support plus double points on numerous baby products for Advantage card holders until your baby's second birthday.

www.pampers.co.uk
Provides money-off coupons, information DVDs and books.

www.huggiesclub.com/uk
Welcome pack with free samples and money-off coupons, regular emails on child's development and free DVDs.

www.tesco.com/babyclub
Seven free magazines for different stages of your child's development, money-off coupons, priority parking at Tesco stores, extra clubcard points and special offers with gyms, the RAC and a professional photographer.

Buying second-hand
www.b-p-a.org/
The Baby Products Association produces a leaflet outlining tips and advice if you are considering buying second-hand.

www.babycentre.co.uk/baby/buyingforbaby/knowhow/secondhand/
General advice on buying second-hand for your baby.

www.babyworld.co.uk/information/baby/what_to_buy/second-hand.asp
Some things to consider when buying second-hand for your baby.

pages.ebay.co.uk/help/ebayexplained/newtoebay/index.html
Beginners guide how to buy and sell second-hand baby goods on eBay.

www.nappyvalley.co.uk
A local online marketplace for nearly new baby items. Most listings tend to be in London or south-east England.

www.mumsnet.com
The social networking site has a classified section to buy and sell baby items.

www.netmums.com
Netmums has a local, classified nearly new section. You can also advertise for 'wanted' items.

www.gumtree.com
Log on to the local area of Gumtree to find second-hand baby items in your area.

www.freecycle.org
Register on the ultimate recycling network, Freecycle, to get baby stuff for free from your neighbours.

The essential kit
www.babycentre.co.uk/baby/buyingforbaby/knowhow/whatyoureallyneed
What you really need for your newborn and what you don't, including a checklist.

Chapter Two: Blooming

Maternity rights and benefits
www.direct.gov.uk
www.direct.gov.uk/en/Employment/Employees/WorkAndFamilies/DG_10029285
Information and guidance on how to obtain your statutory maternity pay.

www.workingfamilies.org.uk
www.workingfamilies.org.uk/asp/family_zone/f_factsheets.asp
Helpful fact sheets detailing your maternity rights and benefits before and after the birth.

www.netdoctor.co.uk
www.netdoctor.co.uk/health_advice/facts/maternity_rights_000618.htm
A comprehensive guide to your maternity rights.

www.worksmart.org.uk
www.worksmart.org.uk/rights/maternity_leave
Details statutory rights that employers must provide for new mothers who work for them.

www.babycentre.co.uk/baby/familyfinance/rightsandbenefits
Information and guidance on all benefits you may be entitled to as a parent, including child benefit, working tax credit, low-income benefit, single parent benefit.

www.askbaby.com/maternity-rights.htm
Useful information on maternity leave, employee pay, returning to work and other pregnancy rights.

What to wear
www.babycentre.co.uk/pregnancy/lookinggood/wardrobe/maternitydirectory
Advice on buying maternity wear, including a pricing guide and stockist list.

www.askbaby.com/maternity-wear.htm
Advice on choosing stylish maternity wear and cheap pregnancy clothing for sale.

www.raisingkids.co.uk/preg/preg_well05.asp
Advice on what maternity wear you *really* need.

www.bumpto3.com
Creative ideas to help you maintain your existing wardrobe, including the 'belly belt'.

www.affordablematernity.co.uk
Stylish maternity wear at affordable prices.

www.more4mums.co.uk
Great selection of affordable, discounted high-street and designer maternity clothes for your pregnancy. Fifty per cent discount on many items.

The high street
www.hm.com
H & M. Fashionable maternity wear and pregnancy basics and underwear.

www.topshop.com
Main collection designs adapted and resized to suit the pregnant figure.

www.dorothyperkins.com
Well-priced maternity wear in line with high-street trends.

www.next.co.uk
Catalogue of maternity and baby wear with mail order available.

www.marksandspencer.com
From basic T-shirts and joggers to outfit ideas inspired by other in-store collections.

www.primark.co.uk
Non-maternity wear but buy bigger for unbeatable value for all styles of clothes.

www.gap.com
Gap Maternity. Stylish maternity wear, look out for the sales.

Lingerie

www.hotmilklingerie.co.nz/uk
Beautiful, sexy maternity bras and knickers.

Buying second-hand

www.becomingmum.com
Online shop selling good-quality, nearly new, predominantly branded maternity wear at affordable prices.

www.budget-bumps.co.uk
Budget Bumps specialises in good-as-new and discount maternity clothes and nursing wear.

www.doesmytumlookbiginthis.com
Second-hand maternity and special-occasion dress hire.

www.maternityexchange.co.uk
Quality new and nearly new maternity clothes at discount prices.

www.ebay.co.uk
Buy or sell; hundreds of maternity wear bundles to suit most shapes and sizes.

Pampering

www.askbaby.com/maternity-beauty.htm
Advice and guidance on everything from skincare to haircare.

www.askbaby.com/new-dad-tips.htm
Hints and tips on how dads can help with pampering.

www.beautyrecipes.co.uk
How to make your own beauty products at home.

www.greenchronicle.com/health_beauty/soapwort_shampoo_recipe.htm
How to make your own shampoo.

www.health.com/health/package/0,23653,1202868,00.html
More home-made spa treatments.

www.bbcgoodfood.com/recipes/2270/homemade-lemonade
Delicious home-made lemonade.

www.nigella.com/recipes/recipe.asp?article=3237
More lemonade recipes.

www.bbc.co.uk/food/recipes/advanced_search.shtml
Search hundreds of yummy and healthy recipes with an added function to help you find pregnancy friendly dishes.

The essential birth kit
www.bbc.co.uk/parenting/having_a_baby/pregnancy_hospital.shtml
When to pack and what to pack in your hospital bag.

www.babycentre.co.uk/pregnancy/labourandbirth/hospitalbag/
Helpful checklist of what you need for the birth for both you and your new baby.

Chapter Three: Nesting

Transforming your boxroom
www.pedlars.co.uk
Great wall stickers.

www.funtosee.co.uk
Hunt online for stylish wall stickers, a cheap alternative to wall-paper and easier than painting your own murals.

www.notonthehighstreet.com
Hunt on this site for inspiration for unique wall murals. London artist, Judith Booth or Mrs Booth, makes beautiful alphabet friezes for nurseries.

www.alternative-windows.com/index.htm
Step-by-step advice on how to make your own curtains, blinds and cushions with a wide range of designs and styles to choose from.

www.dulux.co.uk
Get help choosing paints and colours with useful visualisation and planning tools, plus colour inspirations and product advice.

www.thelaboroflove.com/forum/anndouglas/2.html
Creative ideas, hints and tips on how to decorate your baby's room on a budget.

www.tubtrugs.co.uk
Colourful, plastic storage baskets from pistachio to primrose.

Buying second-hand
www.babycentre.co.uk/baby/buyingforbaby/knowhow/secondhand
What to consider when buying second-hand for your baby.

www.freecycle.org
A grassroots, recycling initiative where people give away unwanted stuff for free.

www.nct.org.uk/home
National Childbirth Trust. Search by postcode for your nearest 'Nearly New Sale', with the opportunity to buy top-quality cots and other nursery essentials at bargain prices straight from their owners.

www.yourbooty.co.uk
www.carbootjunction
Search for details of local car-boot sales on these two websites and plan some serious bargain hunting.

http://popular.ebay.co.uk/ns/Baby/Nursery+Furniture.html
Hundreds of second-hand and new nursery furniture items and accessories at low prices.

www.gumtree.com
A classified site with a wide range of good-quality second-hand nursery furniture.

www.loot.com
Wide range of good-quality second-hand nursery furniture.

www.emmaus.org.uk/shops
Emmaus shops sell a wide range of good-quality, second-hand furniture.

www.dmgantiquefairs.com
Hunt down vintage nursery furniture and toys at an antique fair.

Nursery furniture
www.all4kidsuk.com/childrens_furniture_beds_themed.about.shtml
Lists all UK stockists of nursery and children's bedroom furniture to suit all budgets and styles.

www.ikea.com/gb/en/catalog/categories/rooms/childrens_room/10390
Thoughtful budget solutions for your little ones. Buy a new cot for just £29!

www.nurseryworlde.com
Nursery consultants and winner of Retailer of the Year 2007. Great value furniture and other products for your baby's room under most RRPs.

www.kiddicare.com/_baby/baby-nursery-equipment.htm
Good-value online retailer for nursery furniture.

www.mothercare.com
Knowledgeable, well-priced nursery furniture from cots and changing mats to mobiles and accessories.

www.johnlewis.com
Never Knowingly Undersold; excellent range of cots and nursery furniture with in-store nursery and baby advisers, but it's not cheap.

www.beyondfrance.co.uk
Beautiful vintage rag rugs online for that Scandinavian nursery look.

Chapter Four: Beginning

www.babycentre.co.uk/baby/newborn
Survival guide to those first few hectic weeks; from how to swaddle to caring for the umbilical stump to changing a nappy.

www.babycentre.co.uk/baby/youafterthebirth
Articles on recovering after the birth, dealing with the baby blues and adjusting to life as a new mum.

www.baby.com/view.aspx?pid=196&cid=587
The first ten days. What every new parent should know!

www.bbc.co.uk/parenting/your_kids/babies_index.shtml
Advice and guidance on the common challenges of being a new parent.

www.bounty.com/newarrivals.aspx
www.bounty.com/baby.aspx
A month-by-month guide to caring for your newborn.

www.mumsnet.com/devcal
Development calendar guiding you through the various stages your baby may go through as they grow, including frequently asked questions.

www.gurgle.com
A guide taking you through every week of your baby's first year with hints on what to expect.

www.babycentre.co.uk/baby/buyingforbaby/knowhow/budget
Advice on the essential and non-essential things you need for your newborn; what you can live without, money-saving tips and the golden rules when buying on a budget.

www.mama.co.uk/
Meet a Mum Association UK registered charity, which aims to provide friendship and support to all mothers and mothers-to-be, especially those feeling lonely or isolated after the birth of a baby or moving to a new area. Helpline: 020 8771 5595

www.cranial.org.uk
Seek more information and advice on cranial osteopaths, who can help to soothe newborns.

Chapter Five: Sleeping

Buying the cot

www.babycentre.co.uk/baby/buyingforbaby/cotscribsbedding/mosesbasketcribcarrycot/
The pros and cons of buying a Moses basket, crib or carrycot.

www.babycentre.co.uk/baby/buyingforbaby/knowhow/secondhand
Advice on buying second-hand.

www.babycentre.co.uk/baby/buyingforbaby/cotscribsbedding/tips
Parents' tips on cots, Moses baskets and what bedding to go for.

www.askbaby.com/baby-cots.htm
Advice on cots.

www.askbaby.com/baby-cot-beds.htm
Advice on cot beds.

www.askbaby.com/moses-baskets.htm
Advice on Moses baskets.

www.mumsnet.com/Reviews?v=2
Read cot reviews from real mums before you buy.

www.ikea.com
Buy a new cot for £29.

www.mothercare.com
Well-known and trusted retailer for sleeping accessories, with advice and buying guides to the best mattress.

www.johnlewis.com
Never Knowingly Undersold; excellent range of cots and cribs with in-store nursery and baby advisers.

Buying second-hand cots
(Cot mattresses should always be bought new.)

www.ebay.co.uk
Register to buy or sell new and second-hand cots, Moses baskets, cot beds.

www.freecycle.org
Get a cot for free from your neighbours.

www.nct.org.uk/home
Search by postcode for your nearest 'Nearly New Sale', with the opportunity to buy top-quality sleeping equipment at bargain prices.

www.sids.org.uk
Advice on protecting your baby from cot death from The Foundation for the Study of Infant Deaths.

Lullabies
www.bbc.co.uk/music/parents/yourchild/prebirth_18mnths/rockababy.shtml
Lullabies and accompanying tips to help soothe your baby.

www.kididdles.com/lyrics/index.html
All the lyrics to all your favourite lullabies and nursery rhymes.

Make your own

http://northpoletoyshop.com/Articles/babymobile.htm
Make your own cot mobile.

www.knittinghelp.com
www.learn2knit.com
Both give knitting guidance.

Chapter Six: Travelling

Buying your pram

www.askbaby.com/prams.htm
Useful advice on what to look for when buying a pram, pushchair, three-wheeler or travel system.

www.babycentre.co.uk/baby/buyingforbaby/pramspushchairsbuggies/pram
www.babycentre.co.uk/shopping/prams
Find all the help you need buying a pram for your newborn.

www.babycentre.co.uk/baby/buyingforbaby/pramspushchairsbuggies/reviews
The top ten buggies Baby Centre mums love.

www.pushchair-guide.info
The complete guide to choosing your first pram with details on what choices are available, including the most popular models.

www.thinkbaby.co.uk/
Reviews from parents on the best and most practical travel solutions.

www.buggysnuggles.com
Warm, jazzy sleeping bags that can fit all makes of buggies and prams.

Selecting a car seat
www.askbaby.com/travelling-by-car.htm
Useful information and advice on car seats, car mirrors and car journeys.

www.babycentre.co.uk/baby/buyingforbaby/carseats/stockists
A complete guide to finding the right car seat, listing all the major manufacturers and retailers.

www.childcarseats.org.uk
Includes an advice page offering local advice and help when fitting car seats.

www.thinkroadsafety.gov.uk/campaigns/childcarseats/childcarseats.htm
Government advice listing the most up-to-date car seat rules.

Slings and backpacks
www.babycentre.co.uk/baby/buyingforbaby/slingsbackpacks/tips
Parents' tips on baby slings and back carriers.

www.bigmamaslings.co.uk/zen-cart/page.html?id=12
How to make your own baby sling.

www.naturalmothering.co.uk
Family-run business dedicated to babywearing with advice on the types of baby carriers available, recommended brands and online shopping.

Happy travelling

www.askbaby.com/travelling-on-public-transport.htm
Advice on keeping travelling on public transport with your baby stress-free.

www.askbaby.com/car-journeys.htm
Advice on entertaining your baby on car journeys.

www.babycentre.co.uk/baby/travel/packingchecklistbaby
A checklist of essential travel items.

www.flyingwithkids.com/
Air-travel tips for families travelling with a baby or small child.

www.gurgle.com/articles/Travel/22850/Top_tips_for_travelling_with_a_baby.aspx
Top tips for travelling with a baby.

www.momsminivan.com/babies.html
Games to play with your baby in the car.

www.travellingwithchildren.co.uk
Comprehensive tips and information on child-friendly travel, ranging from the school-run to long-haul flights.

Shopping

www.johnlewis.com/Baby/Travelling/Travelling/SubCategory.aspx
Good selection of car seats and pushchairs to suit all kinds of lifestyles and requirements, plus buying guides to aid your final decision.

www.kiddicare.com
Baby superstore offering a wide range of travel needs, including pushchairs, baby carriers and car seats.

www.mothercare.com
Wide range of pushchairs with a 'help me choose' option based on your budget, how you usually travel and your space restrictions.

www.poppets.ltd.uk
Value-for-money baby and toddler gear, including prams, travel systems, car seats.

www.pramworld.co.uk
Good-value pram retailer with many items at sale prices.

Buying second-hand
(Don't buy car seats second-hand.)

www.ebay.co.uk
Register to buy or sell new and second-hand pushchairs.

www.nct.org.uk/home
Search by postcode for your nearest 'Nearly New Sale', with the opportunity to buy top-quality prams and pushchairs at bargain prices.

www.preloved.co.uk/
From nearly new to really old, Preloved is packed with second-hand bargains in over 500 categories.

Chapter Seven: Feeding

Breast-feeding
www.abm.me.uk
Association of Breast-feeding Mothers. Offers voluntary mother-to-mother support, counselling and information for breast-feeding women. Helpline: 08444 122949.

www.nct.org.uk
The National Childbirth Trust has trained breast-feeding counsellors who can offer individual advice and support. Helpline: 0870 4448708.

www.laleche.org.uk
La Leche League. Helpline offering advice and information on breast-feeding, plus local group meetings.
Helpline: 0845 1202918.

www.breastfeedingnetwork.org.uk
Offers free, confidential telephone information on breast-feeding and one-to-one local support. Helpline: 0844 4124664.

www.babygroe.co.uk
Registered natural parenting charity offering expert advice on breast-feeding, including some natural solutions to breast-feeding problems.

www.nct.org.uk/shop/breast-pump-hire
Hire a breast pump for as long as you need it through the volunteer agents of the NCT.

www.hotmilk.co.nz/uk
Sexy nursing bras and matching knickers.

www.expressyourselfmums.co.uk
Advice on expressing milk, along with details on renting and buying pumps.

www.babycentre.co.uk/baby/buyingforbaby/breastbottlesolids/breastfeedingaccessories
Suggested accessories to aid breast-feeding.

Bottle feeding
www.bbc.co.uk/parenting/your_kids/babies_feeding1.shtml
Advice and guidance on all aspects of breast-feeding and switching to formula.

www.milupa-aptamil.co.uk
The UK's fastest growing infant milk company. Helpline advice from midwives, healthcare professionals, nutritionists, feeding advisers and, of course, mums. Helpline: 08457 623628.

www.ulula.co.uk
Specialists in organic milk formula, suitable from birth.

www.babycentre.co.uk/baby/formula/findrightformula
Advice and guidance on bottle-feeding and helping you choose the right formula.

www.babycentre.co.uk/baby/buyingforbaby/breastbottlesolids/bottlefeeding
Buying guide for bottle-feeding.

www.askbaby.com/baby-bottle-feeding
Bottle-feeding basics, routines, formula milk, problem feeders and mixed feeding explained.

www.infantcaredirect.co.uk
Playtex Baby is an American feeding system that eliminates the need to sterilise bottles.

Weaning
www.greenchoices.org/index.php?page=baby-food
The UK guide to greener living with suggested organic food suppliers to consider when weaning your baby.

www.bbc.co.uk/parenting/your_kids/babies_weaning.shtml
Advice and guidance about weaning your baby, including advice on bought baby food and drinks.

www.babycentre.co.uk/baby/startingsolids/weaningrecipes/beforeyoubegin
Before you begin! Advice on vitamins and nutrients.

www.babycentre.co.uk/baby/startingsolids/firstfoods
Which weaning foods to introduce when.

www.babycentre.co.uk/baby/startingsolids/weaningrecipes/firsttastes
Recipes for babies starting on solids.

www.organix.com
Weaning advice, recipes and meal planners.

www.ulula.co.uk
Free weaning diet plan and home-made organic recipes for babies.

www.annabelkarmel.com/recipes
Nutritional advice, weaning tips and countless recipes.

http://annabelkarmel.tv
An online video service including a series of short films on weaning with recipe ideas.

www.contentedbaby.com/feeding
Gina Ford. One-stop guide to weaning from the routine queen.

www.mumsnet.com/Recipes
Advice on weaning plus tried-and-tested 'first tastes and beyond' recipes from other mums.

www.sainsburys.co.uk/family/tasty+ideas/recipes/babies/babies
Tips to make the perfect purées and some recipes to try.

www.tesco.com/babyclub/
Hundreds of recipes for your baby and you.

www.eatwell.gov.uk/agesandstages/baby/weaning
Government advice on introducing your baby to solids.

www.babycentre.co.uk/baby/startingsolids/babyledweaning
Baby-led weaning explained.

Feeding equipment
www.babycentre.co.uk/baby/buyingforbaby/breastbottlesolids/whatyouneed
Buying guide for weaning.

www.kiddicare.com
Good-value online retailer for all feeding equipment, plus consumer and product reviews.

www.mothercare.com
Knowledgeable, well-priced equipment for feeding your baby; from bottles, sterilisers and highchairs to bibs, bowls and beakers. Website also contains weaning tips from Annabel Karmel.

www.johnlewis.com
Never Knowingly Undersold; excellent range of equipment and products to meet all your baby's feeding needs with in-store nursery and baby advisers.

http://direct.tesco.com/homepage/babytoddler.aspx
Features numerous feeding products from sterilisers to highchairs with excellent savings, plus end-of-line clearances.

www.ebay.co.uk
Buy or sell new and second-hand highchairs and countless other baby products.

www.kelkoo.co.uk
Compare prices for highchairs online before you buy.

www.freecycle.org
Hunt for free highchairs in your local area.

www.nct.org.uk/home
Search by postcode for your nearest 'Nearly New Sale', and try to nab a new highchair.

www.nct.org.uk/shop
Broad range of tried-and-tested products including breast-feeding, bottle feeding and weaning equipment.

www.mumsnet.com/reviews
Read reviews on feeding equipment from real mums before making a decision.

www.lilliput.com
Selection of baby equipment and will hire out specific items. Tel: 020 7720 5554.

www.stokke.com
For Tripp Trapp highchairs, a wooden highchair that grows with your baby and can still be used by a seven-year-old.

www.cathkidson.com
Splurge on beautifully designed wipe-clean bibs.

Chapter Eight: Dressing

Essential items

www.askbaby.com/baby-clothes
Advice on what to look for when buying clothes for your baby, including the essential kit for a newborn.

www.babycentre.co.uk/baby/buyingforbaby/knowhow/whatyoureallyneed
What you really need for your newborn and what you don't, including a checklist.

www.babycentre.co.uk/baby/buyingforbaby/knowhow/layetteguide
Further advice on what to buy for your newborn, plus buying tips including recommended material and how to wash products.

Buying second-hand baby clothes

www.babycentre.co.uk/baby/buyingforbaby/knowhow/secondhand
Advice on buying second-hand clothes for your baby.

www.nct.org.uk/home
Search by postcode for your nearest 'Nearly New Sale', with the opportunity to buy top quality baby clothes at bargain prices straight from their loving owners.

www.ebay.co.uk
Bundles of second-hand baby clothes in age range, from birth onwards.

Make your own

www.knittinghelp.com
Video tutorials for beginners on how to knit.

www.learn2knit.co.uk
Simple step-by-step guide for basic knitting.

www.babyfreebies.co.uk/free-baby-knitting-patterns
Free knitting patterns for baby wear, including hats, booties and cardies.

www.knittingonthenet.com/babies.htm
Excellent range of free knitting patterns for baby wear.

www.nappyhead.co.uk/acatalog/Design_Your_Own.html
Design your own slogan baby T-shirt.

www.thekidswindow.co.uk/personalized-t-shirt-clothing.htm
Create your own personalised baby clothes, including babygros, T-shirts and much more.

www.cheapfabrics.co.uk
Online store for cheap fabric, some material is under £2.50 a metre.

Shopping for baby clothes
www.organic-babywear.com
Organic cotton baby clothes for newborns.

www.buyorganics.co.uk
Dedicated to chemical-free products offering 100 per cent natural clothing and other baby essentials. Ethical shopping made easy.

www.bynature.co.uk
A wide range of green, organic and ethical products as well as advice and tips for a more sustainable lifestyle.

www.kiddicare.com
The online baby superstore offering a wide range of products and accessories for babies, including good-value clothing.

www.mothercare.com
Wide range of well-priced clothes for your baby, from vests and booties to outdoor wear.

www.johnlewis.com
Never Knowingly Undersold; excellent range of clothing from basic to luxury.

www.tkmaxx.com/kids-baby.aspx
Very good value baby clothes from newborn upwards.

www.marksandspencer.com
Good quality starter sets and a full range of baby wear from 0–12 months.

www.matalan.co.uk
Fantastic range of affordable baby clothes from tiny baby to eighteen months.

www.george.com or www.asda.co.uk
Browse online, buy in-store. Enter your postcode to find your nearest Asda for good value clothing for babies from multi packs and all-in-ones to complete outfits.

www.tesco.com/storelocator
Enter your postcode to find your nearest store for good value baby wear from newborn. Clothing unavailable online.

www.sainsburys.co.uk
Enter your postcode to find your nearest store for good value baby wear from newborn. Clothing unavailable online.

www.ukparentslounge.com/index.php?pg=194
Extensive list of baby clothing retailers from UK Parents Lounge; includes an online forum.

Chapter Nine: Washing

Bathing your baby
www.askbaby.com/washing-your-baby.htm
Useful information on all aspects of washing your baby.

www.babycentre.co.uk/baby/newborn/bathingnewborn
Step-by-step advice on bathing your newborn.

www.bbc.co.uk/parenting/your_kids/babies_bathing.shtml
A guide to bathing your baby and what you will need.

www.bbc.co.uk/parenting/play_and_do/babies_bath.shtml
Fun games to play in the bath with your baby.

www.bbc.co.uk/cbeebies/tweenies/songtime/songs/e/elephantsloveabath.shtml
A fun song to sing to your baby in the bath from the makers of *The Tweenies*.

Baby massage
www.iaim.org.uk/
International Association of Infant Massage. For local course information on baby massage.

Cleaning
www.amazon.co.uk/amazing-laundry-ball-washing-powder/dp/B00118W2FG
Invest in eco laundry balls and never use washing powder again.

www.e-cloth.com
Invest in eco cloths and you won't need to use nasty chemicals when cleaning, just water and elbow grease.

www.make-stuff.com/formulas/baby_wipes.html
Recipes for making your own baby wipes.

www.anyclean.co.uk/articles/natural-cleaning-recipes.html
Recipes for natural cleaning products.

www.thefamilyhomestead.com/laundrysoap.htm
Make your own laundry detergent.

www.essortment.com/babyhoodedtowel_riso.htm
Instructions for making your own hooded baby towel.

Nappies

www.babygroe.co.uk/public/features/choosinganappy.aspx
Information and case studies on eco-nappies versus disposable, how to choose the right brand and how to set up a real nappy network.

www.babycentre.co.uk/baby/buyingforbaby/nappies/launderingservice
All you need to know about the pros and cons of a nappy laundering service.

www.bbc.co.uk/parenting/your_kids/babies_nappies.shtml
The pros and cons of disposable and re-usable nappies.

www.realnappycampaign.com
Real Nappy Helpline – 0845 8500606. Provides a list of local cloth nappy contacts countrywide.

www.nappyinformationservice.co.uk
The Nappy Information Service looks at health and environmental aspects, and has an expert medical and technical panel on hand to answer individual enquiries.

www.thenappylady.co.uk
General information and specific advice about real nappies alongside online shop. Helpline: 0845 4566532 or 0845 4562441

www.changeanappy.co.uk
National Association of Nappy Seroices (NANS). Promoting the use of cotton nappies versus disposable, with frequently asked questions and supplier listings by area. Helpline: 0121 6934949.

www.wen.org.uk/nappies/
Women's Environmental Network. Heaps of information on the use of real nappies, including washing instructions, handy tips and a nationwide free brokering service to enable people to sell, donate and buy nappies they no longer need.

www.realnappy.com
The Real Nappy Association. UK Nappy Line gives details of all your cloth nappy contacts, whether you want to wash your own or use a local laundry service. Helpline: 01983 401959.

National real nappy stockists

Baby Beehinds www.babybeehinds.co.uk Tel: 01253 701518
Bambino Mio www.bambino.co.uk Tel: 01604 883777
Cotton Bottoms www.cottonbottoms.co.uk Tel: 0870 7778899
Cottontail Organic Cotton www.thecottontailcompany.co.uk
Tel: 01273 478595
Easy Peasy Bambeasy www.easypeasynappies.co.uk
Tel: 01865 841359
Kushies www.kushies.com Tel: 0870 1202018

Minki Pocket www.nappiesbyminki.co.uk Tel: 01851 870662
Modern Baby www.modernbaby.co.uk Tel: 01992 554045
Nappy Nation www.nappynation.co.uk Tel: 01189 695550
Onelife Cotton Nappy www.onelifeworld.co.uk Tel: 01736 799512
Schmidt Natural Clothing www.naturalclothing.co.uk
Tel: 0845 3450498
Tots Bots Bamboozles www.totsbots.co.uk Tel: 0141 5501514
Tushies www.greenbaby.co.uk Tel: 0870 2406894

Second-hand real nappy stockists
The Nappy Site www.nappysite.co.uk
The Used Nappy Company www.usednappies.co.uk sells through online auction
Women's Environmental Network www.wen.org.uk/nappies/

Local Council Real Nappy Initiatives

Council	Offer
Aberdeen Real Nappy Association 01224 213953	Cashback/incentive
Birmingham Get Real 0121 3031939	Cashback/incentive
Bracknell Smarty Pants 01344 352000	Cashback/incentive
Bristol The Real Nappy Project 0117 930 4355	Free samples/packs
Bromley Real Nappy Campaign 020 8313 4913	Cashback/incentive, free samples/packs
Bucks Real Nappy Initiative 01296 382539	Cashback/incentive
Cambridgeshire & Peterborough County Council 0845 6443045	Free laundry trial, free samples/packs
Carmarthenshire The Real Nappy Scheme 0845 6580445	Free samples/packs

Ceredigion The Real Nappy Project 01545 572572	Free samples/packs
Cloth to Skin – Try Before You Buy 01768 862267	Cashback/incentive
Derbyshire County Council Waste Management Time For Change – Derbyshire 01629 580000 x7051	Cashback/Incentive
Ealing Real Nappy offer 020 8825 6000	Cashback/incentive, free laundry trial
East Ayrshire Real Nappy Network 01563 554770	Free samples/packs
East Renfrewshire Real Nappy Scheme 0141 5773001	Cashback/incentive
Edinburgh & East Central Scotland Cotton Bottoms Nappy Laundry 01259 272082	Cashback/incentive
Essex County Council 01245 437318	Cashback/incentive
Gloucestershire The Real Nappy Campaign 0870 850 8858	Free samples/packs

Hertfordshire – Get Real 07901 984155	Cashback/incentive
Kent Changing Nappies 01622 605972	Cashback/incentive, free laundry trial
Lancashire County Council 01772 531107	Free laundry trial, free samples/packs
Lancashire Nappies – The Real Choice, Waste Management Group 0845 0500 957	Cashback/incentive
Leicestershire County Council Waste Management Department 0116 2658280	Cashback/incentive
Lichfield The Bottom Line 01543 253987	Cashback/incentive
Lincolnshire County Council City Hall Waste Services Beaumont Fee Lincolnshire Real Nappy Campaign 01522 552396	Cashback/incentive
London Borough of Barnet 020 8359 7404	Cashback/incentive
London Borough of Enfield 020 8379 1000	Cashback/incentive

London Borough of Hammersmith and Fulham 020 8753 5686	Cashback/incentive
London Borough of Hounslow 020 8583 5060	Cashback/incentive
London Borough of Islington 020 7527 5157	Cashback/incentive
London Borough of Redbridge Cleaning Services 020 8708 5396	Cashback/incentive
Medway The Real Nappy Scheme 01634 333333	Cashback/incentive, free samples/packs
Milton Keynes MK Get Real Project 01908 227070	Cashback/incentive, free samples/packs
Norfolk Real Nappy Campaign Norfolk County Council Dept of Planning and Transportation County Hall 01603 222259	Cashback/incentive, free samples/packs
Northants County Council 0845 850 0606	Cashback/incentive
Northumberland County Council 01670 534047	Cashback/incentive

Nottinghamshire County Council Waste Management The Notts Nappy Project 01159 772019	Cashback/incentive, free samples/packs
Oadby and Wigston Borough Council 01162 720572	Cashback/incentive
Powys County Council The Powys Re-Usable Nappy Scheme 0845 6076060	Free samples/packs
Preston Environappies 0870 2416313	Cashback/incentive, free laundry trial, free samples/packs
Reading Ready Nappies 01189 390159	Cashback/incentive
Sedgefield Borough Council Sustainable 01388 816166	Cashback/incentive
Sefton Econappy 0151 4796550	Free laundry trial
South Staffordshire County Council 01902 696315	Cashback/incentive
St Helens County Council Bum Deal 01744 456442	Cashback/incentive, free laundry trial

Staffordshire Moorlands County Council 01538 483387	Cashback/incentive
Staffordshire New Nappy Network 01785 244232	Cashback/incentive
Tamworth Real Nappies 01827 709445	Cashback/incentive
Telford and Wrekin React Nappies 01952 202951	Cashback/incentive, free laundry trial
Trafford Metropolitan County Council	Free laundry trial
Wakefield The Real Nappy Campaign 01924 306367	Free samples/packs
Warrington Borough Council Environmental Protection 01925 442604	Free laundry trial, free samples/packs
Warwickshire County Council Cotton on . . . to cotton nappies 01926 418615	Cashback/incentive, free samples/packs
West London Real Nappy campaign 020 8568 4913	Cashback/incentive

West Sussex County Council 01243 642 106	Cashback/incentive, Free laundry trial, Free samples/packs
Wiltshire Real Nappy Network 01380 725670 Ext. 236	Cashback/incentive
Worcestershire and Herefordshire Real Nappy Scheme	Cashback/incentive

Source: www.moneysavingexpert.com

Chapter Ten: Playing

Playing with your baby

www.fisher-price.com/uk/playstages
An overview of what many babies are capable of doing at each age, plus a list of toy types that are appropriate for each age.

www.fisher-price.com/uk/playtime/learn.asp
Step-by-step activities you can play with your baby using materials you have at home.

www.babycentre.co.uk/baby/development/stimulatingdevelopment/toysfornewborns
Comprehensive list of suitable toys for your newborn.

www.babycentre.co.uk/baby/development/letsplay
Fun games for you to play with your baby as they develop week by week.

www.askbaby.com/nursery-rhyme-list.htm
All the lyrics to your favourite nursery rhymes.

www.bbc.co.uk/music/parents/yourchild/prebirth_18mnths/musical_games.shtml
Musical games to play with your newborn baby.

www.bbc.co.uk/music/parents/yourchild/prebirth_18mnths/playing_sound.shtml
Sound games to play with your baby from ten months.

www.kididdles.com/lyrics/index.html
All the lyrics to all your favourite lullabies and nursery rhymes.

www.elc.co.uk/play
Early Learning Centre. Fantastic free play ideas that can be played all year round, incorporating creative, imaginative and active play to help boost your baby's development.

Make your own
www.bbc.co.uk/dna/h2g2/A1134073
Make your own play dough.

www.photobox.co.uk
Print digital photos online and create your own picture books.

Second-hand toys
www.natll.org.uk
National Association of Toy and Leisure Libraries. Found throughout the UK, toy libraries offer services to local families based on regular toy loan for a nominal fee (and sometimes for free). They provide carefully selected toys to borrow, play sessions, and a friendly, informative meeting place for parents and carers. To find your nearest toy library send an email to helpline@playmatters.co.uk.

www.nct.org.uk/home
Search by postcode for your nearest 'Nearly New Sale', with the opportunity to buy toys at bargain prices.

http://baby.listings.ebay.co.uk/
Thousands of good quality second-hand, well-loved toys for babies, usually sold as bundles.

Shopping for toys
www.elc.co.uk/
Early Learning Centre. Well-known toy retailer for babies and children of all ages.

www.argos.co.uk
Well-priced toys for babies categorised by age, brand or budget.

www.babiesrus.co.uk
The UK's largest toy shop, offering thousands of toy and play ideas for young babies at very reasonable prices.

www.letterbox.co.uk
Creative and educational toys for children of all ages.

www.tesco.co.uk
Visit your local store for great value toys for your baby.

Chapter Eleven: Pottering

Local activities

www.babydirectory.co.uk

The Baby Directories are 200-page guides covering pregnancy and life with babies and children under five. Organised into ten regional books they each have thousands of listings, reviews and local ideas. Enter your area into the website to order your local copy.

www.makaton.org/training/baby-signing.php

Makaton signing for babies is provided as a series of sessions where you and your baby learn up to 100 signs and symbols and have fun practising them in songs, games and activities. Send an enquiry form via the website.

www.gurgle.com/groups/Default.aspx

Meet other parents and parents-to-be in your area at the same stage of pregnancy/parenthood.

www.direct.gov.uk

Check online to find your nearest library for details of baby story-time and singing sessions.

www.nctpregnancyandbabycare.com/in-your-area/event-finder

Local NCT branches organise a wide range of events to bring together new parents, including activities for you and your baby like the Cheeky Monkeys Tea Party, coffee mornings, baby massage and first-aid classes, as well as more practical sessions and nearly new sales. Enter your postcode into the website to find details of your local events.

www.netmums.com

An online network for new parents, offering a wealth of information on both a national and local level. Once you have registered on your local site you can access details for local activities, from child-friendly cafés to playgroups and places to go. Chat with local mums in the online coffee house and read other mums' local recommendations.

www.raring2go.co.uk
The definitive guide of what to do and where to go for you and your children, including child-friendly retailers and places to eat. Enter your area into the website to order your local copy.

Swimming
The following listings all offer mother-and-baby swimming classes for young babies:

Company name	Areas covered	Contact
Aquababies	London, Middlesex, Essex, Surrey, Slough, Windsor	info@aquababies-uk.com www.aquababies-uk.com
Aqua Babies	Greater Manchester – Altrincham, Creadle, West Didsbury, Stockport, Wilmslow	info@aqua-babies.co.uk www.aqua-babies.co.uk
Aquarius Swim School	Devon	lisab@aquariusswimschool.co.uk www.aquariusswimschool.co.uk
Aquaschool	Guildford, Surrey	lyane@aquaschool.co.uk www.aquaschool.co.uk

Aquatots	Worcester, Cheltenham, Cirencester, Tewkesbury, Birmingham, Solihull, Stonehouse, Kidderminster, Gloucester	office@aquatots.co.uk www.aquatots.co.uk
Baby Swimming	Surrey, Hampshire, Berkshire, Sussex, Southwest London, West London, Buckinghamshire, Oxfordshire	info@babyswimming.co.uk. www.babyswimming.co.uk
Baba Seahorse	Wolverhampton, Kidderminster, Great Witley, Birmingham	swim@babaseahorse.co.uk www.babaseahorse.co.uk
Birthlight	N.Ireland	info@birthlight.com www.birthlight.com
Born to Swim	London, Middlesex	info@borntoswim.co.uk www.borntoswim.co.uk
The Dolphin Birthlight Baby Swimming School	London, Bishops Stortford	Tel/Fax: 01954 710413 www.dbbss.co.uk.
Flippers Swim Babes	Yorkshire, Derbyshire	swimbabes@tiscali.co.uk www.swimbabes.co.uk

Little Dippers	Wimbledon, Richmond, London Bridge, Redhill, Brighton, Uckfield, Eastbourne, Wilmington, Horsham, Oxford, Staffordshire, St Austell, Plymouth, Burton-on-Trent, Chester, Havant	Tel: 0870 758 0302 www.littledippers.co.uk
Merbabies	Ipswich, Norwich, Huntingdon	enquiries@merbabies.co.uk www.merbabies.co.uk
Pool Babies	York, Stamford Bridge	marjolyn@poolbabies.com www.poolbabies.com
Puddle Ducks	Northwich, Cheshire	Tel: 01477 535527 www.puddleducks-swimming.co.uk
Splash 'n' Swim	Bristol, Bath	enquiries@splashnswim.co.uk www.splashnswim.co.uk
Swimbabies	Worthing, Lewes, Chichester	info@swimbabies.co.uk www.swimbabies.co.uk
Swim Baby Swim	Buckinghamshire	enquiries@swimbabyswim.co.uk www.swimbabyswim.co.uk
Swim Tots	York, Harrogate	info@swim-tots.co.uk www.swim-tots.co.uk
Water Babies	UK-wide	info@waterbabies.co.uk www.waterbabies.co.uk

Music classes

www.gymboree-uk.com

Soft play, music, mum and baby fitness. Classes designed with your baby's development in mind following the ethos of learning through play. Some suitable from birth. Check website for your nearest class. Free trial session available.

www.jojingles.com

Jo Jingles provides fun music and singing classes with an educational slant for babies and children aged from six months to five years of age in more than 500 centres around the UK. Check website to find your nearest class. Free trial session.

www.monkeymusic.co.uk

Thirty-minute classes for babies from three months, introducing music to very young children. Check website to find your nearest class. Free trial session available.

www.musicbugs.co.uk

Music Bugs provides fun and interactive singing and music classes for children aged six months to four years. Check website for your nearest class. Free trial session available.

Exercise

www.buggyfit.co.uk

Outdoor exercise incorporating your buggy in the process! Check website for further information and to find your nearest class.

www.postnatalexercise.co.uk/mothers.htm

The Guild of Pregnancy and Post-natal Instructors. Specialists in exercising for mums-to-be and new murms with suggested gentle exercises you can do from home.

Make your own

www.cakebaker.co.uk/
Countless recipes for delicious cakes, including classic cakes, celebration cakes, easy cakes and children's cakes.

www.elc.co.uk/play/
Free play ideas from the Early Learning Centre.

Chapter Twelve: Juggling

Returning to work

www.babycentre.co.uk/baby/workandchildcare/directories
Useful sources of information and helpful contacts if you are planning to go back to work, including benefits, childcare organisations, support groups and ways to work.

Child Tax Credit and Working Tax Credit

www.taxcredits.inlandrevenue.gov.uk
Full explanations of child and working tax credits with an online calculator to help you determine how much you could be entitled to.

www.hmrc.gov.uk/taxcredits
Another government site explaining child and working tax credits. Helpline: 0845 3003900.

www.childcarevouchers.co.uk
Childcare vouchers are a great way for employers to give working parents help with dependent children. You don't pay tax or National Insurance on childcare vouchers and can save up to £1,195 per year.

www.surestart.gov.uk
Information on Government support for children, parents and communities.

www.dti.gov.uk/workingparents
For information on flexible working including advice on how to ask your boss for more flexible hours. Or call the working families free legal helpline on 0800 0130313.

Childcare

www.aupairs.co.uk
Worldwide service providing a channel for advertising for an au pair.

www.babycentre.co.uk/baby/workandchildcare/costofcare
Guidance and advice on the costs of childcare from childminders versus nannies versus nurseries.

www.babycentre.co.uk/a-z/childcare/
Baby Centre's A–Z list of childcare organisations.

www.bestbear.co.uk
Best Bear offers you the only nationwide listing of vetted and recommended childcare agencies – covering both London and nationwide nanny agencies.

www.childcarelink.gov.uk
Children's Information Service. Comprehensive council service for information about local childcare and activities. Select your area for local help and information. Excellent search function with explanations and advice on all types of childcare available.

www.direct.gov.uk/childcare
Information and guidance on all aspects of childcare including how to locate and choose the right childcare in your area, what provisions and/or benefits could be available to you, plus useful contacts and other helpful hints and tips.

www.daycaretrust.org.uk
The Daycare Trust is a national childcare charity promoting high quality affordable childcare for all.

www.nannyjob.co.uk
Online noticeboard for finding or posting a childcare position.

www.nanny-search.co.uk
Nanny Search places nannies, maternity nurses, temporary nannies and qualified babysitters across the UK. Placements can be from one day to one year plus, residential or daily.

www.ncma.org.uk
National Childminding Association. Promotes and supports quality childminding expertise, providing information and help for parents looking for childminders.

www.ndna.org.uk
National Day Nurseries Association (NDNA) is the national membership association of day nurseries in the UK. NDNA is dedicated to the provision, support and promotion of high-quality care and education for the benefit of children, families and communities.

www.nacis.org.uk
National Association of Children's Information Services. Information on childminders, nurseries, nannies, crèches, playgroups and parent-toddler groups.

www.ofsted.gov.uk
Government-rated reports on prospective nurseries.

www.simplychildcare.com
A childcare listings magazine offering a pack with example contracts and interview questions to help you employ your carer.

www.thenannysharers.co.uk
The Nanny Sharers provide a centralised database where families can team up and share nanny and the related costs. Enter your postcode online to find nearby families.

Other helpful organisations

www.csa.gov.uk
Child Support Agency. Agency ensuring that parents who live away from their children are contributing financially to their upbringing.

www.adviceguide.org.uk
Citizens Advice Bureaux provide free, confidential and independent advice from over 3,000 locations including in bureaux, GP surgeries, hospitals, colleges, prisons and courts.

www.earlysupport.org.uk
The Early Support Programme is the central government mechanism for achieving better co-ordinated, family-focused services for young disabled children and their families across England.

www.earlyyearsequality.org
Early Years Equality. Offer support for ethnic minority parents.

www.maternityalliance.org.uk
The Maternity Alliance is a national charity working to improve support for, and end inequality amongst, pregnant women, new parents and babies under one.

Chapter Thirteen: Healing

www.trusthomeopathy.org/
The British Homeopathic Association has reliable information on homeopathy. The website also has a list of doctors with a homeopathy qualification.

www.a-r-h.org
The Alliance of Registered Homeopaths has an online service to help find a qualified, registered homeopath in your local area.

www.whatreallyworks.co.uk
An informative website written by journalists and health practitioners on natural health and remedies. It includes fact sheets on different conditions.

www.babycentre.co.uk/pregnancy/antenatalhealth/naturalremedies
Advice on beating pregnancy symptoms like morning sickness and stretchmarks with natural remedies and self help.

Chapter Fourteen: Giving

Make your own

www.bbc.co.uk/cbeebies/make/
Make your own gifts for other babies with hundreds of 'make and do' ideas from the BBC.

www.creativekidsathome.com/activities/activity_42.html
Make your own finger paint to create your very own hand- or footprint canvas gift.

www.hobbycraft.co.uk/ideas%5Flibrary
The UK's largest craft superstore, including an online ideas library for making your own thank-you cards complete with step-by-step instructions.

www.moonpig.com
Personalised greeting cards online. Choose from over 7,000 designs; printed and posted in twenty-four hours.

www.pedlars.co.uk
Pedlars sells beautiful word stamp kits for printing letters on home-made cards.

www.photobox.co.uk
Be creative and make your own personalised photo gifts and cards from your favourite digital photo prints, including collage posters, cushions, canvas prints. Print digital photos online and create free online photo albums to store and share photos with friends and family. You can also use your online pictures to send free e cards.

The 1st birthday

www.babycentre.co.uk/baby/traditions/1yrpartyguide
A guide to planning your baby's first birthday party, from getting the timing right and who to invite to party games and choosing food.

www.babycentre.co.uk/baby/traditions/partytoptips/#16
Top ten tips to save time and money when planning a first birthday party.

www.deliaonline.com/recipes/childrens-cake,1790,RC.html
Make your baby's first birthday cake with help from the UK's expert, Delia Smith. Online recipe with full instructions on how to make a large children's party cake.

www.evite.com
Free online invitations with a wide selection of first birthday designs.

www.grizzlybird.net/2007/01/babys-1st-birthday-cake-recipes.html
Healthy sugar-free birthday cakes for babies and toddlers with ingredients and full instructions.

www.kids-party.com/games.shtml
Comprehensive listing of all the games to play at a children's party suitable for a range of ages.

www.smilebox.com/occasions/birthday-greeting-cards
Choose from hundreds of free invitation templates and add your own photos, words or music.

Acknowledgements

I would like to thank my resourceful mums for all their creative and practical advice: Annabel, Abs, Nics, Maria, Monika, Hazel, Amy P, Allison W, Marcela, Alison, Maida, Caroline, Lorna, Lynsey, Shonagh, Susan, Catrin, Rachel and especially Emma Barnsdale for helping with research. Thank you to Michelle Jarvis and Debbie Smith at Rosie's nursery, Aston Pierpoint@HCC for sharing their playing ideas. Also: thanks to Liz Foley for the perfect stepping stone, Lizzie Colcutt and Nicola Taylor for gorgeous illustrations and particularly Rosemary Davidson for her care and attention to detail in shaping the book. Thank you to Mum and Alice for their crafty zing, and to Simon for patience and calm. Finally, a big thanks to Rosie for testing out my ideas and having a lovely, long lunchtime sleep when I could write.

Index